Transnational Ties

Transnational Ties

Cities, Migrations, and Identities

Comparative Urban and Community
Research, Vol. 9

**Michael Peter Smith
and
John Eade,
editors**

Transaction Publishers
New Brunswick (U.S.A.) and London (U.K.)

Second printing 2009
Copyright © 2008 by Transaction Publishers, New Brunswick, New Jersey.

All rights reserved under International and Pan-American Copyright Conventions. No part of this book may be reproduced or transmitted in any form or by any means, electronic or mechanical, including photocopy, recording, or any information storage and retrieval system, without prior permission in writing from the publisher. All inquiries should be addressed to Transaction Publishers, Rutgers—The State University of New Jersey, 35 Berrue Circle, Piscataway, New Jersey 08854-8042. www.transactionpub.com

This book is printed on acid-free paper that meets the American National Standard for Permanence of Paper for Printed Library Materials.

Library of Congress Catalog Number: 2008027790
ISBN: 978-1-4128-0806-4
Printed in the United States of America

Library of Congress Cataloging-in-Publication Data

Transnational ties : cities, migrations, and identities / [edited by] Michael Peter Smith and John Eade.
    p. cm. -- (Comparative urban and community research ; v. 9)
Includes bibliographical references and index.
ISBN 978-1-4128-0806-4 (alk. paper)
    1. Transnationalism. 2. City and town life. 3. Emigration and immigration--Social aspects. 4. Immigrants--Social conditions. 5. Immigrants--Cultural assimilation. I. Smith, Michael P. II. Eade, John, 1946-
HM1271.T72 2008
305.8009173'2--dc22

2008027790

Contents

Acknowledgments ... vii

I. HISTORICIZING TRANSNATIONAL TIES

1. Transnational Ties: Cities, Migrations, and Identities ... 3
   Michael Peter Smith and John Eade

2. Time Matters: Temporal Contexts of ... 15
   Polish Transnationalism
   Kathy Burrell

3. Transnationalism in the Ethno-National City: ... 39
   Migration and Anti-Racism in Belfast
   Peter Geoghegan

II. PATHWAYS TO TRANSNATIONAL URBANISM

4. The Making of Urban Translocalities: ... 61
   Senegalese Migrants in Dakar and Zingonia
   Giulia Sinatti

5. South-South Migration and Transnational ... 77
   Ties between Cuba and Mozambique
   Katrin Hansing

6. Chinese Transnational Entrepreneurs in ... 91
   Budapest and Belgrade: Seeking Markets,
   Carrying Globalization
   Svetlana Milutinovic

III. TRANSNATIONAL RELIGIOUS NETWORKS

7. Spiritual Spaces in Post-Industrial Places: 109
Transnational Churches in North East London
Kristine Krause

8. Spirits in the Marketplace: Transnational 131
Networks of Vietnamese Migrants in Berlin
Gertrud Hüwelmeier

IV. TRANSNATIONAL DIASPORAS AND IDENTITIES

9. A Diasporic Sense of Place: Dynamics of 147
Spatialization and Transnational Political
Fields among Bangladeshi Muslims in Britain
David Garbin

10. Practicing Identities Across Borders: 163
The Case of Bulgarian Turkish Labor Migrants in Germany
Mila Mancheva

Contributors 183

Index 187

Acknowledgments

The contributions to this book are the product of a three-day international conference on "Transnational Identities/Cities Unbound/Migrations Redefined," held at various venues in Krakow, Poland from October 6-8, 2006, at which the editors delivered keynote addresses. We wish to thank the contributors to *Transnational Ties* for their responsiveness to our suggested revisions of their original conference papers, which were aimed at giving greater coherence to the book as a whole. We also wish to thank Leticia Jáuregui for her excellent editorial assistance in the preparation of the final manuscript.

Michael Peter Smith
University of California at Davis

John Eade
Roehampton University, London
& Surrey University

PART I
HISTORICIZING TRANSNATIONAL TIES

1

Transnational Ties: Cities, Migrations, and Identities

Michael Peter Smith and John Eade

Cities are key sites of the transnational ties that increasingly connect people, places, and projects across the globe. They are at once contexts of opportunities and constraints within which transnational actors and networks operate and nodes linking wider social formations that traverse national borders. This book brings together a series of richly textured ethnographic case studies that suggest new ways to situate and historicize transnationalism, identify new pathways to transnational urbanism, and map the contours of translocal, interregional, and diasporic connections not previously studied. The transnational ties treated in this book truly span the globe, giving concrete meaning to the phrase "globalization from below."

How have the contributors to this book conceptualized the wider context informing the conduct of their ethnographically grounded, multi-sited research on the relationship between cities, migration, and transnationalism? Several interrelated contextual dimensions have been singled out as affecting the opportunities and constraints experienced by transnational migrant subjects, mediating their transnational practices, and situating their changing subjectivities and identities in the multiple, interconnected places in which they are orchestrating their lives. Socio-spatially, in several of our studies the political economic context now called neoliberal globalization is shown to be a key driving force creating conditions that necessitate, facilitate, or impede migration, foster trans-local economic ties, and create new inter-regional interdependencies—e.g., new South-South and East-East transnational ties.

In this volume, the changing historical context of both migrating groups and the cities and regions they move across are shown to be central to the study of the interplay of urban change and migrant transnationalism. Changing local political contexts of reception and exit at different historical periods are crucial dimensions of historical context, as are the changing state policy frameworks that affect the practices of transnational migration and migrant inclusion and/or exclusion in new destinations. As Smith and Bakker (2008: 5; see also Smith 2005a and 2005b) have shown, socio-cultural factors are also key elements in the formation and continuity of international migration trajectories in particular locales. As they point out, "the historical particularities of migrant recruitment, migration histories, migratory narratives, and changing gender and class relations all affect the character and geography of transnational migration…, shaping who migrates, where they come from, and where they go." These historical particularities have impacted the social structures of community formation within which new modes of existence across borders are being enacted and lived.

Historicizing Migrant Transnationalism

Although much attention in the transnationalism literature has been paid to the geographical and spatial dimensions of migrant transnationalism, the historical and temporal implications of cross-national activities have been less thoroughly analyzed. Kathy Burrell's chapter, "Time Matters," helps to redress this imbalance by focusing explicitly on the different interactions between time, migration, and transnationalism. Based on ethnographic research undertaken on Polish migration to Britain extending from the Second World War to the enlargement of the European Union in 2004, Burrell offers a nuanced, thoroughly historicized ethnography of the changing temporal contexts of Polish transnationalism in Britain. She identifies and investigates three distinct dimensions of historical context: the nostalgic homeland connections of the post-World War II refugees; the temporal dimensions of Cold War Europe as experienced by subsequent migrant cohorts; and the temporal implications of the increased mobility associated with contemporary migration. Paying close attention to the alternative migration histories experienced by different migrating cohorts from the same country over time, as does Burrell, is one important way to historicize migrant transnationalism.

A second way to approach historical context is to focus upon questions of change and continuity in the politics and society of particular cities that are sites facilitating or impeding the formation of transnational networks. Peter Geoghegan's chapter, "Transnationalism in the Ethno-National City," provides just such a move. Geoghegan offers a careful analysis of the local context of reception for transnational migration to Belfast, Northern Ireland during the past decade. Since the Good Friday Agreement of 1998, Belfast has experienced a growing urban political economy that has become an increasingly attractive site for transnational migration. Accompanying this influx of new migrants, the problem of racism in the city began to receive increased attention. Geoghegan's case study focuses on competing political discourses produced by grassroots anti-racist groups in Belfast. His analysis of the texts produced by these groups shows how anti-racism rhetoric seeks to position migrants in relation to the dominant Protestant-Catholic sectarian division. Drawing on qualitative interview data, his chapter also shows, however, that the new international migrants to Belfast often reject this interpellation and voluntarily exclude themselves from these partisan anti-racist discourses. In sum, the persistent Protestant-Catholic political cleavage in Belfast is shown to be a key political context of reception for transnational migrants that they must accommodate to or resist as they orchestrate new cross border living arrangements.

Translocalities: The Local Pathways to Transnational Urbanism

A substantial literature has emerged over the past decade on the operation of historically specific translocal networks, spaces, and connections and the ensuing formation of "translocalities" as central elements in grounding the study of transnationalism (for key debates on the meaning and impact of translocality, see Appadurai 1996; Hannerz 1996, 1998; and Smith 2001, 2005a, 2005b). Smith's (2001, 2005b) theorization of the relationship between transnationalism and cities, which he terms transnational urbanism, stresses the central role played by cities as key social spaces grounding transnational practices and processes, as arenas for studying the effects of transnational networks on place and vice versa (Smith 2001: 183), and as interconnected sites for the emplacement of the mobile subjects forging transnational ties (Smith 2005b).

Much of the case study literature informed by this perspective has focused on the ties forged and projects pursued by migrants from localities in the global South that closely connect their places of origin to receiving cities in the global North. The chapter of this book by Giulia Sinatti adds another insightful case study to this growing literature on South-North urban translocalities. In her chapter, "The Making of Urban Translocalities," Sinatti demonstrates the usefulness of the concept of translocality for understanding the role played by cities in emerging forms of contemporary migrations. Using the case of Senegalese migration connecting Dakar, Senegal to Zingonia, Italy, Sinatti shows that transnational migratory practices are characterized by the establishment of translocalities, namely cities that are recognized by migrant networks as meaningful sites for collective reference. Through her multi-sited study of processes of place-making initiated in Dakar in the home country and in Zingonia in northern Italy, she reveals how these two cities are socially constructed by the Senegalese as central poles for sustaining transnational relations.

Two other authors in this volume move the study of translocality beyond the South-North migratory trajectory. In Chapter 5 Katrin Hansing assesses a mode of transnational place-making that is now adding an important new spatial dimension to transnational studies, namely the social construction of South-South transnational ties. Hansing's historically and ethnographically grounded case study, "South-South Migration and Transnational Ties between Cuba and Mozambique," examines the well established transnational connections between Havana, Cuba and Maputo, Mozambique forged as the result of the migration of Cuban medical personnel to the previously socialist country of Mozambique, which continued and indeed expanded as the latter's political economy moved in a neo-liberal direction. Her study details key dimensions of Cuba's large-scale state-sponsored aid programs, through which highly skilled Cuban professionals have temporarily migrated to work in other developing countries such a Mozambique. In particular, her chapter focuses on the lives, realities, and changing identities of Cuban doctors, who are based in Maputo, Mozambique, as well as how their experiences feed back into their relations and lives in Havana and Cuba. In so doing she carefully considers the question of whether this particular case of South-South migration differs from more typical South-North and East-West migratory dynamics, motivations and experiences typically found in transnational studies.

Svetlana Milutinovic's chapter, "Chinese Transnational Entrepreneurs in Budapest and Belgrade," focuses on two cities in Eastern Europe that have witnessed a new phenomenon in the last two decades—Chinese entrepreneurial migration, which joins economic processes taking place in sending places with those in receiving places, thereby establishing new East-East translocal and transnational economic ties. The aim of her essay is to show how this phenomenon has played out in these two cities and to shed light on the spread of a Chinese transnational enterprise that links several receiving places across two regions, thereby forging multiple translocalities, linked by their relationships to the enterprise.

Her findings reveal that contemporary Chinese entrepreneurs are new transnational actors capable of merging several localities, not typically thought of as global metropoles, into favorable market relations in the global political economy.

Diasporic Communities, Identity Politics, and Social Integration

When we turn back from these new modes of globalization from below and from the middle, which are signs of *widening* globalization, to the extensive South-North migration trajectory that has characterized the past two decades, we are able to discern some potentially *narrowing* trends occasioned by the spread of diaspora communities in the global North because of growing fears of international terrorism. Initially, the migration of workers from South to North since the end of the Second World War had changed national narratives in Europe, as an early period of temporary migration was followed by permanent settlement with the arrival of wives and dependants. While political elites in the United States, in particular, had long interpreted the nation as a country of immigration, their equivalents in Europe had emphasized the social and cultural homogeneity of their nation-states and presented immigration as a minor issue where minorities would be quickly assimilated. However, the rapid influx of migrants from former colonies between the late 1940s and the 1980s into France, The Netherlands, Belgium, and Britain especially, as well as the far more substantial immigration of guest workers into West Germany, raised the likelihood of permanent settlement by people whose racial and ethnic distinctiveness highlighted the growth of cultural pluralism and hybridity, new ethnicities, imagined communities and diasporic ties with the countries of origin (for key debates on these issues see, for example, Bhabha 1990; Hall 1992; Appadurai 1997; Cohen 1997; Vertovec 2000).

These debates concerning the contribution of immigrants to cultural diversity in Europe were developed before 9/11. The political reaction to 9/11, subsequent terrorist attacks in Spain and Britain, the murder of Pim Fortuyn and the filmmaker Theo Van Gogh in the Netherlands, and the cartoons saga in Denmark are some of the key elements encouraging a backlash by European nation-states against "multiculturalism" and single-issue identity politics. Minorities, including transnational migrants, are now publicly exhorted to focus on what they share with the dominant majority, rather than what makes them culturally and socially distinct. An earlier emphasis on assimilation has revived as the liberal consensus around pluralistic integration weakened in Britain, The Netherlands, and Denmark, and anti-immigrant political sentiment increased in the United States. Muslims were often the targets of assimilationist rhetoric where "faith communities" were encouraged to contribute to "social cohesion" through the generation of "moderate" leaders and adaptation to the nation's "core values."

Transnational Religious Networks

These developments acted as both an encouragement and a constraint to the transnational religious networks, which linked these new ethnic minorities in the West to their religious heartlands. As pilgrimage studies have revealed, European space has been transformed through global migration where diasporic communities have brought their pilgrimage cults with them and established new transnational networks with their countries of origin—a process which has generated vigorous debates within those communities about the changing relationship between these diasporas and their religious and territorial centers (see Coleman and Eade 2004, Badone and Roseman 2004). They have also begun to sacralize local places within Britain itself through the revitalization of established shrines, the founding of new shrines and the sanctification of rivers. This process involves an ideological reinterpretation of the relationship between center and periphery (Eade and Garbin 2007).

The sociological and anthropological analysis of these developments has been heavily circumscribed by nation-state boundaries. This preoccupation reflected a methodological nationalism (see Wimmer and Glick Schiller 2003), which informed the sociological tradition and a focus on debates concerning secularization and the supposed decline of religion drawing on the shapers of that tradition (Durkheim, Weber, and Marx). The secularization debate in Britain, for example, focused on empirical data concerning religious beliefs and practices within mainstream British society such as attendance at Church of England services, the numbers being married, baptized and buried, on differences between people's beliefs and sense of belonging, the development of new age cults and the growth of Christian sects (see Bruce 1995; Davie 1994). Only recently has Davie attempted to broaden the debate by exploring issues of collective memory across Europe but still within the nation-state framework (Davie 1994, 2000).

Research across Europe on ethnic minorities has compensated for the limitations of these debates about mainstream Christian beliefs and practices. They have also alerted us to the global political context outlined above where the rapid growth of Muslim residents, in particular, has been the object of much public concern and suspicion (see Modood and Werbner 1997; Cesari 2004). However, the issues of transnational migration and globalization have been explored through studies of Pentecostal and other charismatic Christian communities (see Coleman 2000), even if developments among Hindus, Sikhs and Buddhists have attracted less attention outside Britain (see Vertovec 2000; Nye 2001; Singh and Singh 2006).

The four chapters in sections III and IV of this book reflect this balance within the academic division of labor since two chapters focus on Muslim groups (Bangladeshis in London and Bulgarian Turks in Germany), while the other two discuss African Christians in London and Vietnamese entrepreneurs in Berlin who draw on Buddhist spirit beliefs and practices. Taken together they raise the following issues relevant to the volume—(a) the relationship between different spatial levels (local, regional, national and global) in globalizing urban conditions; (b) the ways in which the spiritual world is related to local places; (c) the impact of political and economic structures in the context of global economic "liberalization"; (d) the contestation of religious and secular identities, beliefs and practices through networks linking diasporic groups to their countries of origin, other nations and imagined global communities; and, (e) the extent to which social actors use ethnicity as a resource or look beyond ethnic boundaries.

In Section III the focus turns towards transnational religious networks in London and Berlin. Krause examines the performative process of local place-making by socially marginalized African migrants in an industrial area of north-east London. Unlike two other key local social actors—gentrifiers and those engaged in urban renewal—these migrants look beyond the locality to their countries of origin and to an imagined global Pentecostal community. The emptiness, functionality and size of the local space—a disused warehouse—enable these marginalized worshippers to develop an aesthetics and ritual through which they can express their spiritual life with the intensity they desire.

Krause argues that as London becomes increasingly "super-diverse" through the global flows of people, we need to look beyond territorial and ethnic ties to people's involvement with other affiliations, such as religious organizations. She agrees with Glick Schiller's (2005) argument that the transnational character of these kinds of Christian churches shows the importance of looking beyond ethnicity as an analytical framework. However, a shared African background remains important for these worshippers and is strategically deployed according to situations where outsiders may have negative stereotypes about African migrants. The ethnicity card can also be played to build alliances with other non-white people and to take advantage of state support for "ethnic minorities."

In Hüwelmeier's chapter Vietnamese former contract workers from the old East Germany and undocumented migrants have filled their Berlin shops and enterprises with religious meaning through venerating *Ong tho dia*—the "spirit of the place" after the collapse of the "Berlin wall." This process of emplacement breaks down boundaries between local and global, as social relations that have been disembedded through transnational migration are re-embedded in Germany's capital. However, the transformation of places as material and imaginative constructions is not just a spiritual process since religious activities are intimately entwined with economic enterprise and it is this mutual engagement, which helps to bring stability to life outside the country of origin. The spirits of the place both protect the territory and the people from physical misfortune and ensure material success.

This engagement is also shaped by political and economic changes taking place in both Vietnam and Germany, which are bound up with the collapse of communism and the relentless march of "liberalization." The state in both Vietnam and Germany has cut back on economic and social support for its citizens so these migrants are even more marginalized than their African counterparts in London. As a result, the support of the spirit world has become even more important in both Berlin and Hanoi and the changes in both cities are communicated through transnational networks and global flows of people, goods, information, and images.

Transnational Diasporas

In the final section of the book the focus remains on Britain and Germany, but the emphasis shifts towards the complex relationships created by diasporic groups with their countries of origin, with other groups within Britain and Germany, with other nations, and with global imagined communities. Garbin investigates how Bangladeshi Muslims create a diasporic sense of place in London through a process of spatialization that operates through the dialectic between local and global. Drawing on Bourdieu's discussion of "fields" as developed by Glick Schiller (2005), Garbin detects several social fields where diasporic Bangladeshis compete for symbolic capital and status through identity politics. This competition is pursued through translocal and transnational networks and the political construction of imagined (national and religious) communities.

As we have already seen an appreciation of the historical dimension of transnational processes is vital. Garbin underscores this obvious but frequently ignored point by linking his analytical framework to an historical survey of political competition in the east London borough of Tower Hamlets which contains the heartland of the Bangladeshi Muslim community in Britain. During the 1960s and 1970s the first generation of Bangladeshi leaders competed for status and symbolic capital primarily in relation to the country of origin through kinship ties mediated through translocal networks. The second generation drew on the struggle for an independent Bangladesh in 1970-71 to engage with local political struggles in Tower Hamlets and Britain, more generally, while this "secularist" tendency has been recently challenged by Islamist organizations that draw inspiration from visions of a global imagined Islamic community (*umma*). Although these ideological struggles present a powerful image of differences and boundaries between groups and individuals supported by notions of purity and authenticity, they are not so monolithic in reality. Furthermore, their dominance is contested by the hybridized politics of everyday life practiced by young British Bangladeshis.

History plays an important part in this volume's final chapter where Mancheva describes the migration by Bulgarian Turks to Germany, their relations with Turks and Germans in this country, and their continuing links with family and friends "back home." Traditionally this Bulgarian minority either engaged in seasonal internal migration or migration to Turkey, but after the collapse of the "Iron Curtain," they contributed to the movement from other former Communist countries into the European Union, particularly Germany. Here they worked in the less protected areas of the German economy that were dominated by other longer established immigrant groups. In consequence, they kept a low profile and relied heavily on Turks who were already settled in the country. Despite the social and cultural differences between Bulgarian and German Turks, their shared interests and needs lock them into a hierarchical relationship, which Bulgarian Turks seek to subvert through their identity constructions as "modern" Bulgarians and Europeans. This continuing tension and hierarchical dependency is reinforced by German political and institutional hostility towards irregular migration and irregularity in general. Unless they return to Bulgaria or escape into the regular, mainstream economy, Bulgarian Turks need the German Turks.

Interestingly, given the emphasis accorded to religion in the other chapters of sections III and IV, Islam plays a less prominent role in Mancheva's analysis. She describes them as professing a "moderate" form of Islam typical of the Balkans region, which contributes to the tensions with German Turks, who see them as not "proper" Muslims.

Bulgarian Turks, in turn, regard their co-religionists as "backward" and "conservative." As in Garbin's chapter, the language of purity and authenticity shapes the interaction between groups and individuals and reflects the contemporary debates about Islam, which link local, national and transnational identities.

Implications

The studies comprising *Transnational Ties* offer several implications for urban social theory, particularly pertaining to the role of agency in the making and remaking of urban social space. The city is both a medium and an outcome of human agency, including the agency of transnational migrants, their networks, and their projects. As a medium, it is a context of socio-economic and cultural opportunities and constraints unique to its developmental history. It offers a set of structured opportunities and constraints within which those who enter its terrain must operate. At the same time, migrants bring with them historically specific economic, political, cultural, and religious practices and identities. It is the interplay of urban social structure, migrant agency, and identity politics that determines the specific confluence of transnational ties connecting people, places, projects and identities throughout the world.

References

Appadurai, A. (1990). "Disjuncture and Difference in the Global Cultural Economy." In *Global Culture: Nationalism, Globalization and Modernity*, London: Sage.
―――――― (1997). *Modernity at Large: Cultural Dimensions in Globalization*, Minneapolis: University of Minnesota Press.
Bhabha, H. (ed.) (1990). *Nation and Narration*, London and New York: Routledge.
Badone, E. and S. Roseman (2004). *Intersecting Journeys: The Anthropology of Pilgrimage and Tourism*, Champaign, IL: University of Illinois Press.
Baumann, G. (1996). *Contesting Culture: Discourses of Identity in Multi-Ethnic London*, Cambridge: Cambridge University Press.
Bruce, S. (1995). *From Cathedrals to Cults: Religion in the Modern World*, Oxford: Oxford University Press.
Cesari, J. (2004). *When Islam and Democracy Meet: Muslims in Europe and in the United States*, Basingstoke: Macmillan Palgrave.
Cohen, R. (1997). *Global Diasporas: An Introduction*, London and New York: Routledge.
Coleman, S. (2000). *The Globalisation of Charismatic Christianity: Spreading the Gospel of Prosperity*, Cambridge: Cambridge University Press.
―――――― , and J. Eade (eds) (2004). *Reframing Pilgrimage: Cultures in Motion*, London and New York: Routledge.
Davie, G. (1994). *Religion in Britain since 1945: Believing without Belonging*, Oxford: Blackwell.
―――――― (2000). *Religion in Modern Europe: A Memory Mutates*, Oxford: Oxford University Press.

Eade, J., and D. Garbin (2007). "Reinterpreting the Relationship between the Centre and Periphery: Pilgrimage and Sacred Specialisation among Polish and Congolese Communities in Britain." *Mobilities* 2 (In press).

Hall, S. (1992). "New Ethnicities." In *'Race', Culture and Difference* (pp. 252-259). London: Sage.

Hannerz, U. (1996). *Transnational Connections: Culture, People, Places*, London and New York: Routledge.

_____ (1998). "Transnational Research." In *Handbook of Methods in Cultural Anthropology* (pp. 235-256). Walnut Creek, CA: Altamira Press.

Harris, E. (2004). *Theravada Buddhism and the British Encounter*, London and New York: Routledge.

Modood, T., and P. Werbner (eds.) (1997). *The Politics of Multiculturalism in the New Europe: Racism, Identity and Community*, London: Zed Books.

Nye, M. (2001). *Multiculturalism and Minority Religions in Britain: Krishna Consciousness, Religious Freedom and the Politics of Location*, London and New York: Routledge Curzon.

Singh, G., and D. Singh Tatla (2006). *Sikhs in Britain: The Making of a Community*, London: Zed Books.

Smith, M. P. (2001). *Transnational Urbanism: Locating Globalization*, Oxford: Blackwell.

_____ (2005a). "Power in Place/Places of Power: Contextualizing Transnational Research." *City & Society* 17 (1): 5-34.

_____ (2005b). "Transnational Urbanism Revisited." *Journal of Ethnic and Migration Studies* 31 (2): 235-244.

_____ and M. Bakker (2008). *Citizenship across Borders: The Political Transnationalism of El Migrante*. Ithaca, NY: Cornell University Press.

Vertovec, S. (2000). *The Hindu Diaspora: Comparative Patterns*, London and New York: Routledge.

_____ and R. Cohen (2002). *Conceiving Cosmopolitanism: Theory, Context and Practice*, Oxford: Oxford University Press.

Wimmer, A., and N. Glick Schiller (2003). "Methodological Nationalism and Beyond: Nation-State Building, Migration and the Social Sciences." *Global Networks* 2 (4): 301-34.

2

Time Matters: Temporal Contexts of Polish Transnationalism

Kathy Burrell

Transnationalism is now so embedded in the academic discussions of migration that it is almost impossible to remember what came before the pioneering work of the 1990s (Basch, Glick Schiller, and Szanton Blanc 1994; Smith and Guarnizo 1998). Analysis of the cross-national spatial dimensions of migrants' lives is now an established part of the migration literature. In particular, recent scholarship has placed great emphasis upon the varying configurations of social, family, and household life sustained across borders and how it is possible for ordinary lives to circumnavigate national boundaries on a daily basis (Levitt 2001; Bryceson and Vuorela 2002; Gardner and Grillo 2002). While the spatial implications of migration/transnationalism are becoming better understood, it is surprisingly difficult to find research that addresses the temporal aspects of migration and transnationalism. Life-course and life-history research certainly does this to some extent, connecting migration and transnational practices with the particular hopes and pressures of the life-cycle (Plane 1993; Chamberlain 1997). But generally, while space and place dominate understandings of transnationalism, time has been left behind.

Time and Transnationalism

This inattention to time is particularly surprising considering the conceptual connections between the philosophy of transnationalism and observations about the nature of time. While transnationalism sought to revitalize stale migration debates, challenging the insistence of viewing migration as a linear journey starting in one place and ending in another with no deviation, debates about temporality have similarly liberated understandings of time. The differences between "measured" time and "experienced" time, for example, are now widely recognized (Gosden 1994: 2). As Adam (1995: 12) states, "there is no single time, only a multitude of times which interpenetrate and permeate our daily lives." People experience regimented, hegemonic clock and calendar time, but also personal rhythms, remembered and anticipated time. They live in the now, but also simultaneously in different times in the past and future through their memories and aspirations. They abide by ordered routines, but also follow diversely conceived timetables. If the success of transnationalism has been the recognition of the reality of living across multiple spaces, can it also add to understandings of living in these multiple times? As May and Thrift (2001) emphasize, time and space are fundamentally interrelated, space being inherently shaped by temporal contexts. If the reality of the connection between space and time is "less that of a singular or uniform social time stretching over a uniform space, than of various (and uneven) networks of time stretching in different and divergent directions across an uneven social field," as May and Thrift (2001: 5) argue, then perhaps when transnationalism allows people to experience space in a different way, it also does the same for their experiences of time.

Time has not been completely ignored in the migration and transnationalism literature, although it is usually considered implicitly rather than directly. When time is addressed as a factor in migration and subsequent links back home, three points are generally made. First, there is an understanding that for settled migrant populations the homeland represents the past, not just the spatial setting of another life, but the temporal setting too. For Salman Rushdie (1991: 9), for example, a photograph of India reminds him that "it's my present that is foreign, and that the past is home, albeit a lost home in a lost city in the mists of lost time." Any transnational activity maintained is therefore tinged, to varying degrees, with a desire to access that time left behind by accessing those places, going back to the homeland in an attempt to go back in time. The act of migration cannot help but cast the homeland in a specific time zone of the migrants' imaginations.

Second, it is also recognized that while homeland means "past" for many migrants, for many others it is imagined as the site of a future return, the place where the fruits of working abroad can be properly realized, either in eventual retirement or in the more immediate future (Anwar 1979; Ganga 2006). Migration is a life-course strategy, focused on a supposedly fixed, but often elusive, temporal goal. Transnational activity in this scenario is the crucial facilitator in keeping this plan alive, preventing migrants from becoming too disconnected from their future homes.

Finally, bridging these idealized pasts and futures, the change brought about by technological advances in the past two decades has allowed new notions of time and migration to emerge. Utilizing improved travel and communications technology, it has been suggested, has enabled migrants to socially participate in two places *at the same time* (Smith 1998). As Basch, Glick Schiller, and Szanton Blanc (1994: 7) argue, transmigrants are connected "simultaneously to two or more nation-states." The homeland does not have to be either past or future, but can be accessed now, usually through real-time mechanisms such as telephone calls and Internet access.

Much more can therefore be said about the relationship between time and transnationalism. As has been argued more recently, transnational activities need to be located much more firmly in their specific contexts, not just spatial ones, but temporal ones too (Smith 2001; Crang, Dwyer, and Jackson 2003). In particular, the need to historicize transnational practices has been raised, especially taking into account the impact of changing geo-political boundaries on freedom of movement (Smith 2005: 238; Wimmer and Glick Schiller 2002). *When* people migrate is as important as *where* they move to and from. The issue of the simultaneity of transnational lives has also been questioned. Has this changed over time, and how much difference does it make to the lived experience of migration? (Smith 2005: 240). In short, how does timing affect experiences of transnationalism, and how does transnationalism affect experiences of time?

Background to Research

The research for this chapter is based on a series of in-depth interviews with Polish migrants in Britain in the Midlands region; to protect the identities of the respondents pseudonyms have been used throughout. First, I interviewed twenty-six people for my doctoral research in Leicester (Burrell 2006a). I asked questions about their migration experiences, their links back to Poland and their life in Leicester, and also invited them to talk more generally about their lives. Of these people, the first-generation respondents had all settled in Britain as refugees from the Second World War as ex-servicemen, their dependants, or as European Volunteer Workers (Zubrzycki 1956; Tannahill 1958). From Britain's perspective, these refugees provided a timely solution to the severe post-war labor shortages. The Poles were welcomed relatively warmly and resettlement packages were organized to help the newcomers settle in and oversee their labor contributions (Zubrzycki 1956).

The nature of this migration, and the establishment of the Communist regime in Poland after the war, created a strong feeling of exile among the refugees. Traumatic experiences during the war, in particular Soviet deportation to Siberia from eastern Poland, provided a collective focus for Polish identity, which, in turn, has been reinforced by an active diaspora (Burrell 2006b). To a certain extent, this generation of Polish migrants has sustained a historically specific relationship with Poland characterized by loss (ultimately the loss of homes in the westward shifting of the borders after the war) and fear (of the Communist regime and the problems facing Poland in transition). Facets of this relationship have also been inherited by the second generation. The technological "revolution" of the 1990s, coming very soon after the collapse of the Communist regime, perhaps came too late to repair some of this damage for what is an aging and diminishing population. Despite this, extensive and diverse transnational links were maintained with Poland throughout the Communist period and many of these remaining first-generation Poles, and their families, have been enthusiastically utilizing the opportunities recently offered by cheaper telephone connections, satellite television, travel companies and cheap flights to re-engage with the homeland in their old age (Burrell 2006a).

In addition to this research, I have interviewed a further thirty migrants who came to Britain from Poland between 1950 and 2006, asking questions about their life in Poland, why they left, their life here and their connections back. While Britain was never a key destination for emigration before 2004, several thousand Poles came before 1989 for a range of reasons including marriage, short-term professional employment, and the political dangers of Solidarity activism (Sword 1996). Those who married British citizens were sure of permanent residency, but the professional migrants generally still expected to return when their contracts expired, often ending up settling by default.

Leaving during the Communist period created similar barriers for these migrants to those faced by the earlier settlers. The political divide of the Cold War period not only made emigrating difficult, it also placed a strain on transnational activities. Letters and telephone calls could potentially be monitored and censored and crossing the border back into Poland was generally not a pleasant experience. Telephoning was also very expensive and relied on sufficient telephone access at the other end. As with the earlier generation, however, connections were not severed. Having lived in Communist Poland, returning for visits was a less daunting prospect than for the post-war refugees and all of the respondents from this period spoke extensively of the materiality of their ongoing links with friends and family back home, how they posted and took western goods at every opportunity. The impact of technological advances have offered a similar opportunity to connect with home again, facilitating contact with family especially, but many have come to realize that even just twenty years away has fundamentally changed their relationship with Poland.

For the migrants, who left after 1989, the picture is different again. Leaving Poland was easier, but immigration to Britain was still controlled by strict visa requirements, denying those who were here the opportunity to plan to stay permanently. Britain did not become a major focus for the emigration set in motion by the economic and social changes brought by transition until the 2004 enlargement of the European Union (EU), when Britain, Ireland, and Sweden opened their borders to new EU workers. By the time these barriers had lifted, however, a large Polish labor force was already stretching across western and southern Europe, firmly establishing short-term economic migration as a strategy for coping with transition (Iglicka 2001). These are the people perfectly placed to capitalize on the increased mobility of the last decade, the developments in mobile phones, text messaging, emailing and the Internet, and cheaper travel (Larson, Urry, and Axhausen 2006: 9). Now that the political obstacles to mobility have been removed, the strength of these social mobilities can be tested.

It is tempting to see these different movements as clearly distinct "generations" of Polish migration, each reflecting a different stage in Polish and British history. Just as Eckstein and Barberia (2002) identify clear generations of Cuban migrants in the United States as early refugees and later economic migrants, these Polish migrants appear to fall easily into four clear historical categories: post-war refugees, Communist regime *émigrés*, pre-2004 transition migrants, and EU accession migrants. It follows that their transnational activities should mirror these specific temporal contexts of their leaving and arrival. For example, for those who left Poland due to political reasons and were offered the chance to stay in Britain permanently, transnational activities were never realistically focused on a possible return. The uncertainty of short-term contracts for later migrants, however, placed transnationalism at the center of the project of eventual return. EU membership may yet change this pattern again because, although cheap travel facilitates short-term labor migration, it is now easier to stay too. The transnational activities of the post-war refugees and the post-2004 migrants are clearly different, but whether these movements can be so easily divided into categories is open to question. The sheer diversity of transnational practice defies such easy generalization. Just as some post-war settlers have taken to using the Internet to book their trips to Poland, some recent migrants lack easy Internet access. While some migrants who have been away for years feel they are still close to Poland, others who have been away for a much shorter length of time feel the distance more keenly.

The historicity of this Polish example, however, does offer the opportunity to explore in more depth the interactions between time and transnationalism. This chapter will focus on three of these temporal interactions: the homeland relationship of the post-war refugees, the temporal significance of the Cold War for Polish migration and transnationalism, and the possibility of living in two places at the same time for the most recent migrants.

Going Back in Time? Nostalgia and Refugee Transnationalism

At first glance the relationships refugees sustain between homeland and time seems straightforward. First-generation refugee attachments with their homelands appear to be quintessentially about the past, about reaching out to a lost time by reaching out to that place. In fact, as Boym (2001: xv) suggests, nostalgia, a "condition" often associated with refugee longing for home, is less a pining for a place than "a yearning for a different time." It is certainly natural that the life-histories of elderly refugees especially would depict the homeland in a historical framework, the land of the past and the land of youth. Agata, for example, came to Britain at the end of the Second World War having narrowly escaped deportation to a German labor camp by fleeing to Czechoslovakia. In her interview this link between Poland and the past was very clear. It was particularly important for her to stress how beautiful Poland was then. Whether Poland remains a beautiful place in the present was not discussed:

> I remember '38, '39 the New Year ball, and I was the Queen of the ball! I was surprised when I was sitting there where you have the drinks, and the men came and took me, and says you are the Queen! I was so surprised. You know, the life for me was marvelous. It was beautiful. I knew all of Poland well, for holidays we always went somewhere else to see. Poland was very beautiful country, and for me it was really, when I remember now, it was marvelous. My young years were excellent (Interview with Agata, February 2, 2002).

With this correlation between Poland and the past so apparently strong, it seems reasonable to assume that the transnational activities of the post-war refugees should be focused on resurrecting the past, as much as, if not more so, than re-engaging with Poland as a place. As Lowenthal (1985: 259) has argued, wanting to recapture the past is a human instinct: "As the past seems to recede from us, we seek to re-evoke it by multiplying paraphernalia *about* it—souvenirs, mementoes, historical romances, old photos—and by preserving and rehabilitating old relics." To some extent, it is this desire that drives the transnationalism of these exiles. A good example of this can be seen in the transnational travel activities of those who were born in the eastern regions of Poland, but whose birthplaces were integrated into the Soviet Union (Ukraine, Belarus, Lithuania) in the post-war land settlements. In these cases, going "back" to Poland is arguably more a symbolic pursuit of the past than a genuine reconnection with home as a specific place. Original birthplaces may not be within current Polish borders, but the country itself still somehow manages to act as a bridge to life before emigration. Polish satellite television is avidly watched and "homeland" trips to other parts of Poland are carefully planned.

For these people, visiting the real sites of former homes entails traveling beyond Poland. This situation further demonstrates the link between home and past. For example, the language used when discussing these visits illustrates a significant, and perhaps conscious, muddling of place and time, with returnees referring to now defunct place names in their descriptions of their trips. As Hirsch and Spitzer (2003: 79-80) have illustrated, even though the official name of Hirsch's mother's birthplace has changed many times, it is known within the family as Czernowitz, not inter-war Romanian Cernăuți, post-war Soviet Chernovtsky, or current Ukrainian Chernivtsi. Highlighting a similar attachment, Irena, a respondent who had been deported to Siberia as a baby in 1940, telephoned me last year to say how excited she was about her forthcoming trips to "Wilno" and Warszawa where she would be attending a commemoration of the Warsaw Uprising. Despite not originating from the region around "Wilno" herself, she was still looking forward to visiting the area, resolutely calling the capital of Lithuania (Vilnius) by its pre-war Polish name. For many of the post-war refugees it seems that Poland's post-war borders did not change at all; the geography of the homeland continues to be imagined in a specific historical context (Burrell 2006a: 104-5).

Significantly, these visits to "Wilno" and to commemorate the Warsaw Uprising were part of an organized coach trip specifically designed for Poles in Britain. The post-war Polish settlers have benefited enormously from the increase in "roots tourism" (Basu 2005), using cheaper travel and the growth of organized tours to rediscover Poland. On these visits their behavior is arguably closer to that of tourists than transnational returnees as they seek out sites of historical significance or landscapes of natural beauty rather than catching up with family members and becoming re-immersed in "Polish" life. This focus does set these refugees apart from other migrant populations. According to Stephenson (2002), for example, Jamaican return trips are equally sacred, but typical tourist activities are assiduously avoided by the returnees when they visit. It is possible that the experience of being refugees for so long has severed the "real" ties (social, familial) that the Poles would need to sustain similar trips, with new, very different ties being created in their place. It could be argued that their visits, therefore, do not succeed in locating them back in time as much as highlight how much time has passed since they left.

Analyzing the character of Polish first-generation transnationalism is important because this transnationalism reflects the wider impact that technological advances have on personal experiences and perceptions of time. For settled migrants, enhanced travel opportunities and Internet access especially are used to try to bring the past closer to the present; they are used essentially as rooting technologies. Transnationalism, therefore, allows people to access different times *at* different times. Through a variety of transnational activities immigrants can revive different memories at different points in the present and be regularly transported back in time in different ways. Significantly, this historically focused transnationalism is not limited to first-generation migrants, but has been inherited by their children. In all of the interviews I undertook with second-generation respondents the association of Poland with the past was even more noticeable. Most started their interviews by recounting some background about their parents' migration to Britain and almost all spoke explicitly of Poland as being the place of their family's and their own "roots." Trips to Poland were arguably more important for these respondents than for the original migrants; visits were recounted with great reverence and framed as events that finally made their personal histories make sense. As Hirsch and Spitzer (2003) have demonstrated, these visits offer a connection with the past that cannot be achieved any other way. Only the places themselves can animate the familiar yet unknowable stories of the past. Kasia, born in Britain with two Polish parents, spoke of her trips to Poland:

> The summer before last we took the children to show them, I definitely felt different. The way of life. I went just before Solidarity started, life was so difficult then. I went over for Christmas and there was one moment when we went to church for Christmas

Eve, and sang all the carols and things that we have always done here, and I got this sense that this is what it is all about. I suppose it is that sort of personal connection, my experience, their experience. (Interview with Kasia, February 9, 2001.)

Halina, another second-generation respondent, voiced similar sentiments and spoke particularly of the need to take the next generation again to Poland, so that they too could feel more connected to their roots. Visiting Poland, therefore, is viewed as a trusted means of transmitting family history and identity:

> I'd like to, because I haven't been for a long time, I was 21 last time I went. I'd like to go because I'd like the boys to go, and it is my mum's dear wish that they should go. (Interview with Halina, July 3, 2000.)

These links are perhaps most significant for the migrants who were born in Poland, but were forced to migrate before they were old enough to form a strong consciousness of their environment. Zena was deported to Siberia as a very young child and has no memory of living in Poland. Her trips to Poland are ultimately an attempt to find a sense of belonging *somewhere* and recreate an attachment that was severed over fifty years ago:

> My mother did, I do go on holidays but I don't keep in touch with the family, they are very distant family, and when I do go back to Poland I usually go to do some sightseeing and see the country. I still have a very strong desire to live there for a while, very strong. I feel very much that I don't belong anywhere, although I was born there it is not like the country I grew up in and I very much feel that I don't have the sense of belonging. I'd like to go and spend more time there ... You don't know where your roots are. I feel quite at home when I go to Poland, and I often think, oh I wouldn't mind staying here. I went for two holidays this year, and I would love to spend the whole summer in Poland. But then your family is in England, so you are really torn. (Interview with Zena, November 22, 2000.)

The numerous Polish diaspora genealogical Internet sites (for example, Polishroots.com and Rootspoland.com) demonstrate the depth of this quest for identity among first-, second-, and even third-generation Poles abroad. These sites promise a closer connection to family history through intensive research in specific locations, again tying past and place together and utilizing modern technology to try to go back in time.

In many respects these attempts to re-engage with Poland have been successful. There are certainly significant movements of second-generation British Poles "returning" to Poland to take advantage of the economic opportunities offered by transition for highly skilled westerners (Gorny and Osipovic 2006). The continued presence of Poland in family life, even through memories, has equipped many of the second generation with enough confidence in their Polish connections to move there to work. This tendency to view Poland through a historical lens, however, has received considerable criticism both from other Polish migrants and from academic observers. Temple (1996: 93) has argued that British Poles are "stuck in the past" and are disconnected from the present realities of Poland. Breytonbach (1991: 70) has challenged the tendency of exiles in general to "wallow in self-pity" in the "suspended state" created by the refugee experience. "On auspicious occasions," it is charged, exiles "bring forth the relics and sing the cracked songs and end up arguing like parakeets about what 'back home' was really like." More recent arrivals from Poland have been particularly struck by the antiquated Polishness they have found among the post-war settlers. Julia, who migrated to Britain in 1999, was especially critical of the favored Polish satellite channel *TV Polonia*, the station deliberately aimed at the diasporic audience:

> Now I only have one proper channel which is *TV Polonia* which is for ex-pats. But I would say it is a program for older people, for older people who are really not much in touch with Poland, or haven't been to Poland. There are lots of sentimental programs that I am just not interested in, or some repeats of old films that I have seen millions of times. When I still lived in Poland two years ago I used to watch Polish soap operas, so when I am in Poland I still watch it, but those episodes they have on *TV Polonia* they are still the ones that I used to watch in Poland when I used to live there. I just don't even watch it any more because I get confused. (Interview with Julia, May 5, 2005.)

Barbara, who came to Britain in 1988, was shocked by the level of patriotism she encountered among those post-war settlers who could not even remember Poland:

> This patriotism, this probably was such an atmosphere of patriotism because this woman Ania, she never remembered Poland, she had never been, she was taken as a child, and she never remembered Poland, and she learnt the Polish that she speaks without any accent, you cannot recognize, it sounds like any Polish accent from people that live there. And she goes there, for each holiday she goes to Poland, she had never been there before, and she goes there and she enjoys holidays there even now. That for me is really something. (Interview with Barbara, February 8, 2006.)

Several of the first-generation respondents were sensitive about this issue, clearly aware that their intense longing for Poland has been viewed negatively. Danuta also came to Britain as a child refugee, having spent most of her youngest years in a camp in Africa. She raised this matter unprompted in her interview, feeling moved to defend the strength of attachment maintained by the exiles:

> We have lived here a long time and yet we have the feeling, I don't know whether it is inborn, inside, we have a feeling. I care about what is happening there, I care about

the politics, that they do a proper job and help people. It is such a big country, and a third of them live abroad. There are lots of Polish people. Most of them care. Some of them in Poland said they didn't understand Polish people coming to Poland from abroad, and longing and feeling nostalgia for the country, and then they themselves went and lived in Germany, or other countries, and they have the same feeling now so they understand that. (Interview with Danuta, August 8, 2002.)

But is the charge of being "stuck in the past" a justified observation of the post-war refugees, and even of long-established refugee populations in general? First, nostalgia and disconnection with the present homeland are issues that *all* migrants potentially have to navigate, regardless of when they left and even in many cases regardless of the circumstances of their leaving. While refugees are perhaps more likely to cling to past ideas of home, a need created by traumatic departures, these sentiments are not exclusive to these types of migration movements. Katarzyna left Poland to come to Britain in 1988 to join her mother who had already moved here. She was not forced to leave and has returned many times since. In her interview, however, she spoke about the temporal disconnection of the post-war generation and *also* of her own temporal distance from Poland:

> They got stuck in the time that they left, and this is the danger where I'm going to be probably the same, because I am stuck in the time I left, I know the Poland from when I left, everything that is new now, it is very strange for me ... sometimes it is funny because you are having a conversation and they are *telling* you how it is in Poland, and you are thinking "no it's not, it's not." That's how it is. I can see the same pattern repeating. People that came like I did almost 20 years ago, they have detached themselves from society, so you don't know what's going on. Even when I watch TV, sometimes it's OK, but sometimes it aggravates me, the sayings, the new words that they have, usually from English and they are saying the Polish way, and I am thinking "no, no," it just doesn't sound right. (Interview with Katarzyna, February 3, 2006.)

Second, to simply label the post-war generation's transnational activities as nostalgic, and therefore somehow less authentic, also misunderstands the fundamental impact of these connections on the temporal experiences of the exiles. Even if the intention behind these transnational activities is to try to go back in time, it is impossible to engage with any transnational links without being exposed to the contemporary realities of the homeland. For all the emotion of Hirsch and Spitzer's (2005: 83, 92) trip to Czernowitz, their account of this visit is interspersed with observations about the present landscape and even the noise of the traffic. If the past is accessed at all, the access itself takes place in the present.

It is better, therefore, to understand this transnationalism as bringing the past and the homeland together into the present, rather than enabling some sort of traveling backwards in time. Poland can be embedded in the daily lives of the settlers *now* and as such is also fundamentally part of future plans too, perhaps not permanent return, but upcoming trips and connections. It is also significant that the Polish respondents have built much of their transnationalism on new relationships with Poland. How can they be going back in time if their behavior does not even try to emulate the life they left behind? These new bonds may be "touristy" in nature, but they are a powerful way of healing old wounds. As Stephenson (2002: 397) comments on Jamaican homeland travel, leisure visits are an important way of overcoming traumatic experiences of migration. If Jamaican travel promotes new mobilities in a historical context of forced slave trade migration, Polish travel also illustrates the new power of the migrants to control their own movements across borders. As Ehrkamp (2005: 346) notes regarding the proliferation of Turkish travel agents in Germany, homeland tourism demonstrates above all that the relationship maintained with "home" is not static.

Polish refugee transnationalism, therefore, is far more than nostalgia. The most common activities of telephoning and sending letters to friends and family are not even explicitly nostalgic in themselves. The links maintained with Poland have allowed the respondents the luxury of accessing multiple times in addition to multiple places. They permit them to go back in time, but crucially, these journeys into history are placed in a contemporary context, anchored firmly in the present. This ability to access different times and places is so important because it enables migrants to find continuities with their past lives, but also forces them to confront change. In fact, most of these respondents and their children have developed ambiguous, contradictory relationships with Poland, aware of the gap between the present-day Poland and the place of their memories and stories. Second-generation Halina demonstrated her conflicting views of Poland when she described the country's landscape in her interview: "But it's grim, it's very picturesque, very scenic, but the towns, there is a lot of pollution."

Temporal Dimensions of Geo-Political Divides

Any temporal dislocations between the post-war *émigrés* and Poland cannot be properly understood without considering the wider geo-political contexts of the post-war world. The distances that developed between Poland and the post-war population especially appear to have been exacerbated by very negative perceptions of the Communist regime. From their exilic vantage point, the Poles in Britain were able to focus on the worst aspects of the Communist establishment and, tying personal and national biography together, could continue to view the regime as an aberration and a deviation from Poland's intended progression. Thus, when presented with "free" Poland in 1989 many could only focus on what the country could have been and should have been, measuring Poland's development against an imagined ideal. Stefan, an ex-serviceman and key community figure, was incredibly disappointed with the state of Poland after communism:

> Unfortunately my country being behind the Iron Curtain, it's economically poorer than it should be. Western Europe was progressing, and Eastern Europe under the Russian rule just couldn't make any progress. Everything was dominated by the stupid ideology of communism... the country is very poor in general. We need autobahns, the country was neglected for fifty years and they are trying to catch it up now and that is rather difficult. They need to rebuild this country but it will take time. The problem is not only economically, but mentally. There were two generations brought up under the communist system, and I'm afraid it left a heavy toll on the two generations. They just cannot think properly. When you talk to the young Poles, educated and so on, their idea of justice in the world, they just can not understand, "what are you talking about?" When I talk to my family, my nephews, we are not thinking on the same level, so it will take time for the two generations to come to the idea of democracy and the way of living as Poland used to be. The two generations grew up and were educated under that system, and I'm afraid they are the lost generation, so we need a young new generation to start in a different way. (Interview with Stefan, January 26, 2001.)

From a temporal perspective, these sentiments are particularly significant because they suggest a reversal in the assumed relationship which migrants form between homeland and time. Usually the homeland is charged with "changing," an implied recognition that time has moved on *there* while the exiles have been left stranded in a temporal vacuum. Stefan, however, clearly does not feel that *he* has been left behind; rather Poland itself has lagged behind, blighted by years of a "backward" regime.

The spatial dynamics of east and west in Europe have been infused with temporal significance since at least the eighteenth century. While "the west" was considered synonymous with civilization, travel writers were able to describe journeying from west to east as "like traveling back in time" (Hagen 2003: 492). These constructs are still clearly visible with "east-west" continuing to be conceptualized through a "past-future" axis. Second-generation Grazyna's impression of Poland on her first visit there illustrates this very well. She "couldn't help notice the amazing difference in the standard of living, walking down the street it was quite obvious you were from the West."[1] Just as many theories of transition have implied (Burawoy and Verdery 1999: 4), in the eyes of the interviewees Poland needs to be brought up to date. The country is visualized as being on a temporal journey that will see the country eventually meet the norms of "western" economies and democracies and "return to Europe" (Hagen 2003). Ziegler (2002: 685) has demonstrated how this vision has underpinned transitional political positioning in Poland, with various governments emphasizing their "new" cartographical situation in Europe, closer to west than east. Importantly, these associations were voiced as strongly in the interviews held with very recent migrants as with those held with the post-war refugees. Gosia came to the Midlands in 2005 and was very keen to talk about Poland's temporal challenges:

> That is the thing in Poland, it is so messy, all about bribery, and I don't really want to talk about it. That's the next thing they really run away from, the political system in Poland is just hopeless, and I think a lot of the other problems, the economics, it all comes out from that side of the Polish system, and I hoped that the new election would change everything but it looks like nothing is going to change. So I think that we need the next generation, 50 years or something, to change the mentality of people, but now it's just hopeless. I am glad to be here and not being worried and thinking about the how the political system in Poland influences my life. I can do what I want in my life, so I don't really care about that now. (Interview with Gosia, November 18, 2005.)

The respondents were almost unanimous in their suggestion that Poland has failed, or has at least not yet fulfilled, the temporal aspect of this return to Europe. For Gosia, as for Stefan, migration has repositioned her temporal relationship with Poland. She too has left her homeland behind.

These disparities between East-West in Europe had the greatest impact on those migrants who left Poland during the time of the Communist regime. During the Cold War, going back and forth between Poland and Britain was a difficult experience spatially (visas, border guards), but it also exposed the temporal dislocation between the two countries. First, before the travel "revolution" return journeys were very long, usually involving more than one day's solid driving; Poland was not close to Britain in terms of traveling distance. The situation in Poland on arrival, furthermore, catapulted the migrants back in time in more than one way, through family dynamics, but also in lifestyle, living standards and daily uses of time. Just as Boym (2001: xv) found that her first return trip to Russia was like "traveling into another temporal zone," transporting her from a time-pressured western environment and reintroducing her to a society which did not appear to regard time as a precious commodity, these Polish migrants found themselves re-immersed in different temporal practices when they went back. Iwona, who migrated at the age of 19 in 1961, found herself spending much of her return visits queuing for hours for household goods with her mother, a normal part of life in 1970s and 1980s Poland, but utterly removed from her life in Britain:

> When I went back, from England, when I went back on holiday, I used to stand in the queue. Sugar, they used to sell only a kilo of sugar for one person, so my mum, and I was next to my mum to get another kilo. And whatever, salt, whatever. Not for myself, because I knew I was coming back, but for them. (Interview with Iwona, June 26, 2006.)

This divergence in living standards, coupled with the strong association between "west" and "best" in Poland, was an important driving force fuelling the transnational connections sustained by the migrants who left at the time of the Communist regime. As Iwona's testimony demonstrates, it is often family and social circles that act as the main sites of these larger geo-political manifestations. She spent much of her interview detailing the demands her family and friends in Poland had placed on her to keep sending western goods, and spoke about her assumed responsibility for bridging the same divide that she had managed to cross for those left behind. Her family and friends' perceptions of the United Kingdom placed so much pressure on her that it ultimately damaged her relationship with them:

> After my daughter was two, after about four or five years I went back for the first time for two months, I went back to Poland. For two months, to my mum's. Everybody was jealous, "oh you are in England", and at that time I had to borrow the money to go to Poland because I missed it so much that I had to borrow the money to go and visit my family. And everybody was so jealous, "you are from England, a different class, a different standard of living", and I worked here so hard, I cried so much, and I couldn't say anything. (Interview with Iwona, June 26, 2006.)

When migrants leave, therefore, clearly has a fundamental impact on the type of transnational connections maintained. In this case, the Polish migrants emigrating at the time of communism found that the divide they had to negotiate between Poland and the UK was as much a temporal one as a spatial one.

The Limits of Simultaneity

If the timing of migration is so important for migrant transnationalism, it is evidently significant that the most recent migrants leaving Poland are doing so in a different temporal context again. The last fifteen years has been a period of rapid political and technological change. Not only have the political barriers of the Cold War ostensibly dissolved, confirmed by the 2004 EU enlargement, but global time-space dimensions also have diminished substantially through intensifications in travel and communications links. Izabela came to the UK in 1990 and has seen these changes transform her ability to "go home":

> So we are there quite often now. Every summer, at least five to six weeks and now in half terms and sometimes when there is Christmas or Easter break we quite often go, especially now that the cheap airlines are going… Our entire family is there… I think you gather a circle of friends in the very early years in your life, so all of these are still in Poland for us. So yes sometimes I feel very lonely, but now with the cheaper fares, Internet, cheaper phones, because they introduced fantastic phones for 2p per minute, I can afford to phone, if I would like to, to phone every day, it is much cheaper. You have a double income and you have all this communication possibility. In the beginning we didn't have the money and there was nothing like that, the Internet, it was introduced a bit later, and even if we had had access to Internet, they don't have it back in Poland. Flights were expensive. So all these circumstances worked against us you see, now everything is for us. (Interview with Izabela, October 3, 2005.)

Transnationalism, although clearly not a new activity (Morawska, 1999), is now embedded as an ordinary aspect of migrants' lives. All of the more recent migrants spoke about the ease of travel between Poland and the UK and in particular the proliferation of low-cost flights offered by easyJet, Ryanair, and Wizz Air. This is one way in which the temporal distance between the two has dramatically been reduced. According to Rafal, who left Poland in 2005:

> I have to go back to Poland even more often, every month, it is so easy to travel right now. It is very cheap. From Stansted there is a direct flight to Wrocław, I paid, how much did I pay, from Stansted to Wrocław it takes two hours and I paid only £33 twice. (Interview with Rafal, November 19, 2005.)

Advances in telephone connections and wider accessibility to the Internet have similarly reduced the time lag between the two countries in terms of information exchange. Again, the testimonies collected from the newer migrants placed heavy emphasis on how easy it is to maintain close links with Poland. Rafal talked about his daily cyber activities:

> Every day, chatting with my girlfriend, parents and friends over the Internet via audio messaging programs like Skype. I also visit Polish Internet portals to read the news a few times a week. (Interview with Rafal, November 19, 2005.)

Joanna, who came in 2005, was pleased that staying in such intimate contact with Poland has proved to be so straightforward. She starts her day by checking Polish news over the Internet and is in close telephone contact:

> Everyday I check my favorite newspaper on the Internet, it's the start of the day to check Polish newspaper on the Internet, to be orientated a little bit with what is hap-

pening now. And my dad keeps me, he emails me all the news, the political news, our new president, things like that.

Q: Do you get to phone regularly?

Yes, because it is quite cheap, to my surprise, to phone Poland. So I am in touch by email and phone. (Interview with Joanna, December 10, 2005.)

As Vertovec (2002: 222) has noted, transnational telephone calls are incredibly significant in migrants' lives: "The personal, real-time contact provided by international telephone calls is transforming the everyday lives of innumerable migrants." Regular calls to friends and family in Poland are integral to life in Britain and offer a renewable up-to-date connection with the social and emotional home environment. The same point can be made about instant messaging, email exchange and even access to Internet sites.

In general, the interviews offered very positive portrayals of the level of mobility facilitated by these developments. The huge diversity of transnational options ensures that the migrants can "travel" to Poland in numerous different ways: physically, imaginatively, virtually and through direct communication with people there (Larson, Urry, and Axhausen 2006: 59-60). Certainly in academic discourse the notion of being in two places at the same time has helped to sustain a celebratory stance on the social possibilities of transnational connections. As M. P. Smith notes (2005: 239), simultaneity and speed are now anticipated characteristics of transnationalism. He observes especially how commentaries on transnationalism have helped to create a new perception of time: "Co-presence in more than one spatial location (place/country/locality) is viewed as occurring in the postmodern 'now' rather than, as in earlier times, in sequenced stages of time (before/after), space (sending/receiving), and place (here/there)" (Smith 2005: 240). But, as he suggests, the simultaneity experienced by migrants is possibly overplayed, clearly has limits, and potentially brings with it new strains and costs.

This apparent ability to live in two places at the same time does not necessarily translate well into the lives of ordinary people. High speed Internet access and cheap airfares do not always prevent migrants from experiencing the old fashioned sentiment of missing home. Migrants, in fact, are often more firmly emotionally rooted in specific places than over-emphasis on mobility allows for. Longing for home is also not exclusive to refugees and elderly migrants. Many of the young post-2004 migrants interviewed counterbalanced their discussions of mobility with comments about how *distant* they feel from Poland. As Clarke (2005:

312) has observed of British gap year travelers in Australia, close contact often highlights just how far away home is. You can phone home, but you cannot touch the people on the other end of the line. In her interview, Gosia spoke both about missing specific people and places and about how she tries to alleviate this distance. Her assertions that "it's fine" and that there is "no problem" staying in close contact reinforce her open admission of missing home:

> I miss people, and I miss places, my places. I'm here and I'm fine, as I told you I'm open to new places and new people, that's fine. But they are not my places and my people. I can meet people, I can talk to them, I can even have fun doing this, but it is not emotional. I miss people and I miss my places...
>
> *Q Is it easy to keep in contact with Poland?*
>
> Yes, it's very nice because the cost of, we have got cheap number so we can call Poland for 1p a minute, sometimes cheaper than calling different English people. No problem. We have got the Internet and emails everyday and we spend all the weekend on the phone in fact, talking to everybody. So no problems. We get letters and we send letters sometimes. Yesterday I got a CD with pictures from my friend. (Interview with Gosia, November 18, 2005.)

Similarly, Adriana, who migrated in 2005, explained that despite good Internet and telephone connections, "Of course it is not the same, like I sit here with you and talk. Still it is relatively good." (Interview with Adriana, November 24, 2005.)

If spatial and emotional distances have not been fully eroded by the speed and ease of transnational connections, there are also further temporal implications resulting from these difficulties. Ultimately, it takes time to be transnational. However mundane transnational activities are, they still require a long-standing temporal commitment to their upkeep and force adaptations to the daily rhythms of life. The biggest casualty of attempted simultaneity is therefore spontaneity. Transnational connections usually have to be planned in advance and carefully orchestrated to take into account personal timetables in two countries (Larson, Urry, and Axhausen 2006: 94). Crucially, the homeland is accessed *at certain times* not *all the time*. With the possible exception of marathon satellite television viewing, temporal connections can only ever be short-lived. When these various activities end, the migrants are left in one place knowing that time is moving on in a different direction in the other place. It is therefore impossible to live in one country and be *continuously* connected into another. This perhaps explains the importance attached to these moments of connection in the collected interviews. Transnational time is precious time and is treated and narrated accordingly. Before an

Internet connection was even installed in her flat, Elzbieta, who came to Britain in 2006, was anticipating the prospect of a new routine involving Friday night Internet parties with friends and family in Poland:

> When I get finally the Internet connection, my parents have the Internet as well, and all my friends, so we will organize some kind of Internet party every Friday, stuff like that. (Interview with Elzbieta, May 5, 2006.)

In spite of the plethora of mechanisms in place to maintain transnational links, being away from Poland ultimately means missing out on real-time experiences. New connections with friends and family have to be remanufactured, fundamentally altering the character of these relationships. One of the most important temporal implications of this is the time needed to adjust to this situation. More settled migrants have already gone through a process of accepting this reconfiguration in their homeland interactions. The current post-2004 migrants, in contrast, are still learning to cope with the changes migration inevitably brings. Several respondents, for example, expressed surprise at how quickly they have lost touch with Poland. For Elzbieta, six months away from Poland has been long enough to make her feel more disconnected than she expected:

> I want to. I want to know, maybe I feel quite connected but I am not quite as connected as I was in Poland, and I have the feeling that for some stuff I look now from a different point of view. There was excitement about a couple of things that happened in Poland, and I found out about it one or two weeks later, and I thought "oh my god" again, "stupid things in Poland." (Interview with Elzbieta, May 5, 2006.)

These issues of temporal detachment are closely related to the fundamental mechanisms of time and life-course. As the data collected for the Home Office's Worker Registration Scheme suggests (Home Office 2006: 10), most of the post-2004 migrants are relatively young (82 percent aged 18 to 34) and as such are at a point in their lives when distance from Poland and the need to undertake time consuming transnational activities do not have such a significant impact on their lives and family roles. At this point in their life-cycles they can juggle family demands in Poland and forge a new life in Britain at the same time.

However, while their lives may be balanced between the two places now, the real durability of this transnationalism will be tested in the future as they become older. For those who do not yet have children, where will they choose to live when they have their own families? How will they negotiate the needs of their Poland-based family when their parents age and become more dependent? These are the problems that the emigrants of the 1980s are now facing. Many of these respondents spoke about the guilt they feel at not being able to look after elderly parents and even discussed the dilemmas they face about a possible return to Poland for retirement. Izabela has been in the UK for thirteen years and is already thinking about how to resolve these tensions:

> My husband has mentioned quite often that on our retirement we have to go back, but then I think about our kids. Do we want to be parted from them? But the idea of being cremated in the local crematorium and staying here after life is just killing me, so I really don't know. It is a dilemma. (Interview with Izabela, October 3, 2005.)

Living across two nations may be sustainable in life, but death ultimately forces a declaration of belonging to one country or the other. These issues, which preoccupy the Communist-era migrants who are now in their forties and fifties, are yet to feature in the life strategies of the vast majority of the most recent migrants. Regardless of how far technology advances again in the next twenty years, it is still unlikely that these concerns will be resolved for those migrants who decide to stay in Britain.

It is clear that these recent migrants are enjoying unprecedented freedom of movement within Europe and are actively exercising their new rights of mobility. The 2004 enlargement of the European Union was an extremely important event in terms of the symbolism of east and west in Europe. As Adriana commented, "When we entered the Union you could just go then, provided you have the money." Since 2004 the only real obstacles to movement and transnationalism are economic and social in nature, rather than political. What the interviews have demonstrated, however, is just how important these obstacles continue to be in perpetuating temporal and spatial distances between different countries. Even in the twenty-first century migrants' lives still seem to revolve around the navigation of borders and obstructions.

Conclusions

This chapter has demonstrated how time, as much as space, is at the heart of the transnational experience. Moving to another country and then sustaining ties back again fundamentally reconfigures the temporal lives of migrants in many different ways. The Polish example used here has highlighted three key scales of this temporal repositioning.

First, the experiences of all the Polish migrants interviewed have demonstrated the significance of the wider historical and political contexts of the initial migration and subsequent transnationalism. War, Cold War and now EU membership have all dominated Polish mobility, governing the divides created between the migrants and their homeland. The acts of leaving and returning were, in turn, traumatized, politicized and liberalized. Individual acts of migration and transnational contact have therefore changed over time along side these broader shifts. Key moments in time have had inordinate influence over the transnational connections maintained between the two countries; the 1947 Polish Resettlement Act; the establishment of the Communist regime in Poland; the collapse of the regime in 1989; and Britain's decision in 2004 to accept Polish workers. Transnationalism is therefore shaped both by the historical context in which it is located and the historical contexts it traverses.

Second, the interviews have also revealed how closely transnational activities are tied to life-course time and rhythms. Just as transnationalism operates in a historical framework, it also works within the parameters of personal expectations of the life-cycle. Transnational activities therefore reflect the life stages of the actors, whether satellite television viewing among elderly refugees or instant messaging among young Internet-literate migrants. Transnational decisions are influenced by life-cycle considerations, taking advantage of not having dependants to spend money on flights back, choosing where to spend retirement, or going to Poland to reconnect with a lost childhood. Ordinary people's transnationalism changes with the passing of life-course time.

Finally, this chapter has demonstrated the enormous impact that transnationalism exerts over personal experiences of time on an even smaller scale. For the most recent migrants, transnationalism is a time-consuming part of everyday life, seeping into daily decisions and structures. Now it is easier to access another place, migrants find themselves spending considerable amounts of time doing so. The ability to go back has particularly important implications for the experiences of time among the settled refugee population. Through transnational pastimes these people can seek to revive their memories of life before migration, but also at the same time become better acquainted with present-day Poland. By facilitating spatial travel transnationalism has in some senses aided time travel, at least emotionally.

Collectively, however, these different temporal contexts all highlight the continued spatial limitations of transnationalism. It is still impossible to be physically in two places at the same time and it still takes time to travel and to plan transnational exchanges. The spatial dimensions of transnational activity are ultimately still shaped by temporal constraints.

Note

1. The interview with "Grazyna" was recorded for the *Millennium Memory Bank Archive*, 10.3.99. Ref: 1CDR0016353 NSA. It may be accessed at: http://www.bl.uk/collections/sound-archive/millenni.html.

References

Adam, B. (1995). *Timewatch: The Social Analysis of Time*. Cambridge: Polity Press.
Anwar, M. (1979). *The Myth of Return: Pakistanis in Britain*. London: Heinemann.
Basch, L., N. Glick Schiller, and C. Szanton Blanc (1994). *Nations Unbound: Transnational Projects, Postcolonial Predicaments and Deterritorialized Nation-states*. Basel: Gordon and Breach.
Basu, P. (2005). "Roots-Tourism as Return Movement: Semantics and the Scottish Diaspora." In *Emigrant Homecomings: The Return Movement of Emigrants, 1600-2000* (pp. 131-50). Manchester: Manchester University Press.
Boym, S. (2001). *The Future of Nostalgia*. New York: Basic Books.
Breytonbach, B. (1991). "The Long March from Hearth to Heart." *Social Research* 58 (1): 69-83.
Bryceson, D., and U. Vuorella (2002). *The Transnational Family: New European Frontiers and Global Networks*. Oxford: Berg.
Burawoy, M., and K. Verdery (eds.) (1999). "Introduction." In *Uncertain Transition: Ethnographies of Change in the Postsocialist World* (pp. 1-17). Lanham, MD: Rowman and Littlefield.
_____ (eds.) (1999). *Uncertain Transition: Ethnographies of Change in the Postsocialist World*. Lanham, MD: Rowman and Littlefield.
Burrell, K. (2006a). *Moving Lives: Narratives of Nation and Migration among Europeans in Post-war Britain*. Aldershot: Ashgate.
_____ (2006b). "Personal, Inherited, Collective: Communicating and Layering Memories of Forced Polish Migration." *Immigrants and Minorities* 24 (2): 144-63.
_____ and P. Panayi (eds.). (2006). *Histories and Memories: Migrants and their History in Britain*. London: I.B. Tauris.
Chamberlain, M. (1997). *Narratives of Exile and Return*. London: Macmillan.
Clarke, N. (2005). "Detailing Transnational Lives of the Middle: British Working Holiday Makers in Australia," *Journal of Ethnic and Migration Studies* 31 (2): 307-322.
Crang, P., C. Dwyer, and P. Jackson (2003). "Transnationalism and the Spaces of Commodity Culture." *Progress in Human Geography* 27 (4): 438-56.
Eckstein, S., and L. Barberia (2002). "Grounding Immigrant Generations in History: Cuban Americans and their Transnational Ties." *International Migration Review* 36 (3): 799-837.
Ehrkamp, P. (2005). "Placing Identities: Transnational Practices and Local Attachments of Turkish Immigrants in Germany" *Journal of Ethnic and Migration Studies* 31 (2): 345-364.
Ganga, D. (2006). "Reinventing the Myth of Return: Older Italians in Nottingham." In *Histories and Memories: Migrants and their History in Britain* (pp. 114-30). London: I.B. Tauris.
Gardner, K., and R. Grillo (2002). "Transnational households and ritual: an overview." *Global Networks* 2 (3): 179-90.
Gorny, A., and D. Osipovic (2006). *Return Migration of Second Generation British Poles*, Centre of Migration Research Working Paper No. 6/64. Warsaw University: Warsaw.

Gosden, C. (1994). *Social Being and Time*. Oxford: Blackwell.
Hagen, J. (2003) "Redrawing the Imagined Map of Europe: the Rise and Fall of the 'Center'." *Political Geography* 22 (5): 489-517.
Harper, M. (ed.) (2005). *Emigrant Homecomings: The Return Movement of Emigrants, 1600-2000*, Manchester: Manchester University Press.
Hirsch M., and L. Spitzer (2003). "'We would not have come without you:' Generations of Nostalgia." In *Contested Pasts: the Politics of Memory* (pp. 79-95). Oxford: Routledge.
Hodgkin, K., and S. Radstone (eds.) (2003). *Contested Pasts: the Politics of Memory*. Oxford: Routledge.
Home Office, Department for Work and Pensions, HM Revenue and Customs and the Department for Communities and Local Government (2006). *Accession Monitoring Report May 2004- September 2006*. Accessed at: http://www.ind.homeoffice.gov.uk/aboutus/ reports/accession_monitoring_report.
Iglicka, K. (2001). *Poland's Postwar Dynamic of Migration*. Aldershot: Ashgate.
Larson, J., J. Urry, and K. Axhausen (2006). *Report to the UK Department for Transport: Social Networks and Future Mobilities*. University of Lancaster, Institute for Transport Planning and Systems, Swiss Federal Institute of Technology Zurich.
Levitt, P. (2001). *The Transnational Villagers*. Berkeley, CA: University of California Press.
Lowenthal, D. (1985). *The Past Is a Foreign Country*. Cambridge: Cambridge University Press.
May, J., and N. Thrift (2001). "Introduction." In *Timespace: Geographies of Temporality* (pp. 1-46). London: Routledge.
―――――― (eds.). (2001). *Timespace: Geographies of Temporality*, London: Routledge.
Morawska, E. (1999). *The New-Old Transmigrants, Their Transnational Lives, and Ethnicization: A Comparison of 19th/20th and 20th/21st Century Situations*. Florence: European University Institute.
Plane, D. A. (1993). "Demographic Influences on Migration." *Regional Studies* 27 (4): 375-83.
Rushdie, S. (1991). *Imaginary Homelands: Essays and Criticisms 1981-1991*. London: Granta.
Smith, M. P. (2001). *Transnational Urbanism: Locating Globalization*, Malden, MA: Blackwell.
―――――― (2005). "Transnational Urbanism Revisited" *Journal of Ethnic and Migration Studies*, 31 (2), 235-44.
―――――― and L. E. Guarnizo (eds.). (1998). *Transnationalism from Below*. New Brunswick, NJ: Transaction Publishers.
Smith, R. C. (1998). "Transnational Localities: Community, technology and the politics of membership within the context of Mexico and U.S. migration." In *Transnationalism from Below* (pp. 196-238). New Brunswick, NJ: Transaction Publishers.
Stephenson, M. (2002). "Traveling to the Ancestral Homelands: The Aspirations and Experiences of a UK Caribbean Community." *Current Issues in Tourism* 5 (2): 378-425.
Tanhahill, J. A. (1958). *European Volunteer Workers in Britain*. Manchester: Manchester University Press.
Temple, B. (1996). "Time Travels: Time, Oral Histories and British-Polish Identities." *Time and Society* 5 (1): 85-96.
Sword, K. (1996). *Identity in Flux: The Polish Community in Britain*. London: SSEES University of London.

Vertovec, S. (2004). "Cheap Calls: the social glue of migrant transnationalism." *Global Networks* 4 (2): 219-24.

Wimmer, A., and N. Glick Schiller (2002). "Methodological nationalism and beyond: nation-state building, migration and the social sciences." *Global Networks* 2 (4): 301-334.

Ziegler, D. J., (2002). "Post-communist Eastern Europe and the Cartography of." *Political Geography* 21 (5): 671-686.

Zubrzycki, J. (1956). *Polish Immigrants in Britain: A Study of Adjustment*. The Hague: Martinus Nijhoff.

3

Transnationalism in the Ethno-National City: Migration and Anti-Racism in Belfast[1]

Peter Geoghegan

Sectarian division is such an integral, though unfortunate, part of the lived experience of Belfast city that it has long been considered a subject of mirth as well as conflict. A popular Belfast joke concerns a tourist walking through a no man's land between Protestant and Catholic neighborhoods. The unsuspecting *flâneur* is grabbed by a masked man who asks: "Are you a Protestant or a Catholic?" The tourist answers: "I'm a Jew." Without a moments hesitation the masked man enquires whether the tourist is "A Catholic Jew or a Protestant Jew." While the ridiculousness of trying to force a Jew into the Catholic/Protestant binary serves to mock this distinction it also attests to the power, and relative impermeability, of sectarian division. This joke has been recycled many times with different ethnic, religious and racial groups, but the denial of the existence of "other traditions" in Northern Ireland remains the salient point (McVeigh 1998).

Belfast has been often described as a contested city divided between Catholics and Protestants, but rarely, if ever, as a transnational city.[2] Minority ethnic communities were rendered invisible during "the Troubles" and the history of small-scale migration to the city was rarely mentioned in public discourses (McVeigh 1998). The tensions between Catholics and Protestants in Northern Ireland have not gone away, but since the signing of the Belfast Agreement in 1998 the conflict in the region has stabilized. As confidence in the peace process has grown, the region has experienced a minor economic resurgence and numbers of people immigrating to Northern Ireland have increased substantially (Mussano 2004). Although this migration has occurred across Northern Ireland, the greatest numbers have moved to its only major city, Belfast. At the same time as there has been a transnational movement of people to the city, evident in the presence of different languages and specialty shops on the streets of Belfast for the first time, there has also been a noticeable increase in racism and racist attacks (Jarman 2002). In response to a series of highly publicized, mendacious racist attacks, anti-racism has recently emerged as a prominent discourse across the political spectrum in Northern Ireland and, in particular, in Belfast.

Anti-racism is a remarkably diffuse and contested concept.[3] Recent work has highlighted the diversity of discourses and practices that might be termed anti-racist (Lentin 2004; Lloyd 2002). Bonnett (1993: 136) argues for empirically grounded accounts of "how and why anti-racist commitment has emerged differently in different places." This focus on the context and location of anti-racism mirrors the promulgation by writers on transnationalism that "local sites of global processes do matter" (Guarnizo and Smith 1999: 12). Anti-racism and transnational practices both develop, and are expressed, within specific contexts and societal structures. Beginning with a discussion on the importance of attending to the receiving location for transnational migration, often the city, this paper shall go on to discuss the changing demographic and social structure of Belfast. While the transnational movement of people to Belfast has contributed to the growth of anti-racism at both government and civil society levels, this paper shall interrogate anti-racist discourses, which have been produced by "grassroots" groups in areas of the city strongly associated with territorialized sectarianism. An analysis of texts produced by these groups illustrates how these emergent anti-racist discourses construct and position migrants in relation to the dominant sectarian division. This paper shall then look at how migrants in Belfast receive and position themselves in terms of these anti-racist discourses. Anti-racist practice in Belfast is structured by the social and cultural context of the city, most notably sectarian division, but the concluding section of this paper argues that migrants still have the power to disrupt pre-existing power structures by choosing not to engage with partisan anti-racist discourses.

Grounding Transnationalism

Transnational migrants have been characterized as transgressive, liminal figures speaking, and acting, beyond the margins of the society in which they live and work. Bhabha (1994) famously proclaimed the migrant as located "in-between" hegemonic discourses of race and nation and best placed to resist the domination of these hegemonic narratives. Mitchell (1997a) cautioned against the assumption that fluid and hybrid subject identities are necessarily counter-hegemonic, and suggested that liminal locations and subject positions are often used in capital accumulation rather than resistance. Some scholars on transnationalism have gone even further and have argued that the putative liminality of the spaces occupied by migrants can be both fictive and misleading. Migrants are not free-floating ciphers of identity moving through space, they are situated in specific social and historical conditions which are not of their own making. In highlighting the "emplacement" of mobile subjects in specific locations Smith (2005: 238) stresses the need for research, which is grounded in the "historical context in which transnational processes take place."

Transnational migration is an inherently spatial phenomenon and it is of paramount importance that research accounts for the social and historical characteristics of migratory spaces. Grand claims such as Castells' (1996) notion of the globe as a "space of flows" have limited utility for empirical studies and risk ignoring the grounded, material sites in which global processes take place. Global conditions are made relevant in specific times and places, as Mitchell (1997b: 111) notes in highlighting the relevance of geographical context in developing a fuller understanding of transnational processes. Since most migrants move to cities (Beaverstock 2005), transnational studies must engage with the urban social, cultural and historical context within which transnational processes occur. This involves an awareness of both the repositioning of cities and states within wider global restructuring as well as the local specificity of the city itself.

The pre-existing societal configurations and power structures of the transnational city provide migrants with both "opportunities and constraints" for engagement (Guarnizo and Smith 1999: 12). Transnational migrants may interact with, and sometimes disrupt, the pre-existing social organization of the city in a myriad of ways, from engaging with local politics to altering the residential make-up of the city. New patterns of migration might also disrupt old patterns of inclusion and exclusion and lead to radical changes in the organization of social life in the city (Evergeti and Zontini 2006). On the other hand, migrants may be interpellated in quite specific ways by dominant discourses of identity and belonging already embedded in the social space(s) of the city. Consequently, studies need to engage with both the pre-existing social organization of the transnational city and the effect that transnational practices are having on these pre-existent social structures. Grounding transnational migrants within the social milieu of the city forces a necessary focus on the historical and cultural context where transnational processes take place. It also allows for the appreciation of the effects of these processes and the agency of migrants themselves.

Belfast: Transnational Migration Before, During and After "the Troubles"

A once prosperous Victorian city of roughly half a million people nestled on the north-east corner of the island of Ireland, during "the Troubles" Belfast became a byword for ethnic violence.[4] The city was home to a large proportion of the 3,000 people killed in the conflict and scene of some of the most violent excesses of "the Troubles" (Coulter 1999). Since Belfast first began to develop from a minor settlement to a major urban center sectarian division has been a crucial structuring factor in social organization, even at the micro-level (Anderson and Shuttleworth 1998). Endemic segregation along religious lines led Boal (2000) to describe Belfast as "the Ethno-National city" and to this day over 80 percent of its residents live in segregated areas. Territorial markings such as murals, flags, and curb paintings play a crucial role in the maintenance of sectarian division on the streets of Belfast (Shirlow and Murtagh 2006).

Despite the common depiction of Northern Ireland as a land divided between "Two Traditions," groups who do not fit easily, if at all, into Nationalist and Unionist blocs have always existed (Hainsworth 1998). Irish Travelers have resided in the territory of Northern Ireland since before the foundation of the country in 1922 and a small Jewish community has existed in Belfast for several centuries (McVeigh 1998). Images of bombs and riots beamed around the world unsurprisingly made Northern Ireland an unattractive site for migration. Post-war levels of migration were not as high as in the rest of the United Kingdom, however, there was some migration from Commonwealth areas to the main urban centers in Northern Ireland with significant numbers of migrants from India and China (mainly Hong Kong) settling in Belfast from the 1960s on (Jarman 2006). In a qualitative study of the four main minority ethnic groups at the time Irwin and Dunn (1997) estimated that between 6,270 and 8,270 minority ethnic persons resided in Northern Ireland. The largest group, the Chinese, was thought to number some 3,000, of whom the vast majority, like all migrant groups, lived in Belfast.

Irwin and Dunn's study was conducted in 1996, during a particularly precarious moment in the then emerging Northern Irish peace process. The paramilitary ceasefires which followed the publication of the Downing Street Declaration in 1994 were unraveling and there was widespread mistrust on both sides of the sectarian divide. Since then the political climate has improved considerably. The Good Friday Agreement, signed in 1998, established a power-sharing Assembly between Nationalists and Unionists. Paramilitary ceasefires were reinstated and provisions made for the release of paramilitary prisoners. Despite a series of political setbacks, and the maintenance of sectarian division in everyday life, the levels of violence have dramatically declined.[5] Northern Ireland is now the site of a "normalization" process as efforts are made to regularize social and economic life in the region (Shirlow and Murtagh 2006). Economic investment in the area has increased and flagship developments like the Laganside regeneration project in Belfast have been undertaken. The increased proliferation of multinational companies in and around Belfast illustrates how Northern Ireland, for years considered "a place apart," is now, along with the rest of the UK, being repositioned as part of global restructuring. Over the last ten years the peace process has made Belfast a more attractive site for transnational migration at the same time as global changes have placed the city within new patterns of migration.

Traditionally a region of net out-migration, since 2001-2002 Northern Ireland has witnessed net in-migration (NISRA 2006). The 2001 census was the first to include a question on ethnicity, identifying 26,659 people living in Northern Ireland that were born outside the United Kingdom or the Republic of Ireland. Of this number 14,276 identified themselves as belonging to an ethnic minority. In the following years, the volume and patterns of migration have changed as migrants from countries without a strong history of immigration to either the UK or Ireland have begun to come to Northern Ireland (Jarman 2006). As a constituent region of the UK, all citizens of new member states joining the European Union (EU) in the last expansion (May 2004) are entitled to freedom of employment in the UK and there has been a significant movement of people from the A8 countries of Eastern Europe to Northern Ireland. A substantial number of Portuguese nationals have also migrated to Northern Ireland, primarily to work in the food processing industries of mid-Ulster (Soares 2002). Similarly healthcare workers from South Asia and the Philippines have begun working in a number of hospital trusts, including a number of Filipino nurses in the Royal Victoria Hospital in Belfast (Bell, Jarman, and Lefebvre 2004).

The size of the migrant population in Northern Ireland is difficult to ascertain (Rogers 2006). Jarman (2006) uses applications for National Insurance Numbers to suggest that the largest new migrant group in Northern Ireland is made up of people coming from Poland, followed by those from Lithuania, Portugal, Slovakia, India, and the Philippines. Migrant workers in Northern Ireland are mainly employed in administration/management, the manufacturing sector, construction, and hospitality (Jarman 2006).[6] The Accession Monitoring report suggests that Northern Ireland, at 0.72 percent of total population, has a higher proportion of migrants than the rest of the UK (Home Office 2006). Almost two-thirds of migrants in Northern Ireland are male, the bulk under thirty-five with no dependants and working full-time in lower-end occupations (Rogers 2006). Although these new migrants are spread across Northern Ireland between 25 and 33 percent live in Belfast, suggesting an in-flow of approximately 7,000 new migrants to Belfast in the last three years (NISRA 2006). These migrants have come to Belfast as a result of demand from public and private sectors created by a lack of skilled workers as well as a lack of opportunities in sending countries (Jarman 2006). The comparative ease of movement allowed to A8 nationals has also encouraged many East Europeans to migrate, often along similar lines to those evidenced in the rest of Ireland (Devine 2006).

Racism and Anti-Racism in the Ethno-National City

On March 20, 2006 seven men armed with baseball bats, their faces covered by scarves, smashed in the door of a house on Donegall Road in South Belfast. The only person in the house, a 51-year-old Polish man, was viciously assaulted with a hammer (McCambridge and Moulton 2006). Depopulation, coupled with an excess of cheap rental accommodation, has made the Donegall Road, which is in a staunchly Protestant/Loyalist area, an attractive place for migrant workers, mainly from Poland and Lithuania. Racist attacks in Loyalist areas of South Belfast have increased dramatically in recent years (Lentin and McVeigh 2006: 154). During the afternoon of March 20, posters were attached to lampposts warning that "The Community of the Donegall RD and the Village WILL NOT TOLERATE attacks on women and familys off (sic) the area, drug houses, brothels." Although the text does not refer directly to migrants, it became clear that they were the target when, at eight o'clock that evening around thirty residents gathered on nearby Fortuna Street to protest against perceived "anti-social behavior" by migrant workers. Within two hours of this protest the racist attack took place and scores of windows were broken at the homes of other migrant workers on Fortuna Street and adjacent Coolfin Street.

Racism in Northern Ireland is not a new phenomenon, but in recent years there has been a significant increase in public discussion about the issue (Lentin and McVeigh 2006). Research suggests that levels of racist prejudice in Northern Ireland have grown since 1994 (Gilligan and Lloyd 2006). Over half of all migrant workers reported having experienced some form of racism or racial abuse (Bell, Jarman, and Lefebvre 2004). The Police Service of Northern Ireland (PSNI) recorded an increase in racist attacks from 634 in 2004-05 to 746 the in 2005-06 (PSNI 2006) and a significant minority of victims of racist incidents were migrant workers from A8 Accession countries.[7] Over 25 percent of attacks occurred in the Belfast area and racist incidents, like the attack on the Polish man in South Belfast, have earned Belfast the unfortunate label of "Race Hate Capital of Europe" (BBC News Online 2004). Recently Sir Hugh Orde, the chief constable of the PSNI, highlighted the link between paramilitarism and racist attacks, suggesting that racist violence is the biggest threat to stability in Northern Ireland (Kampfner 2006).

The pernicious attack on Donegall Road occurred on the first night of European Anti-racism Week 2006. Previously such events had little impact due to the popular perception that racism did not happen in Northern Ireland (McVeigh 1998). However, given the increased public attention on "race" and racism, it is not surprising that voluntary and community groups have begun to mobilize around the issue. During European Anti-racism Week a host of events were held in Belfast, ranging from exhibitions and public discussions about racism to the launch of an Irish Football Association campaign to "Kick Racism out of Football." Race relations has also emerged as an issue of governmental concern in Northern Ireland for the first time.[8] The aims of the recently published *Racial Equality Strategy for Northern Ireland* include the development of strategic planning and policy around new migrants and the introduction of measures to try and prevent racist attacks (OFMDFM 2005).

At the same time as anti-racism has emerged as a concern for government and NGOs, grassroots groups based in areas of Belfast strongly associated with Loyalism and Republicanism have also begun to prioritize anti-racism. Founded in 2003, in the wake of a series of violent racist attacks in South Belfast, the Anti-Racist Network (ARN) is a protest group operating throughout Belfast. The West Against Racism Network (WARN), the group's branch in the west of the city, is "a grassroots anti-racism campaign based in West Belfast ... to challenge individualized and institutionalized racism and to build a genuinely anti-racist culture in West Belfast" (WARN 2005a). West Belfast is an area synonymous with sectarian division and tensions have resulted in violent clashes in the area since the foundation of Northern Ireland (Boal 1969). A ten-foot high corrugated iron "peaceline" divides the Protestant Shankill from the larger Catholic Falls where most of WARN's small team of anti-racist activists are based.

In 2005 WARN organized the painting of an anti-racist mural on Divis Street at the entrance to Republican West Belfast (see Figure 1). This wall painting depicts two guesthouse windows side by side; "London 1966" and "Belfast 2005." In the mural the link between anti-Irish racism in London in the 1960's and racism in Belfast today is highlighted. The Celtic motif on the right hand side is WARN's symbol. The edge of the window is painted in green, a color associated with Republicanism, and Irish nationalism more generally. Irish is a language used by some people in the Falls area and the use of Gaelic words and symbols overtly, and cleverly, links anti-racism with an Irish Republican agenda.

The painting coincided with the launch of a campaign to promote West Belfast as an anti-racist "Republic of Conscience." A checkpoint was constructed on the Falls Road and A6 size "passports" for this fictitious "Republic" were produced and distributed to people in the area. The text of this passport draws attention to attacks against Filipino nurses working in the local Royal Victoria Hospital and anti-Muslim graffiti daubed on a fast food restaurant on the Falls Road. The narrative also stresses that the experience of anti-Irish racism, Loyalist attacks, and state oppression should make anti-racism a natural position for the people of West Belfast; "it stands to reason that our solidarity with people from black and minority ethnic communities should be automatic, because we know what it is like to be on the receiving end of such bigotry, whether from individuals, from mobs, or from the state" (WARN 2005a: 7). Although the occurrence of racist attacks in Nationalist areas is referred to racism is defined as something Loyalists do: "You don't need to be a politics professor to work out the connection between loyalists burning out Catholics in North Belfast ... and loyalists driving out Africans, Moslems, Filipinos, Portuguese and Chinese in South Belfast, Ballymena, Antrim and Dungannon" (WARN 2005a: 7). The putative identification of Republicans with migrants as the victims of aggression is reiterated throughout this anti-racist text.

Toward the end of 2005, WARN received funding from the Office of the First Minister and the Deputy First Minister (OFMDFM) to compile

Figure 1
WARN mural, Divis Street, Belfast.

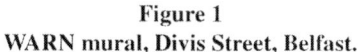

a Welcome Pack for migrants coming into West Belfast. In the information booklet that accompanied the pack, only Catholic churches in the West Belfast area were listed. The booklet also advised minority ethnic people that the police were not trusted by the people of West Belfast and they should avoid calling the police "unless it is a necessity, e.g. for insurance purposes" (WARN 2005b: 7).[9] These anti-police sentiments reflect Republican opposition to the PSNI in areas of West Belfast and when these statements were noticed government funding for the pack was withdrawn. This anti-racist text incorporates migrants into the dominant Catholic and Republican narratives of the area. Constructing all migrants as Catholic effectively denies ethnic, racial and religious differences just as instructing migrants not to contact the police draws migrants into a particular position in relation to the highly politicized Northern Irish policing debate.

The assumed links between far-right groups in the UK and Loyalist paramilitaries in Northern Ireland have often been overstated, but the fact that the majority of racist attacks have occurred in Loyalist areas suggests that the "elective affinity between Loyalism and racism" described by Lentin and McVeigh (2006:162) has some validity. There have, however, been some attempts by groups identifying themselves as Loyalist to produce anti-racist discourses and practices. In 2005 a Community Restorative Justice group in the Shankill Road area of West Belfast commissioned a local artist to work with children in a nearby school on an anti-racist mural (see Figure 2).[10] This mural, entitled "Declare War on Racism," appears to be set in a World War I graveyard. On some of the gravestones are inscribed the names of dead servicemen while on other stones words like "Paki," "Chink," and "Nigger" are daubed. The poppy and the red hand are commonly associated with Ulster Loyalism and the use of these symbols in this anti-racist mural is important. Since the Battle of the Somme is a pivotal event in the discourse of Ulster Loyalism, the setting of an anti-racist mural in a World War I graveyard is important. Loyalism is depicted as inherently anti-racist and racism is constructed as something that can be "fought" under the watchful gaze of the red hand.

Around the same time as the Shankill mural was unveiled, and in response to accusations of paramilitary involvement in racist attacks in Belfast, the Loyalist Commission launched its own anti-racist campaign.[11] A glossy pamphlet entitled "Loyalist or Racist? You can't be both" was distributed to community groups and bars in Loyalist areas of Belfast. On the front cover a woman of Indian appearance sports henna tattoos and a Union flag t-shirt with "Made in Britain" emblazoned across her chest. Surrounding the image is a number of slogans such as "Ulster says no" and "Ulster will fight," phrases synonymous with Loyalist opposition to the 1986 Anglo-Irish Agreement. Inside the pamphlet a vision of empire and imperialism as benign and benevolent is produced: "the world owes much to the British empire—freedom of political choice, thought and belief" (The Loyalist Commission 2005). Colonial-era photographs and military images are used to associate anti-racism, and racialized difference, with a Loyalist political position. In another publication anti-Pol-

Figure 2
Declare War on Racism Mural, Ballygomartin Road, West Belfast.

ish racism is criticized on the grounds that Poles fought in the Second World War alongside the British army. In contrast to the texts produced by WARN, which call on migrants to identify with the suffering of the "local" Catholic community, the Loyalist campaign is targeted at the perpetrators of racist violence. This paternalistic imperial discourse appeals to Loyalists to protect migrants as they previously protected the colonies and the empire.

Attempting to raise awareness of racist attacks in Belfast is a laudable aim given the current situation in the city. However, in order to produce their anti-racist message these groups rely on images and narratives, which are strongly associated with sectarian division. While it is debatable whether an anti-racist campaign, which did not utilize popular images and stories, would be able to succeed in effecting attitude and behavior change in Loyalist and Republican constituencies in Belfast, these anti-racist discourses and practices are open to the charge of (re)producing sectarian division. Loyalist and Republican anti-racist discourses differ in terms of the subject to which they are appealing, and the way in which they seek to incorporate migrants, but both position migrants within pre-existing structures of sectarian division and contestation.

Receiving Anti-Racisms

The content of anti-racist discourses produced by grassroots groups in Belfast clearly demonstrates the importance of the historical and social context in which transnational processes and practices occur (Guarnizo and Smith 1999; Smith 2005). In Belfast sectarian division, and the fractured, contested, legacy of "the Troubles," circumscribes social organization at every level. The unique context of the city shapes both the medium (e.g., the use of wall murals) and the anti-racist message directed at new transnational migrants, especially those moving into areas closely associated with Loyalist or Republican political identities. These emerging anti-racisms socially and spatially situate migrants in different relations to the dominant tropes of sectarian division. However, migrants may contest, and reject, their interpellation within these discourses and it is important to investigate how, and why, migrants are positioning themselves in terms of these anti-racist discourses.

During "the Troubles," migrant communities generally tried to draw as little attention to themselves as possible. For example, the Northern Irish Muslim community, mainly based around the only mosque in South Belfast, consciously distanced itself from Protestant/Catholic issues (Marranci 2003). This strategy was also adopted by other groups; "despite all of the Troubles in Northern Ireland, the Indian community kept their heads down and never took part in any of the sectarian troubles... [but] carried on living a normal life" (ICC 2004). Since the ceasefires, and the increase in migration to Belfast, migrants have become the subject of both racism and anti-racism. Many migrants, however, contest the interpellations of the grassroots anti-racist discourses identified in the previous section and choose to avoid anti-racist groups and their actions. As the CEO of a large minority ethnic umbrella organization commented:

> After the high profile [racist] attacks in Donegall Road... certain people, especially from the local community, hijack the issue. And then it is polarized; it is the Unionist side or the Republican side who are the worst perpetrators. It hijacks the whole issue. And certain people, they are keen to do this. It just becomes the politician playing the game and it totally takes away the whole race issue. It becomes sectarian politics. That is why we boycott all those, WARN and all those things. They just hijack the issue.

This interviewee has been active in anti-racism in Belfast since migrating to the city from Hong Kong. Although in the past he conducted anti-racism training in statutory bodies, as well as with the police, he suggests that an awareness of racism in Northern Ireland only emerged in the wake of "the high profile attacks in Donegall Road." Many actors in representative organizations believe that the anti-racist efforts of groups like WARN focus on which side of the sectarian divide is most racist and are simply an extension of sectarian politics. The perception that the issue of racist attacks has been hijacked to make sectarian political capital has led many migrants in Belfast to avoid the discourses and practices of emerging anti-racist groups.

During the research the level of participation by migrants in anti-racist initiatives was very low. Only a small group of Chinese and Indian dancers attended the unveiling of the Loyalist anti-racist mural in Figure 1. Similarly the "Republic of Conscience" passport distributed on the Falls Road was only stamped by a couple of local Irish Traveler Groups and not by any migrant representative groups. Although the Filipino Association in West Belfast has been involved in some WARN events, in the main new migrants in the area have largely shown little interest in their activities. A project worker, and anti-racist activist, engaged in a South Belfast multicultural initiative, suggests that, amongst other issues, low participation is due to migrant's fears of being made visible:

> There are very few individuals active [in anti-racism] who would be local minority individuals…If it is people who have newly arrived they have a whole load of issues to deal with, the last thing they will want to be is visible. If it is people from the settled minority communities who are already involved in the NGO sector then they are not going to be the most political. There is a real shortage of people who would be both political and from a minority ethnic background.

The failure of anti-racist discourses produced by groups like the West Against Racism (WARN) and the Loyalist Commission to address the often quite specific interests and needs of different migrant groups has also led to many migrants choosing to avoid these initiatives. In positioning all those not definable as Catholic or Protestant in the Northern Irish context as "Other," these anti-racisms construct a monolithic group of victims of racism as the subject of their anti-racist interventions. This symbolic violence denies divisions within the "Others" based on such indices as, religion, class, gender and ethnicity.

Many interviewees referred to the differences between "settled minority communities," most notably Cantonese-speaking Chinese and Indian, and more recent arrivals to Belfast from Poland, Lithuania, and mainland China. Migrants, who arrived in Belfast before and during "the Troubles," developed their own mechanisms for dealing with their situation and many became involved in founding, and running, representative organizations outside the margins of formal electoral politics.[12] As an activist from the Anti-Racist Network (ARN) noted, these older migrant communities are wary of becoming involved in anti-racist campaigns around issues like asylum and immigration:

> Some of these groups think that "we have been here a long time, it took us a long time to claw out a position for ourselves that we are a respectable part of the community and we don't want anything to do with those asylum seekers."

In contrast more recent migrants who have arrived in Belfast over the last five years have generally come from countries without a history of migration to Northern Ireland (Jarman 2006). These new migrants have arrived in Belfast without the support system provided by representative organizations and most new migrant communities have yet to form such organizations.[13] In the absence of formal organizational structures most newcomers to Belfast are too busy with personal issues like work and family to become involved in anti-racism. While one Polish woman interviewed became involved in the ARN after seeing a poster on a bus shelter in the city center, most first generation migrants to Belfast are either unable or unwilling to participate in emerging anti-racist discourses, regardless of their content or producers. That many new migrants in Belfast choose to avoid these partisan anti-racist discourses reflects both their alienation from the sectarian nature of these discourses and the limits of their own circumstances.

Conclusion

The presence of Polish delicatessens and African hair salons in Belfast visibly illustrates the emergence of transnational practices in a city synonymous with sectarian division and violence. New migration patterns have opened up along different pathways, and in different volumes, from previous small-scale migration. That new migrants would choose to travel to Belfast in search of work and other opportunities stands as a testament both to the changes which have taken place in the city, most notably the cessation of armed conflict, and the city's new found position within wider UK flows of labor and capital. However, these transnational processes are occurring within the specific social structures of the "Ethno-National city." In emphasizing how pre-existing sectarian configurations of the city impinge on anti-racist practice the case study of anti-racism in Belfast presented here highlights the importance of attending to the local specificities of the sites at which transnational practices are taking place.

The empirical focus of this paper has been on the content of, and receptions to, anti-racist discourses produced by grassroots groups based in areas of Belfast which are strongly associated with territorialized sectarianism. The territorial markings, such as murals and posters, which are used to create, and maintain, sectarian division on the streets of the city are now also being used to produce an anti-racist message. Just as transnational migrants coming to Belfast are situated within the contested social and historical context of the city these anti-racist messages are also structured by the sectarian context in which these anti-racist groups are situated. Loyalist anti-racist images and texts draw on identifiably Loyalist themes and iconography in constructing their message. On the other hand anti-racist groups based in Republican areas of Belfast emphasize the Catholic experience of sectarianism and the struggle against British rule. Each of these conflicting discourses attempts to claim affinity with the racialized "Other" as the sole preserve of either Loyalists or Republicans, in the process positioning migrants, and all "Others," within an overtly sectarianized gaze.

While migrants are located or, following Smith (2005), emplaced within these partisan anti-racist discourses the majority eschew these efforts made on their behalf. The perception that anti-racism is an extension of sectarian politics has led some of the main representative groups in Belfast to boycott these actions. Many migrants continue to keep a consciously low profile, a tactic employed by earlier migrants who came during "the Troubles." The tacit assumption made by many anti-racists that there exists a unified "migrant community" ignores a number of deep structural divisions both within and between migrant groups. More established groups in Belfast, like the Cantonese-speaking Chinese and the Indian communities, have little in common with more recent arrivals from A8 countries and South East Asia. Migrant groups are also divided internally and externally along gender, religious, class, racial, and ethnic lines. The one dimensional discourse produced by many grassroots anti-racist groups fails to appreciate the specific needs and goals of different constituent groups, leading many migrants to ignore and avoid these emerging anti-racist practices.

The presence of new migrant groups, and the occurrence of racist attacks, has prompted the mobilization of grassroots groups around anti-racism in Belfast. This development attests to the effects that transnational practices and processes are having on the social organization of the city. Although migrants are hailed in specific ways within these anti-racist discourses they also posses the agency to receive and position themselves in relation to these emerging discourses. This paper has shown that many migrants in Belfast have elected to avoid these anti-racist practices for a range of reasons, reflecting the limits of these anti-racist efforts and their failure to engage fully with the migrants' real concerns. This absence of engagement undermines these anti-racisms since effective anti-racist action requires the active involvement of those it purports to represent (Lentin 2004). New migrants from areas like the A8 Accession countries, Portugal and South East Asia have only recently arrived in Belfast and it remains to be seen whether significant numbers choose to stay long-term and begin to self-organize on a similar scale to older migrant communities. Perhaps, in the coming years, these new migrants shall be at the forefront of anti-racist initiatives that aim not to sectarianize "Others," but to positively affect the social organization of the city by moving beyond sectarian binaries and championing the specific concerns of transnational migrants.

Notes

1. An earlier version of this paper was prepared for the Transnational Identities: Cities Unbound, Migrations Redefined conference, Saturday 7th October 2006, organized by the Center for Research on Nationalism, Ethnicity and Multiculturalism (CRONEM). This paper arises out of my doctoral research on anti-racism and race relations in Northern Ireland and is based on eight months of ethnographic fieldwork and over forty interviews conducted in Belfast and Lisburn from December 2004 to August 2006.
2. The terms Catholic/Protestant and Republican/Loyalist are both used in this chapter. The religious breakdown of Northern Ireland is roughly 55 percent Protestant, 45 percent Catholic. The vast majority of Catholics are Nationalists (i.e., support a united Ireland) and the bulk of Protestants are Unionists (i.e., support the maintenance of the union with Great Britain). Republicans can be defined as Nationalists who support the use of force and Loyalists their Unionist equivalent, though these definitions are less than ideal (see Coulter 1999 for more detailed discussion on these distinctions).
3. Debates about what does, and does not, constitute anti-racism abound in the literature (see Bonnett 2000). For the purposes of this chapter grassroots groups self-defining as anti-racist are treated, but a more complete picture of anti-racism in Belfast will be provided in my doctoral thesis which investigates anti-racism conducted by NGOs in Northern Ireland as well as racial equality policy and practice in government.
4. "The Troubles" is the name commonly assigned to the conflict between Catholics and Protestants in Northern Ireland, which endured from 1969 to the signing of the Good Friday Agreement in 1998.
5. The Agreement introduced a consociational model of government into Northern Ireland. Under this system an Assembly was constituted on the basis of local elections in 1998 and all representatives designated themselves Nationalist, Unionist or Other. The Assembly was dogged by problems between the Nationalist and Unionist blocs and, after four previous suspensions, was suspended again in October 2000 following allegations of a Sinn Fein spy ring operating in Stormont, the seat of the Assembly. The Assembly has remained in suspension since this time, though talks aimed at reinstating it were ongoing at the time of this writing.

Paramilitary ceasefires, despite some breaches, have generally held since 1998. Although, as Shirlow and Murtagh (2006) illustrate, sectarian division on the ground in Belfast has actually increased since the signing of the Good Friday Agreement.
6. According to Jarman (2006) from 2003 to January 2006 there were 12,020 applications for National Insurance numbers from Polish nationals, 4987 from Lithuanians, 3605 from Portuguese, 3469 from Slovakians, 2486 from Indians, 1524 from Filipinos, 1358 from Latvians, 1338 from Czechs, 1317 from Chinese and 867 from Ukrainians. The A8 migrants are employed in the following industries, arranged in order of greatest number: admin/management, manufacturing, construction, hospitality, food processing, agriculture, health, retail, transport and entertainment (from Jarman 2006).
7. The ethnic origin of all victims of racial attacks is not recorded by the PSNI, but a report in *The Belfast Telegraph* used figures obtained under Freedom of Information legislation to show that out of 736 racist crimes recorded in Northern Ireland in 2006, 335 were committed against so-called "White Europeans." "It is believed that the vast number of these crimes are against east Europeans, particularly members of the Polish community who have come to Ulster to work" (McCambridge 2007).
8. While legislation outlawing racial discrimination existed throughout the UK from 1965 on it was never extended to cover Northern Ireland. Only after prolonged campaigning from anti-racists and minority ethnic groups was the Race Relations Order (NI) passed in 1997. However, in the aftermath of the Good Friday Agreement a Racial Equality Unit and an Equality Commission were quickly established, both with a remit around "race" issues (for more detail on this emerging state anti-racism see Lentin and McVeigh 2006: 149-151).
9. Policing in Northern Ireland is a highly politicized issue. Throughout the history of Northern Ireland, and particularly during "the Troubles," The Royal Ulster Constabulary (RUC) was perceived to be the coercive arm of the Protestant state (Weitzer 1985). Despite radical changes in policing since the Good Friday Agreement, at the time of this writing, Republicans had yet to endorse the policing board, a skepticism reflected on the ground in Republican areas, like the Falls, where the police still lack legitimacy in the eyes of many.
10. Community Restorative Justice (CRJ) is a form of social/community criminal justice that focuses on crime as an act against another individual or a community rather than the state. CRJ groups have been active on both sides of the West Belfast "peaceline." However, in Northern Ireland CRJ has been quite a contentious issue and recently funding was withdrawn from most groups.
11. Loyalist Commission is an unelected body representing all the main Loyalist paramilitary groups: the Ulster Defense Association (UDA), the Ulster Volunteer Force (UVF), the Ulster Freedom Fighters (UFF) and the Red Hand Commando (RHC). Lentin and McVeigh (2006:153) implicate members of groups represented by the Loyalist Commission in racist attacks, arguing that by meeting with members of the Commission British and Irish governments are effectively sanctioning racist violence.
12. Notable examples of such groups include the Belfast Islamic Centre (founded in 1977), the Indian Community Centre (1980) and the Chinese Welfare Association (1986). These groups later also became members of larger umbrella organizations such as the Multicultural Resource Centre (founded in 1991) and the Northern Ireland Council for Ethnic Minorities (1994) and all played an influential role in lobbying for the extension of race relations legislation to Northern Ireland.

13. A Polish Association was founded in Belfast and Derry in 2004 and has since published a regular newsletter in Polish and organized a festival of Polish culture in the Botanic Gardens in July 2006. However, this grouping (and others like the Hungarian United Network) is still in its infancy.

References

Anderson, J., and Shuttleworth, I. (1998). "Sectarian demography, territoriality and political development in Northern Ireland." *Political Geography* 17 (2): 187-209.
BBC News Online (2004). "Race Hate on the Rise in NI." Accessed at: http://news.bbc.co.uk/1/hi/northern_ireland/3390249.stm.
Beaverstock, J. (2005). "Transnational Elites in the City: British highly-skilled intercompany transferees in New York City's financial district." *Journal of Ethnic and Migration Studies* 31 (2): 245-268.
Bell, K., N. Jarman, and T. Lefebvre (2004). *Migrant Workers in Northern Ireland.* Belfast: Institute for Conflict Research.
Bhabha, H. (1994). "DissemiNation: Time, Narrative and the Margins of the Modern Nation." In *Nation and Narration: The Location of Culture* (pp. 1-8). New York: Routledge.
Boal, F. (1969). "Territoriality and the Shankill/Falls divide, Belfast." *Irish Geography* 6 (1): 30-50.
Boal, F. (2000). *Ethnicity and Housing: Accommodating Differences.* Aldershot: Ashgate.
Bonnett, A. (1993). *Radicalism, Anti-racism and Representation,* London: Routledge.
Bonnett, A. (2000). *Anti-racism.* London: Routledge.
Castells, M. (1996). *The Rise of the Network Society, the Information Age: Economy, Society and Culture Vol. 1.* Oxford: Blackwell.
Coulter, C. (1999). *Contemporary Northern Irish Society: An Introduction.* London: Pluto Press.
Devine, T. (2006). "Migrant Workers in Northern Ireland: Responding to the Challenge." In *Labour Market Bulletin No. 20* (pp. 241-247). Belfast: Department of Education and Learning.
Evergeti, V., and E. Zontini (2006). "Introduction: Some critical reflections on social capital, migration and transnational families." *Ethnic and Racial Studies,* 29 (6): 1025-1039.
Gilligan, C., and K. Lloyd (2006). *Racial Prejudice in Northern Ireland.* Accessed at: http://www.ark.ac.uk/publications/updates/update44.pdf.
Guarnizo, L. E., and M. P. Smith (1998). "The locations of transnationalism." In *Transnationalism from Below* (pp. 3-34). New Brunswick: Transaction Publishers.
Hainsworth, P. (1998). "Politics, Racism and Ethnicity in Northern Ireland." In *Divided Society: Ethnic Minorities and Racism in Northern Ireland* (pp. 33-51). London: Pluto Press.
Home Office (2006). *Accession Monitoring Report May 2004-December 2005.* London: Home Office.
ICC (2004). *An Introduction to the Indian Community Centre.* Belfast: Indian Community Centre.
Irwin, G., and S. Dunn (1997). *Ethnic Minorities in Northern Ireland.* Coleraine: University of Ulster.
Jarman, N. (2002). *Overview Analysis of Racist Incidents Recorded in Northern Ireland by the RUC, 1996-1999.* Belfast: Office of the First Minister and Deputy First Minister.

Jarman, N. (2006). "Diversity, Economy and Policy: New Patterns of Migration to Northern Ireland." In *Shared Space: A research journal on peace, conflict and community relations in Northern Ireland, No. 2* (pp. 45-61). Belfast: Community Relations Council.

Kampfner, J. (2006). "Divided in Peace." *New Statesman*, 20 November.

Lentin, A. (2004). *Racism and anti-racism in Europe*. London: Pluto Press.

Lentin, R., and R. McVeigh (2006). *After Optimism? Ireland, Racism and Globalisation*. Dublin: Metro Eireann Publications.

Lloyd, C. (1998). *Discourses of Anti-racism in France*, Aldershot: Ashgate.

McCambrige, J. (2007). "The truth about Ulster's hate crimes." *Belfast Telegraph*, 12 January.

McCambridge, J., and M. Moulton (2006). How Ulster marked international day against racism. *Belfast Telegraph*, 22 March.

McVeigh, R. (1998). "There's no racism 'cause there are no black people here: Racism and Anti-racism in Northern Ireland." In *Divided Society: Ethnic Minorities and Racism in Northern Ireland* (pp. 11-32). London: Pluto Press.

Marranci, G. (2003). "'We Speak English': Language and Identity Processes in Northern Ireland's Muslim Community." *Ethnologies: Language and Culture* 25 (2). Accessed at: http://www.erudit.org/revue/ethno/2003/v25/n2/008048ar.html.

Mitchell, K. (1997a). "Different diasporas and the hype of hybridity." *Environment and Planning D: Society and Space* 15 (5): 533-553.

Mitchell, K. (1997b). "Transnational Discourse: Bringing Geography Back." *Antipode* 29(2): 101-114.

Mussano, S. (2004). "Citizenship Education policies in Northern Ireland and the recognition of ethnic and racial diversity in the wake of new immigration." *Migration Letters* 1 (1): 2-10.

NISRA (2006). Long-term International Migration Estimates for Northern Ireland (2004-05). Accessed at: http://www.nisra.gov.uk/archive/demography/publications/NI_Migration_Report(2005).pdf.

OFMDFM (2005). *A Racial Equality Strategy for Northern Ireland, 2005-2010*. Belfast: OFMDFM.

PSNI (2006). *Hate Crimes and Incidents*. Accessed at: http://www.psni.police.uk/3._hate_incidents_and_crimes-4.pdf.

Rogers, D. (2006). "Migrant Workers in Northern Ireland: What is the Current Situation?" In *Labour Market Bulletin No. 20* (pp. 239-240). Belfast: Department of Employment and Learning.

Shirlow, P. and B. Murtagh (2006). *Belfast: Segregation, Violence and the City*. London: Pluto Press.

Smith, M.P. (2005). "Transnational Urbanism Revisited." *Journal of Ethnic and Migration Studies* 31 (2): 235-244.

Soares, A. (2002). *Relatório Sobre Trabalhadores*. Accessed at: http://www.mcrc-ni.org/publications/pub_peng/rst_eng.htm.

The Loyalist Commission (2005). *Loyalist or Racist? You can't be both*. Belfast: The Loyalist Commission.

WARN (2005a). *Comhar na Gcomharsan: West Belfast Welcome Pack*. Belfast: Print.com.

WARN (2005b). *Passport: Republic of Conscience*. Belfast: Print.com.

PART II

PATHWAYS TO TRANSNATIONAL URBANISM

4

The Making of Urban Translocalities: Senegalese Migrants in Dakar and Zingonia

Giulia Sinatti

Since it was first suggested in a groundbreaking book by Glick Schiller, Basch, and Szanton Blanc (1992), transnationalism has been recognized as an increasingly diffuse feature of contemporary migration flows. The growing ease with which even ordinary people can access the means of communication and travel (Portes 1999), has favored the establishment of migrant networks that are organized across borders and allow people to maintain significant connections in the country of origin (Vertovec and Cohen 1999). The political and economic situation of sending and receiving countries, furthermore, often puts contemporary migrants in a position of "sojourners" who will eventually return to their country of departure, rather than of "settlers" who wish to stay permanently in the country of reception (Grillo 2007: 208).

Transnationalism: An Emerging Character of Contemporary Migrations

The debate on migrant transnationalism has generated a new enthusiasm, as if the mere existence of this new perspective for the understanding of migrations had the power to suddenly liberate migrants from the difficulties of dealing with uprootedness and re-settlement. Thanks to constant mobility and transnational connections, migrants are able to be simultaneously present here and there. Whilst it is undoubtedly useful to highlight some of the emerging features of contemporary migrations, transnational theory has often been accompanied by excessive claims about migrants breaking free from the confines of the local and being able to move freely in broader arenas above and beyond the multiple places in which their everyday lives are lived.

I will argue in this chapter that while transnational migration makes migrants' multiple presence and engagement possible, it should still be viewed as strongly emplaced. Transnational movement relies strongly upon certain sites, which constitute a reference point within a complex crisscrossing of individual migratory paths. Put differently, instead of constituting a mere flow of circulating and mobile people, resources and images, transnationalism inhabits "translocalities."

After I have defined what I mean at the theoretical level, I shall push my argument further and will provide two examples of urban translocalities established by the Senegalese diaspora in its homeland and abroad.

The Nodes of Transnational Migration: Translocalities

Appadurai (1995, 1996) was the first to use the term "translocality." In his definition he emphasizes the influences of transnational processes on specific localities. According to him the production of locality has become an increasingly difficult task. Translocalities "create complex conditions for the production and reproduction of locality, in which ties of marriage, work, business and leisure weave together various circulating populations with kinds of "locals" (1995: 216). Hannerz's approach (1998) is similar to Appadurai's (1998). He also emphasizes that translocalities are "intensely involved in mobility and in the encounters of varied kinds of mobile people" (1998: 139).

My understanding of translocality differs from or is complementary to the definitions outlined above. I believe the focus should not only be on the issues of mobility, but also on the importance of the local dimension. In this sense, my notion of translocality is closer to that offered by Smith (2001 and 2005), who places greater emphasis on aspects of emplacement: translocalities are the places in which mobile subjects are locally grounded.[1]

As I have argued elsewhere (Sinatti 2006), place still plays an important role in the identification and homing of transnational migrants who, along their routes, strongly refer to specific and locatable places as sources of belonging. It is therefore essential for the notion of translocality to restore the importance of the local, to indicate the places "in which transnational relations anchor themselves to the ground, i.e., they become regularized or institutionalized" (Sinatti 2006: 31). As I will show in the coming pages translocalities are more than places for migrant identification—they offer the basis for transnational living itself. As the term trans-national suggests, these places incorporate both mobility and emplacement. Trans-*localities* introduce the idea of place as a setting for interaction, where people are brought together in bodily co-presence. *Trans*-localities, however, are also connected through transnational flows to other, distant places. They are not simply places of origin or of destination, therefore, but are significant and meaningful stops along people's many and diverse transnational routes.

The relevance of cities for networks has been stressed by numerous authors. Hannerz (1980), for example, convincingly argues that networks are embedded in cities to the extent that we should speak of networks as a mode of urban life. Regardless of their size or location, cities are places of transit, exchange, consumption and flow of information. As a result they are also likely to occupy an important position with regard to transnational phenomena. It is these features that make them the most suitable places where translocalities may be hosted. When it comes to migrants, it should be added that cities also host invisible spaces, such as the suburbs, townships and *favelas* inhabited by many of these migrants. These intermediate zones are the settings for new types of relations and spatial occupations (Agier 1999), where the issue of actors' agency becomes highly visible.

Smith, in particular, has explored the relationship between the locations of transnationalism and cities (see 2001; 2005). In his pursuit of transnational urbanism he emphasizes the central role played by cities as localities where the transnational is grounded. Cities are also theatres where researchers should investigate the effects of transnational networks on places and on the lives of those occupying those places (Smith 2001: 183). Considerable research has followed up this suggestion,[2] and this chapter seeks to add to this by drawing on my study of Senegalese migrants in the translocalities that they have constructed as collective sites of reference.

Senegalese Migration and its Translocalities

It should now be clear what I mean by the notion of translocality. I next wish to invite the reader to travel virtually to the field. I shall illustrate how two cities have come to occupy the role of translocalities for Senegalese migrants.[3] The Senegalese have often been depicted as having strong transnational characteristics shaped by their religious, commercial and family networks (Bava 2003; Carter 1997; Diouf 2000; Kane 2002; Riccio 2001 and 2003). The average Senegalese migrant, in fact, prefers temporary residence to long-term settlement in the country of immigration. Most leave their families in Senegal and they regularly visit their homeland and dream about returning to it.

My exploration of the commonalities and differences between translocalities led me to identify two very diverse settings: Dakar, the capital city of Senegal, and the industrial area of Zingonia, an urban settlement in northern Italy where a significant Senegalese community has established itself. Since the end of the 1980s Italy has become one of the privileged destinations for Senegalese migrants (King and Black 1997). The restrictions to entry, introduced by the countries in continental Europe to which Senegalese had traditionally migrated, were the main factor favoring the initial explorations of their networks in this country and now almost 60,000 Senegalese are officially resident in the country.[4]

Dakar

The capital of Senegal, Dakar, is a vast and heterogeneous city, occupying a peninsula that marks the most western point of the African continent. Flanked by the sea to the west, this city has expanded eastwards towards the mainland. It now hosts over two million urban dwellers, a figure almost equal to the total number of Senegalese estimated to be currently living outside their country (between one and two million people, based not only in Italy, but also in France, Spain, Germany and, more recently, in the United States). Although Dakar is the place of origin of only some Senegalese migrants, this city still occupies a position of vital importance in the lives of all of them.

Node of Migrant Passage, Gateway to the West

For a long time Dakar has been the prime magnet for internal migration flows from rural areas of Senegal. In the process, the peripheral neighborhoods of Dakar's *banlieues* have grown at a rapid pace, housing people from all regions of the country. More recently, unable to offer the living conditions expected by those seeking better opportunities, the city has started exporting migrants directly to international destinations. The Region of Dakar, in fact, has currently come to account for the major part of emigration flows from the country (Eurostat 2000).

Today's emigrants from Senegal—be they of rural or urban origin—are all linked to Dakar, where they have either left their homes and families or have spent some length of time, drawing on the hospitality of some relative in preparation for their own exodus after having left their region of origin. Since Dakar is the point of departure and of arrival for all major transport routes to and from the country, the statement just made may appear all too obvious. However, alongside its strategic geographic position, the city has gained a role as a veritable stepping-stone for emigration. As they come and go between Senegal and Italy or other destinations, migrants rarely use Dakar as a mere stopover on their way to the airport.

For some, the journey to Dakar prior to international migration has involved their whole family and may date back many years. One of the migrants, whom I got to know during my fieldwork, proudly declared that he came from a village in one of the interior regions. What is surprising is that this assertion was made despite the fact that he had spent most of life in Dakar, where he had joined his parents when he was still a young child. Assan (this and other names used in these pages are fictitious) had grown up in the city, gradually growing familiar with what he initially saw as a vast metropolis. In Dakar Assan grew familiar not only with city life, but also with the idea of migration as an appealing option like many in his neighborhood, who relied on the support of family members abroad. As a young adult, he also headed for Italy.

The migration routes followed by Assan and his family are similar to those of many other people: while one or more family members have moved on to international destinations, the linkages between a village of origin and Dakar still remain very strong. In these cases, Dakar is able to attract and hence connect both the rural village and the various destinations in which members of the network have settled or traveled to. Throughout his childhood and youth, Assan recalls his home in Dakar as being a haven for those who came and went from the home village to other towns, countries or continents. Some of them stayed for months or even years, making it difficult to establish whether they should be considered guests or members of the household. The movement back and forth between the village and Dakar was not limited, of course, to those coming and going internationally and plenty of people spent periods of time in town without ever traveling beyond it. It is, however, significant that when questioned about this, Assan found it hard to distinguish between the two: his family home in Dakar simply represented a link in the chain, which tied the village to the many places its diaspora is scattered across.

Assan is similar to many other migrants. For all of them, Dakar facilitates transnational communication across countries, thanks to the continuous coming and going of people as well as to the greater accessibility of telephone facilities and other communication technologies. Indeed, it is not uncommon for those who expect to spend their working lives abroad, to move their whole household to Dakar in order to ensure greater ease of contact.

Thanks to its role as a communication hub and gateway to the West, Dakar is the place where the many paths of families or larger groups meet. Consequently, the city features strongly in the imagination of many people, and is frequently perceived as a window to the outside world. Dakar is pictured by many as having the flavor of foreignness: it is the point of departure for any aspiring transnational migrant, a place where people are exposed to the outside world and where their migratory paths and projects take shape.

Place of Investment and Return

Dakar is also a place in which migrants invest from overseas, hoping one day to return to their home country. Migrants' assets are extremely visible in a city that has been hit by a construction boom and infused with new commercial vigor. According to many people I talked to, Dakar has a strong hold on many migrants: for many it is where their future is envisaged on their return to the homeland. Housing is the first and foremost sector in which migrants choose to invest (Tall 1994): building a home in Dakar demonstrates that they have made it in the migratory challenge. In certain areas of the city, where out-migration is particularly strong, construction activities on behalf of migrants have resulted in processes of genuine urban makeover. The taste and style of construction fully reflects the scale of migrants' ambitions. Years of transnational coming and going, of overcoming the difficulties of maintaining contact with family and kin across distances, of remittances sent back to acquire brick after brick for the building site, mould the shape of the final edifice. The greater the efforts involved in the project, the bigger and more sumptuous the final outcome.

Talla was among the many migrants I visited during his holidays in Dakar. Born in a distant neighborhood of the *banlieue*, migration allowed him to upgrade his situation and he has built a family home. It is still in the Dakar suburbs, but much closer to the city center. Work on the house is far from being complete. However, the ground floor is already fully inhabited by the family members he has chosen to transfer here: his parents, wife and children and a couple of other members of the extended family. Talla has negotiated an arrangement with the factory where he works as a welder in Italy: he is granted a two-month leave every two years and he spends this time entirely in Dakar. "One month a year is not worth it," he states. "It's not enough time here, plus you have the cost of the journey."

When I first started visiting his home, I feared "stealing" some of his short and precious time in Dakar. Yet he soon made it quite clear that my visits represented for him a way of exhibiting to the researcher he had first met in Italy what he had achieved back home. He manifested an obvious glee in showing me around the house, making sure I caught more than just a glimpse of the rich furnishings of the bedrooms and lounge, offering to switch on stereos and televisions not so much for my entertainment as a guest, but to put the material accomplishments of years of transnational living to use.

Talla's ongoing project, however, envisaged the addition to the existing building of a second or even a third floor. Organizing the building into separate apartments would ensure living space for his family and would secure a regular flow of income by way of rent. Like Talla those with at least one migrant member typically build multi-storey buildings as opposed to ground-level dwellings, radically transforming the landscape in certain parts of the city. With the values of property rapidly rising and the margins of profit offered by rental rates also increasing, many migrants like Talla are progressively turning towards investment in housing also as a potential source of speculation (Tall 1994).

Alongside the housing sector, commerce has become another area of speculation for Senegalese migrants in this urban translocality. Thanks to the importance of its port and airport, Dakar has always been a major hub in national and international trade routes (Sy, Ba, and Ndiaye 1999). That the transnational networks of Senegalese merchants are strongly rooted in Dakar's city center or *Plateau*, is a fact that has been established by much literature on the commercial activities of members of the Murid Islamic brotherhood (Ebin and Lake 1992; Ebin 1996; Sarr 2004).[5] Relying upon contacts between retail sellers in Dakar and members of the diaspora overseas, these itinerant Murid traders have contributed to the transformation of the city center (Ebin and Lake 1992). They mark space as they appropriate it by sending out visible messages of their religious affiliation and migrant status. The shop, boutique or warehouse of a Murid merchant always brazenly exhibits images of the saint or religious guide of its owner, hence declaring membership in the brotherhood.

As a result of the development of mass transnational migration from Senegal, however, Dakar's role as a commercial hub has been further revitalized by redevelopment beyond the city center. The availability of migrant remittances in the *banlieue* has generated new demand, so that commercial activities *in situ* are sure to find local buyers. Entire sectors of the *banlieue*, once bare and served only by local street markets and mini-bazaars, are now jam-packed with small retailers able to offer an entire range of new products and wares which, until very recently, people were obliged to look for in the town center.

Besides servicing the purchasing power of buyers, migrants who regularly come and go between Senegal and some Western destination often play an important part also in responding to the new demand that they themselves have generated. They are, in fact, in a privileged position to start up new commercial activities. The tradition of importing vehicle parts and accessories, such as tires and mechanical components from Europe, is a longstanding practice. In recent years, however, a whole new range of products has been added to this list. From their Western destinations, migrants have specialized in the trade of raw materials for construction, tiles, furniture, electronic goods and household appliances, literally monopolizing these sectors of activity. Not surprisingly, the new commodities for sale are all house-related and therefore linked to the migrants' own investment in the housing sector.

The Route des Niayes, a main artery cutting through the *banlieue* of the city and heading out of town, has come to symbolize the economic and commercial vigor of Senegalese migrants. The number of commercial activities recently established along this road is bewildering. A great many are run by migrants and, more frequently, by their family and kin during their absence. A careful observer can often trace the transnational routes and linkages behind these economic initiatives: shop signs, messages on the origin of the goods for sale, posters, calendars, national flags and other imagery used for decoration inside and outside shops often disclose (or ostentatiously announce) the country in which migrants have attained their fortune. Alongside the country of immigration, shop owners frequently exhibit their gratitude to the religious leaders and spiritual guides whom they believe have protected them in achieving their success. The Murid, in particular, are strongly committed to expose their portraits, with the purpose not only of expressing gratitude for what they have currently achieved, but also of ensuring blessings and protection for the future.

For many migrants engaged in commercial trade, coming and going transnationally becomes a permanent way of life. Most of them alternate between spending time in the home country with medium- and long-term periods overseas, where they often work to accumulate the earnings needed to purchase a new shipment of merchandise. Constant mobility between the home country and an overseas base is a strategy, which ensures the sustainability of economic activities set up in Dakar and spurs an increasing number of people towards entrepreneurial engagement. The rapid succession of migrants' shops and the ever-growing number of their stores and warehouses along the Route des Niayes turns this road into a demonstration of their overseas success.

Thanks to its capacity to attract and concentrate transnational investment, migration becomes almost tangible in this and other areas of Dakar. The city embodies migrants' dreams as well as the accomplishments of those who have succeeded. Along the routes of most Senegalese migrants, this urban translocality represents an important stepping-stone towards departure as well as an anchorage encouraging return. The continuous flow of migrants, their resources, symbols and aspirations contributes to the social construction of this city as a shared translocality.

Zingonia

While stressing the importance of Dakar in the sending country, I have said little so far about the places in between departure from and return to this African translocality. The strong transnational character of their migration has favored the clustering of Senegalese migrants in certain overseas areas, which attract newcomers through religious, commercial and family networks. In Italy many migrants have clustered in the northern industrial districts where blue-collar employment opportunities for largely unskilled workers are concentrated.

Zingonia, located between the cities of Milan and Bergamo, saw its birth during the 1960s. It was at this time that work started for the development of what should have become a model industrial town, inhabited by a workforce drawn from southern Italy. Today, while its local industries are fully operational and still attract a low-skilled workforce, many neighborhoods are neglected and decaying. Zingonia displays, therefore, the typical features of a disadvantaged suburban neighborhood. Foreign workers have gradually taken the place of Italians who have left over the years. Official data does not indicate how many foreign migrants are currently living in the tall blocks of flats that are still standing and fully inhabited. Unofficial data collected among various informants, however, suggests that foreign immigrants constitute between 40-50 percent of the total population. The Senegalese are the largest foreign national group in the area and have grown consistently in size and importance since the first arrived towards the end of the 1980s. Well over a thousand Senegalese are officially resident in this urban development today. This figure might at first appear low and is, in fact, an underestimate since a large number of Senegalese are undocumented migrants and many others are housed here without having taken up legal residence or commute here daily for work.

Over the years Zingonia has become a landmark along the diversified routes of many Senegalese in Italy. It is not so much the presence of resident Senegalese that makes this town a translocality, but rather the capacity it has developed to attract a constant flow of people who spend more or less extended periods of their time here for a variety of reasons. For the Senegalese of Italy, Zingonia has been socially constructed as a shared spatial reference. Through the diversified range of reasons that may draw people to it, the role of Zingonia as a translocality has become institutionalized. In contrast to the model of an indigenous industrial town that gave it its birth, Zingonia is now famous as a "Little Senegal."

A Place of Passage

When arriving in Zingonia, the first thing that catches the visitor's eye is its high-rise residential blocks. Numerous satellite dishes decorate their crumbling external walls. They reveal Zingonia's role as a place where information is continually circulating and contacts are maintained in an attempt to narrow the gap between Zingonia and the homeland. At street level, the town reveals a world of formal and informal activity created by Senegalese and other immigrants. Entering the intricate web of lanes and porches between the buildings, a long line of shops and services cater for the migrants: grocery stores, international phone centers, money transfer desks, job placement cooperatives advertising short- and long-term employment. These and other shops are regularly used not only for their specific purposes, but also as meeting places, where people often spill out onto the road outside. In the streets of Zingonia Wolof is the predominant spoken language.

Less immediately visible, a lot of informal economic transactions also take place in Zingonia's streets. Shipments of goods heading for Senegal are organized and collected here; air tickets are traded with no need to make reservations through a formal travel agency; hairdresser salons are improvised in the back of shops engaged in some other activity; Senegalese music and video productions are stocked in the suitcases of door-to-door informal merchants and offered for sale in the shops and numerous apartments inhabited by Senegalese migrants. This long range of services is at hand not only for those who live in Zingonia, but it acts as a magnet which daily attracts flocks of Senegalese from neighboring areas.

Assan and Talla, as I have shown, still have strong linkages with Dakar, despite the fact that they now spend most of their time in Italy. It was here in Zingonia that their paths crossed for the first time. They have become close friends and spend their time together at weekends or after their factory shifts. Assan had first arrived here following the footsteps of other emigrants from his home village of origin. When he arrived in Italy, he could already count on a copious list of acquaintances and an address where he was sure to find refuge and assistance in settling into a new place. Talla, in contrast, decided to leave Senegal against his family's will and prepared his departure in great secrecy. After arriving in Milan, he sought the advice of a group of Senegalese whom he met by chance at the Central Station and they directed him to Zingonia. "I was given instructions on how to get here by train. They told me that it is a Senegalese place and that this is where everyone can easily find hospitality."

Talla's life in Italy, therefore, started in Zingonia. A few years later he decided to move to a quieter and less crowded village nearby, where he also holds a regular job. Zingonia, however, still remains the town that he turns to in his spare time. It is here, he insists, that he is kept up to date with developments in Senegal, where he meets up with people with whom he discusses the latest news and political events, where he can purchase the latest *mballax* (rhythmic music of Senegal) release.

It is here that Talla has left his closest friends, one of whom is Assan. They had first met at the desk of an informal money transfer service, set up by an enterprising group of Senegalese who collect euros in Italy and dispense CFA francs to recipients at the other end, thanks to an agreement with a transnational merchant whose business is based in Dakar. Because of their weekly appointments to send remittances home and then to phone from the international phone center to give their relatives the instructions to collect the money at the other end, Talla and Assan had met many times. Week after week they gradually got to know each other and now spend most of their weekends together in Zingonia, where they both feel that they have recreated a Senegalese environment. During the cold months they spend their time in the apartment Assan shares with five other Senegalese, enjoying conversation and drinking *attaya* (Senegalese tea). In the summer they prefer to stay outdoors, lingering under the porches of the buildings, outside local shops and in the few public gardens that decorate Zingonia's landscape.

During their meetings, Assan, Talla and their friends not only spend time remembering distant Senegal, they also renew their image of homeland and keep up with its developments. In the long series of formulae that are exchanged upon greeting each other, many revolve around the latest update from the family back home. *"Ana waa Senegal? Gëj nga dégg Senegal? Naka sa soxna? Sa doom bi tane na"* (tr.: "How's everyone in Senegal? Has it been long since you last heard from them? How's your wife doing? Is your son feeling better?"). The conversation then moves from the private sphere to lively debates on more general themes. On these occasions, Assan and Talla both maintain that: "We can forget our everyday lives here in Italy and close the door on its hard work and factory shifts. It is like going home for a while...."

Besides the regular get-togethers I have just described, Zingonia also constitutes a port of passage for many transnational merchants, who stop here for the mere time necessary to accumulate and organize their wares for their next shipment to Senegal. In Zingonia they find a base for frequent brief returns. Others, who are more strongly based in Italy, come here for their weekend shopping at the Senegalese grocery, to phone, to find a job, to find out about the latest news. Zingonia offers numerous occasions to remind people of the temporary nature of their life-projects in Italy and to recreate a more familiar environment. This translocality allows migrants to renew their feelings of involvement in a broader design: of being Senegalese and working towards return.

A Sacred Town

A strong symbolic value is attributed to Zingonia also in the name of its cultural, and especially religious, initiatives. A key role in making Zingonia a Senegalese town is played, in fact, by its *Daara*, the seat of the local Murid association.

Assan and Talla are not assiduous frequenters of the *Daara*; they prefer exercising their faith in the private space of the home. Assan and Talla, however, are exceptions. Most of the initial settlers in Zingonia were strongly associated to the Murid brotherhood and have turned Zingonia into one of Italy's Islamic enclaves. As a result, even today many Senegalese pass a large part of their spare time at the *Daara*, where weekend prayer sessions are regularly organized. Here the Murid followers (*taalibe*) not only fulfill their religious obligations, but also take decisions which concern the entire "community" and consolidate social ties.

Thanks to the *Daara* acting as a mosque, religious association and Koranic school, the Murid of Zingonia have diffused the fame of this place of prayer and worship far beyond the borders of town. During the numerous religious meetings, celebrations and visits by religious guides (*marabut*) from Senegal, busloads of pilgrims are attracted to Zingonia from even very distant places. It takes a certain familiarity with the town's layout to reach the *Daara*, since it lies hidden away in the industrial quarters of Zingonia. From the outside, it looks more like an anonymous warehouse than a place of worship. What makes it distinctive, however, is the colorful presence of Senegalese in their traditional dress—the only human presence in an otherwise deserted area of town.

The *Daara* also has an important role in channeling resources and directing them to Senegal. Zingonia is one of the collection points where it is always possible to pay the yearly offering that each Muslim is expected to give to the religious community (or *àddiya*). These funds are mostly reinvested in Senegal, where they are contributing to the spectacular growth of the Murid religious capital of Touba. Other material, such as religious publications, video recordings of prayer and chanting sessions and other celebrations, are also produced in Zingonia and regularly supply shops and market stalls selling religious items across Senegal. Thanks to these initiatives, the fame of Zingonia as a pious town has spread beyond the confines of Italy and has become also well known in Senegal itself.

It is interesting to observe that the role assumed by Zingonia as a religious center extends also to the followers of other Islamic brotherhoods in Senegal. The presence in Italy of members of the Tijaniyya, Qadiriyya and Layène brotherhoods, in fact, is gradually growing and they often enthusiastically participate in the religious happenings organized by the Murid. Zingonia, according to many Senegalese migrants, has become a sacred town, which exudes a protective power over those who live here and visit.

Secular events are also increasingly organized in Zingonia. Alongside the transnational success of religious initiatives, a rich calendar of concerts, street parties, and football tournaments is often announced on satellite radio, so that listeners in Zingonia as well as in Senegal are kept informed. In promoting religious as well as secular initiatives and in extending their reach across both Italy and Senegal, Zingonia creates the common ground that allows the Senegalese to feel part of the same transnational game, regardless of where they are momentarily located. In the words of many respondents in the field, this industrial town has been restored by the Senegalese, who have literally conquered its land and turned it into a Senegalese center.

Conclusion

The central role played by cities within transnational migration processes clearly emerges in the case studies of Dakar and Zingonia. Urban translocalities, I have argued, occupy an important role not merely as places of departure or of temporary and long-term residence, but also as places of transit and passage. Thanks to their position along the routes of many people, translocalities have become institutionalized and they are recognized as important steps along the migrants' diverse paths. The coming together of circulating and sedentary migrants in translocalities makes them places where people negotiate between pressures for emplacement and the drive for continuous transnational mobility.

The stories of the Senegalese in Dakar and Zingonia that I have collected in these pages epitomize the places where, as a result of transnational migration, identity and belonging are re-defined and transnational living across different countries is facilitated. Using translocalities as a tool to interpret social processes associated with migration also highlights the difference that exists between transnational migration and mobility. As Riccio (2006) points out, being a *transmigrant* is not synonymous with being a *nomad*: the first does not automatically lead to the latter, as migrants and their networks still remain strongly emplaced.

The picture I have just outlined portrays the main features shared by translocalities across a country of origin and a country of immigration. Dakar is a city that opens up to the outside world, insofar as it is strongly linked to foreign localities through trade, migration and media. It is from Dakar that the migrant's relationship with place is broken and the transnational voyage begins. Departure from the homeland marks an act of place-breaking that is followed by processes of place-making in the country of immigration. Zingonia, in this sense, is a place socially constructed as a locus where people come to terms with being migrants. It acts as a decompression chamber, allowing each individual to readjust to the new condition and facilitating insertion in the host country. Zingonia, however, is also the place where the home country is redefined from a distance, recreated through memory and nostalgia and through the reproduction, abroad, of familiar cues. In turn, Dakar is also recreated through the many investments resulting from migrants' transnational living. Dakar is not merely an intangible symbol of a distant homeland or an icon of dreams about return; it occupies a significant part in the re-materialization of the entire migratory experience.

Notes

1. Basic references to Smith's notion of translocality are offered in his classic *Transnational Urbanism* (2001). In later writing (2005), he offers a critical confrontation of the use made of the concept of translocality in his own work and in those of the other two authors just mentioned.

2. A special issue of the *Journal of Ethnic and Migration Studies* edited by Conradson and Latham (2005), for instance, gathers the contributions of various authors engaged in research that incorporates both mobility and emplacement.
3. The data used in the coming pages was collected mainly during research I conducted for my PhD in the period 2004-2005. Research was based upon ethnographic observations in Senegal and in Italy and interviews with Senegalese migrants and their families.
4. This figure is derived from data published by the Istituto Nazionale di Statistica (ISTAT), updated to the end of the year 2005.
5. This Senegalese Islamic brotherhood traditionally has a strong tie with commercial trade activities. For general readings on the issue see Bava (2003), Diouf (2000), Salem (1991).

References

Agier, M. (1999) *L'Invention de la Ville: Banlieues, Townships, Invasions et Favelas*. Paris: Editions des Archives Contemporaines.
Appadurai, A. (1995) "The Production of Locality." In *Counterworks: Managing the Diversity of Knowledge* (pp. 204-255). London: Routledge.
_____ (1996) "Sovereignty without Territoriality: Notes for a Postnational Geography." In *The Geography of Identity* (pp. 40-58). Ann Arbor: University of Michigan Press.
Bava, S. (2003) "De la 'Baraka aux Affaires:' Éthos Économico-Religieux et Transnationalité Chez les Migrants Sénégalais Mourides." *Revue des Migrations Internationales* 19 (2): 69-84.
Carter, D. M. (1997) *States of Grace: Senegalese in Italy and the New European Immigration*. Minneapolis, London: University of Minnesota Press.
Conradson, D. and A. Latham (2005) "Transnational Urbanism: Attending to Everyday Practices and Mobilities." *Journal of Ethnic and Migration Studies* 31 (2): 227-233.
Crang, M. (1998) *Cultural Geography*. London: Routledge.
Diouf, M. (2000) "The Murid Trade Diaspora and The Making of a Vernacular Cosmopolitism." *Public Culture* 12 (3): 679-702.
Ebin, V. (1996) "Making Room versus Creating Space: The Construction of Spatial Categories by Itinerant Mouride Traders." In *Making Muslim Space in North America and Europe* (pp. 92-109). Berkeley: University of California Press.
Ebin, V. and R. Lake (1992) "Camelots Sénégalais à New York." *Hommes et Migrations* 1160: 20-26.
Eurostat (2000) "Facteurs d'Attraction et de Répulsion à l'Origine des Flux Migratoires Internationaux. Rapport National—Sénégal." *Eurostat Working Papers* Population et Conditions Sociales 3/2000/E/12.
Glick Schiller, N., L. Basch, and C. Szanton-Blanc (eds.) (1992) *Toward a Transnational Perspective on Migration*. New York: New York Academy of Sciences.
Grillo, R. (2007) "Betwixt and Between: Trajectories and Projects of Transmigration." *Journal of Ethnic and Migration Studies* 33 (2): 199-217.
Hannerz, U. (1980) *Exploring the City: Inquiries toward an Urban Anthropology*. New York: Colombia University Press.
_____ (1998) "Transnational Research." In *Handbook of Methods in Cultural Anthropology* (pp. 235-256). Walnut Creek, California: AltaMira Press.
Kane, A. (2002) "Senegal's Village Diaspora and the People Left Ahead." In *The Transnational Family: New European Frontiers and Global Networks* (pp. 245-264). Oxford-New York: Berg.

King, R. and R. Black (eds.) (1997) *Southern Europe and the New Immigrations*. Brighton: Sussex Academic Press.

Portes, A. (1999) "Conclusion: Towards a New World. The Origins and Effects of Transnational Activities." *Ethnic and Racial Studies* 22 (2): 463-477.

Riccio, B. (2001) "From 'Ethnic Group' to 'Transnational Community'? Senegalese Migrants' Ambivalent Experiences and Multiple Trajectories." *Journal of Ethnic and Migration Studies* 27 (4): 583-99.

_____ (2003) "More than a Trade Diaspora: Senegalese Transnational Experiences in Emilia-Romagna (Italy)." In *New African Diasporas* (pp. 95-110). London: Routledge.

_____ (2006) "Transmigrants mais pas 'Nomades.' Transnationalisme mouride en Italie." *Cahiers d'Etudes Africaines* 46 (1): 95-114.

Salem, G. (1991) "De la Brousse Sénégalaise au Boul'Mich: Le Système Commercial Mouride en France." *Cahiers d'Études Africaines* XII: 267-288.

Sarr, C. (2004) "Émergence de Nouveaux Acteurs Locaux et Recomposition des Territoires Urbains; Appropriation de la Centralité des Villes par les *Moodu Moodu*: Exemples de Dakar, Saint-Louis et New York." In *Gouverner les Villes du Sud. Défis pour la Recherche et pour l'Action* (pp. 125-129). Actes du Colloque International du PRUD, Programme de Recherche Urbaine pour le Développement, 5th-7th May. Paris: Unesco.

Sinatti, G. (2006) "Diasporic Cosmopolitanism and Conservative Translocalism: Narratives of Nation among Senegalese Migrants in Italy." *Studies in Ethnicity and Nationalism* 6 (3): 30-50.

Smith, M. P. (2001) *Transnational Urbanism: Locating Globalization*. Oxford: Blackwell.

_____ (2005) "Power in Place/ Places of Power: Contextualizing Transnational Research." *City and Society* 17 (1): 5-34.

Sy, M., A. Ba, and N. Ndiaye (1992) "Demographic Implications of Development Policies in the Sahel: The Case of Senegal." In *Migrations, Development and Urbanization Policies in sub-Saharan Africa* (pp. 112-152). Dakar: Codesria.

Tall, S. M. (1994) "Les Investissements Immobiliers à Dakar des Émigrants Sénégalais." *Revue Européenne des Migrations Internationales* 10 (3): 137-151.

Vertovec, S. and R. Cohen (eds.) (1999) *Migration, Diasporas and Transnationalism*. London: Edward Elgar.

5

South-South Migration and Transnational Ties between Cuba and Mozambique

Katrin Hansing

Over the past decades the social sciences and humanities have been greatly influenced by the effects of and discourses on globalization, migration and transnationalism. In so doing scholars have tried to theoretically understand and explain the complexities involved in a world of increasing movement, interconnectedness and mixture of cultures (Appadurai 2001; Castells 2000; Hannerz 1996; Kearny 1995; Rosaldo and Inde 2002; Smith and Guarnizo 1998; Trouillot 2003; Vertovec 1999). Despite these efforts much of the research on migration and transnationalism has tended to be conducted and conceptualized along traditional geographical axes. Whether it is research on types of migration or specific migrant communities, (Anderson 2000; Mahler 1995; Killingray 1994), remittance-sending practices (Lozano Ascencio 1993; León-Ledesma and Piracha 2004; Orozco 2002), transnational politics (Glick Schiller 2001; Ong 1998; Østergaard-Nielsen 2003) or the multifarious social and cultural phenomena that occur in and/or between diasporas and their countries of origin (Caglar 1995; Karim 2003; van der Veer 1995; van Hear 1998), the focus continues to be overwhelmingly North-South and East-West. In contrast, research on migration and transnational links between countries in the global South is still relatively limited.[1]

This chapter intends to break away from these more established research and theoretical norms and contribute to the discussion on South-South migration within the context of globalization. This will be done through a case study of Cuba's large-scale state-sponsored aid programs, through which highly skilled Cuban professionals temporarily migrate to work in other developing countries of the South. Based on anthropological field research in Havana, Cuba and Maputo, Mozambique, the chapter will focus on the lives, realities, and changing identities of Cuban doctors, who are based in Maputo as well as their transnational ties to Cuba. Particular attention will be paid to how Maputo, the capital of one of the world's poorest yet economically fastest growing African nations, is perceived, experienced and lived by these professional migrants who, for the most part, have never left socialist Cuba before and how, in turn, their experiences feed back into their lives in Cuba. In so doing, the overriding question whether this particular case of South-South migration differs from North-South and East-West migratory dynamics, motivations and experiences will also be considered. The chapter will start with an overview of Cuba's aid programs, in general, and to Mozambique, in particular, before examining the lives of the Cuban doctors in Maputo and their transnational ties back home.

Cuban Social Assistance Programs

Since the 1960s, Cuba has offered social assistance in the form of education, health care and technical aid to dozens of developing nations (Eckstein 1985; Feinsilver 1993). Based on the revolutionary government's ideological principle of helping poor countries to strengthen their own human capital resources, Cuba's assistance has mainly consisted of: (a) sending Cuban professionals to other developing nations in order to temporarily help fill their skilled labor gaps, as well as to train locals in various applied professions, and (b) offering scholarships to nationals from these countries to study in Cuba. The Caribbean island has been able to offer this type of aid because of its own strong emphasis on and policy of free education at home, which has over the years produced large numbers, even surplus numbers of high skilled professionals.

As a result, over 140,000 Cuban technical and professional personnel, including doctors, teachers, engineers, agronomists, construction workers, sports trainers, agricultural and fishing experts, have been sent on *misión* (a mission) and served as so-called "proletarian internationalists" in over 150 countries.[2] During this time Cuba has also offered scholarships to over 50,000 students from dozens of developing nations.[3]

These aid programs emerged in a Cold War context where Cuba not only made a decisive break with the dominant patterns and hierarchies of globalization, then predominantly understood in terms of capitalism, imperialism and the United States, but also attempted to create an alternative model based on relations to socialist, non-aligned and developing nations, many of which are located in the global South. In this process a sophisticated Third World, Southern hemispheric solidarity discourse was developed in which poor, developing countries came to be represented as a united group of nations, sharing a common socio-economic plight and struggling against the same global injustices.

Cuba's assistance programs have played an important role in the construction of this image. Since their emergence, the Cuban government has embedded them in an official language of South-South solidarity and Third World brotherhood, characterizing them as an alternative form of globalization (as in the current popular political slogan "*globalicemos la solidaridad*" [let's globalize solidarity]) and hailing its aid workers as selfless, caring, humanitarian volunteers, who are proof that "*un mundo mejor es possible*" (a better world is possible).[4]

Until the late 1980s, when Cuba's economy was largely subsidized by the Soviet Union, the island was able to pay for its aid programs. However, with the fall of communism in the eastern block Cuba fell into a deep economic crisis and began charging for its aid.[5] Based on bilateral agreements, Cuba now provides the recipient countries with the number of requested specialists in return for a fixed fee per person, of which the aid worker only receives a small percentage in the form of a stipend/salary. Despite having now to pay for the aid, many developing countries welcome this scheme as it is still much less expensive than importing specialists from elsewhere. Over the past few years the assistance programs have become one of Cuba's most important sources of badly needed hard currency. As a result, the number of aid programs and professionals being sent abroad has increased dramatically. In so doing, the Cuban government not only profits monetarily, but has also created a handy mechanism to temporarily get rid of a large part of its arguably most frustrated surplus labor.

Cuba's Aid to Africa and Mozambique in Particular

Over the past four decades Africa has by far been the largest recipient of Cuba's aid. Since the 1960s, over 45,000 Cuban doctors and nurses and thousands of other professionals have worked on various development projects on the Continent, while more than 30,000 African students have studied and graduated in Cuba. Moreover, Cuba has and continues to build and staff numerous hospitals and medical schools in several African nations. To date Mozambique and Angola have been the largest beneficiaries of this aid.

When Mozambique gained its independence in 1975, it not only lost the majority of its skilled labor force,[6] but also inherited a land void of schools, hospitals, roads, and other modern infrastructure, and had an illiteracy rate of 93 percent. Given these conditions and a looming civil war that would last for almost twenty years, the Cuban government offered the then-socialist government of Samora Machel to send Mozambican schoolchildren to study in Cuba and Cuban professionals to work in Mozambique. It was during this time, in the late 1970s, that the first Cuban doctors started arriving in Mozambique, which until the mid-1980s had almost no indigenous health care workers and only one major hospital with medical specialists in the capital, Maputo. The Cubans came to work as doctors and to teach medicine. This scheme has remained in place until today. For although there is now a growing group of Mozambican health care workers, there are still not enough indigenous doctors to serve the population so that the government needs to import foreign doctors. Today 55 percent of all doctors in Mozambique are foreigners, of which over 40 percent are Cuban.[7]

Profile of Proletarian Internationalists

Currently there are 245 Cuban doctors on the state-sponsored aid programs in Mozambique.[8] They are men and women, aged between 35 and 60, who come from all parts of Cuba and represent a wide range of medical specializations. Although some have been on a Cuban medical mission abroad before, for many this is their first time outside of Cuba and away from their families, including their spouses and children, who are not allowed to come. They are initially sent out for a period of three years, during which time they are allowed to return home once a year on vacation. Known in Cuba as "proletarian internationalists" these doctors can also be defined as highly skilled temporary labor migrants.

The doctors, who are based in Maputo, are usually specialists and work at the main, central hospital, while most general practitioners are sent out to the rural areas. Working conditions are quite challenging, especially given the lack of modern medical equipment and supplies and the overwhelming amount of patients of which at least 70 percent are HIV/AIDS infected.

In Mozambique each doctor receives an average salary of US$500 a month plus free housing and local transport to and from work.[9] In comparison to other foreign aid workers or even most Mozambican doctors, their salary is considered quite low. Given these conditions, what motivates these Cubans to go and work abroad, thousands of miles away from their homes and families?

Motivations for Going *en Misión*

For the past forty years the Cuban government has described and praised its aid workers as altruistic internationalists, who have "voluntarily" gone out into the world, leaving behind their own families, friends, homes and workplaces, in order to help others less fortunate than themselves. Without a doubt many Cuban aid workers have, in part, been motivated to go abroad by these noble principles and in so doing, have helped many people to live a better life. Unfortunately it cannot be stated that Cuban professionals have always gone abroad voluntarily—if by voluntarily we mean based on their own free choice and will to do so. Instead, people have had the "choice" to decline going abroad once they have been chosen. Few have, however, dared to decline, except in urgent cases such as ill health, out of fear of potential negative repercussions that are never publicly uttered, but of which everyone is aware, such as not being promoted or having one's children not get into university. In a society where everything is managed and controlled by the state these are very real barriers, which, in practice, have led most people to outwardly conform to the status quo.

Since the beginning of Cuba's economic crisis in the early 1990s this culture of fear has been joined by economic and material necessities. Going on an international mission is one of the few legal ways for Cubans to make somewhat of a better living. In Cuba a medical specialist, such as a gynecologist or heart surgeon, earns the equivalent of US$25 a month that, despite government subsidies, is not enough to live on and, therefore, most people need to engage in the informal, black market economy to get by. Thus although US$500 may be a relatively low salary for most doctors and other aid workers, it is a huge salary increase for Cubans, especially given that their rent is paid for and most of their fixed costs are confined to household related expenses, such as electricity, gas, food, toiletries and personal/leisure items.

In other words, they can save and send some money home. As a result, going on a mission is now so popular that using connections and bribes to do so have become standard practice. Although these Cubans might be considered lucky to be able to go abroad where they can earn dollars, they can still not be said to be doing so voluntarily. We are thus presented with a fascinating example of a massive, state-sponsored involuntary/voluntary highly skilled labor migration.

Cuba vs. Mozambique

Although most doctors nowadays are eager to go on a mission for the reasons discussed, most have never left Cuba before and thus have no idea what awaits them. Although they have heard many stories from family, friends, colleagues, or neighbors who have been abroad, seen foreign movies, spoken to tourists or other foreigners in Cuba and perhaps contemplated, fantasized or even tried to emigrate, most have very little concrete understanding of what it means to live and work in a completely different culture, society and politico-economic system from that of their own.

Moreover, most of the ideas and images which people harbor in relation to life abroad are connected to what they think life is like *en la yuma*, as Cubans refer to Miami, the U.S. or the North more generally, namely images and ideas of modern houses, cars, highways, household appliances, satellite television, beautiful shopping malls and mountains and mountains of goods to choose from. In short, this reflects a desire for comfort associated with consumption. However, Cuba's doctors and other international workers are not sent to *la yuma*, but rather to countries such as Haiti, Pakistan, and Mozambique.

A decade after the end of its long and bitter civil war, which left the country physically and humanly ravaged, Mozambique has recently turned from its former one party, socialist system to a multi-party democracy and market-oriented economy. Western luxury items, Chinese consumer goods, modern shopping centers, sidewalk cafes colorful advertisement and mobile phones can now be found in most urban areas. Many former state-owned companies have been privatized and private enterprise and foreign investment are growing and turning the country into one of the fastest growing African economies. Nevertheless, Mozambique remains one of the poorest countries in the world, with an official unemployment rate of over 30 percent, 42 percent illiteracy, and an average life expectancy of thirty-seven years. HIV/AIDS is rampant as are cholera, tuberculosis and malaria. Basic housing, sanitation and clean and safe drinking water are considered a luxury by most.[10]

From afar, Maputo's mix of colonial, socialist and more modern buildings set alongside the Indian Ocean makes it look like a picturesque city. On closer observation however, one is struck by its many peripheral shanty towns, mountains of overflowing garbage sites and loud and busy streets filled with peddlers, beggars, and streetchildren trying to make ends meet by competing for the attention of the few tourists, expatriates and privileged locals.

All this contrasts dramatically with Cuba's relatively slow pace, where there is little competition and rush, but instead endless lines of people waiting for everything from food rations to being able to make a phone call from a public phone booth. Moreover, despite Cuba's authoritarian political and dire economic situation, Cubans have been used to a cradle-to-grave social security system and semi-egalitarian society which, despite the current major shortages and increasing social inequalities, does still guarantee and provide them with a roof over their head, basic foodstuffs, free access to medical care and education. Furthermore, the island has a low crime rate, almost 100 percent literacy and one of the highest life expectancies in the world.

Plunged from one socio-economic and political reality into the other, how do the Cuban doctors perceive and experience these differences? How do they orchestrate their lives in Maputo and to what extent have they been able to integrate themselves locally? To answer these questions we must look at how the doctors actually live in Mozambique, particularly in comparison to their lives in Cuba.

Life in Cuba and Maputo

Paulo[11] is a 43-year-old pediatrician from Guantánamo City in the eastern part of Cuba and has been working in Maputo for almost two years. This is his first medical mission although not his first time abroad, having been sent to Angola as a soldier at age seventeen. At home he worked at a local polyclinic for many years and earned the equivalent of US$23 a month. In order to support himself and his family he had to buy and resell things in the black market, as well as often spend his day off in the countryside in order to barter consumer goods for food with farmers. Together with his wife, two teenage children and ailing mother he lives in a small, run-down house on the outskirts of town. In good periods they have running water every six to seven days and cooking gas that lasts for three weeks of the month. Power cuts are part of daily life. It was the desperate need to repair his roof and outer walls as well as a desire to be able to buy certain basic domestic appliances and scarce consumer goods that initially made Paulo decide to try and go on medical mission. In order to do so, he entered the Cuban Communist Party (CCP) and bribed a series of people in charge of deciding who gets sent abroad.[12] Two and half years later he was told that he would be sent to Mozambique.

In Maputo, Paulo has his own apartment. Although by no means luxurious, it is a lot more modern, well equipped, and spacious than his home in Guantánamo. He also rarely has power cuts, always has running water and has someone who comes in several times a week to clean and cook. At the central hospital Paulo is the head of the pediatric ward. Unlike in Cuba where, due to the large number of health care workers and free health care system a doctor's position entails no special social status, in Mozambique Paulo's profession brings him both status and respect. Moreover, Cuban doctors in Mozambique enjoy enormous popularity. This is not only because they are considered professionally highly competent, but also because of their perceived open, non-hierarchical and sociable manner.

Paulo is also the Cuban Communist Party secretary in Mozambique. In practice, this means that he is in charge of all CCP affairs in Mozambique, such as keeping the doctors informed of political developments at home, organizing political and ideological meetings and other events, and collecting party dues. He did not choose this position, but was appointed CCP secretary a few weeks after his arrival in Mozambique. To have declined would have raised suspicions and perhaps cost him his job. Like so many of his colleagues, Paulo thus plays the game and consequentially lives with the daily contradictions of having to celebrate the values of the Cuban Revolution and its altruistic aid to Africa, when in fact he admits that his main reason for coming to Mozambique was to be able to earn a decent salary and save enough money to fix up his house.

Two years into his mission, Paulo still misses many aspects of his life in Cuba, especially his family, neighborhood and the general comfort and familiarity of his own home and culture. He admits that it was difficult at first to get used to his new surroundings, work routine, colleagues, the local mentality and, above all, that suddenly everything had a price tag. He was also overwhelmed by the levels of extreme poverty and wealth as well as the never-ending lines of patients, many of whom he cannot really help given that they are HIV/AIDS infected. However, like many if not most of his colleagues, Paulo has adapted well and made a life for himself in Maputo. In this the similarities in climate, languages (Portuguese and Spanish), and culture (Mozambique and Cuba both share an Afro-Latino heritage) are an advantage. Beyond having his own space, good living conditions and the respect he gets through his job, Paulo mostly enjoys earning his own money and being able to live a standard of living and lifestyle he could only dream of in Cuba. As he put it: "What I can earn in one month here would take me about three years in Cuba and there I could not even save one penny."

Making and saving money is Paulo's main priority. Apart from his monthly salary of US$500 he, like most Cuban doctors, tries to earn an extra income by taking overnight shifts from his Mozambican and other foreign colleagues. Depending on the month, he can increase his monthly salary by US$300 to US$400 in this manner. Working for a monetary rather than ideologically-based incentive and then having the power to spend their own money on goods and activities of their own choice is a novelty for most Cubans—a novelty, which accompanied by their relative freedom of movement and access to information, is perceived as a form of personal freedom. This is a "relative freedom" because, although the doctors are geographically far away from the daily hardships of life in Cuba, their lives are still controlled by weekly CCP and other political activities, as well as the omnipresent eyes and ears of embassy and fellow medical staff, some of whom are said to be Cuban state security informants. This produces a sense of unease and distrust in most doctors as well as discreet and careful behavior even among each other.

Despite these constraints, the doctors move around the city with ease. On their days off many can be found scouting out good deals in the wholesale stores and local markets. Given that the doctors are allowed to send home unlimited amounts of cargo freight at a reduced cost, many use their savings to buy extra appliances and cheap goods, which they then resell once they are back in Cuba. Due to the dearth of consumer goods on the island, they can make a handsome profit on items such as microwaves, televisions, VCRs, and DVDs, but also underwear, socks, make-up, pens and other lightweight goods, which they buy in bulk at wholesale prices.

Apart from shopping and managing and reinvesting their savings, the doctors also spend their free time taking advantage of the different leisure opportunities on offer in Maputo such as going out to nightclubs, restaurants, bars, and theatres. Given that most of these activities are only available to tourists or people with hard currency in Cuba, it is often the first time for some of the doctors, especially the younger ones, to experience them. Although much of the socializing occurs among the Cubans themselves in the form of meals, parties, and joint excursions, it is not uncommon for them to meet and engage in friendships as well as more intimate relationships with locals and other foreigners.

Paulo, for instance, has a Mozambican girlfriend, Isabel, who is a successful, middle class businesswoman. They have been together for over a year and have lived in Paulo's flat ever since. Through his relationship with Isabel, Paulo has become exposed to Mozambican culture and society in a much more intimate and personal way. Apart from becoming involved in local activities, such as playing on a football team and going to a local church, he has also grown close to Isabel's friends and family members. Having a Mozambican partner despite being married and having a family in Cuba is very common among Cubans abroad. Even though this often leads to major interpersonal difficulties, it is one of the ways the doctors integrate themselves more easily into Mozambican society.

It is through such relationships and activities, but also through their access to the Internet and cable television, which are illegal in Cuba, that the Cuban doctors are continually confronted with new ideas, experiences and possibilities that not only broaden their own horizons, but also make many reflect more critically on their political and economic situation at home. Although some may have done this long before going abroad, they can now compare and contrast the different realities through their own lived and embodied experiences. "It is like being thrown from savage socialism into savage capitalism," as Paulo described his experience of leaving Cuba and coming to Maputo, "but here I can see, hear and explore so many different things and for the first time I have options and can make my own decisions. It's like I can finally breathe."

Although most doctors find it hard to be away from their families and to live and work in a society with such enormous socio-economic discrepancies, it is this first-time experience of relative personal freedom, economic comfort, and choice that make most doctors perceive Maputo not as a peripheral, marginalized developing city, but rather as a dynamic, globalized urban space. In fact, in comparison to their lives in Cuba as well as most people's lives in Maputo, their relatively privileged status and what could be defined as middle class standard of living and lifestyle makes them perceive their lives in Mozambique as akin to being in the North or West. Equated with economic opportunities, freedom of choice and movement and consumer culture, the North or West can thus also be found in the South, depending on where one is coming from and what socio-economic status one has in the host society.

Transnational Ties between Mozambique and Cuba

Unlike many migrant communities in the North and West, which owing to relatively inexpensive telecommunications, air fares and remittance sending opportunities, can keep fairly strong and ongoing transnational ties with their home communities, this is not the case with the Cuban doctors in Mozambique or most other countries they are sent to on missions. In large part this has to do with the fact that given the unreliable Cuban mail service, the Cuban government's monopoly on international phone calls to and from the island, and Cubans' lack of access to the Internet, contact and communication with Cuba from any part of the world (including the North/West) is challenging and expensive. Added to this are all the potential challenges and difficulties that can arise when trying to communicate between two countries of the South, such as Mozambique and Cuba. Last but not least, many moneygram agencies located in the South do not offer sending but only receiving remittance services. Such is the case with Western Union, the only moneygram agency in Mozambique.

As a result, the Cuban doctors in Mozambique have had to find and create alternative mechanisms to stay in touch with their families and friends at home. Apart from occasional phone calls and emails that are rerouted via someone in Cuba who has an email account, the main avenues of communication between the doctors and their loved ones are the doctors themselves. Given that all doctors return home once a year on vacation and do so at different times of the year, there is usually a small group that comes and goes every five to six weeks. Being the most direct and reliable as well as cheapest form of communication to and from Cuba for all, all doctors at some point serve as "mules" carrying hundreds of letters and photographs, thousands of dollars and other small items back and forth between southern Africa and the Caribbean. In this the individuals are not only bearers of goods, but also of news, stories, and gossip.

Impact and Consequences of the Transnational Ties in Cuba

The letters and remittances enable families to stay in touch, but also have an enormous impact on the local Cuban economy. According to recent studies remittances are currently Cuba's main source of hard currency, of which a large percentage is said to come from the international workers. Through these remittances, individual families are able to improve their standard of living considerably. However, in so doing, a culture of dependence on Cubans who are abroad has arisen, as have signs of the emergence of new social classes and inequalities, given that not all Cubans receive remittances.

Despite the irregularity and limitations of these South-South transnational ties, they also allow for new and different ideas to enter Cuba. In their letters but, more importantly, on the doctors' annual return visits and their final return to Cuba, they not only bring with them their amassed savings and highly priced consumer goods, but also new experiences, habits, ideas, dress codes, and the like. In contrast to the Cuban government's ideologically driven images and discourses of the developing world, which tend to focus predominantly on the socio-economic inequalities in such countries and pin the blame for these on the West/North, especially the United States, the doctors' stories and anecdotes portray a much more multifaceted and complex reality of life in places like Maputo. These include both the downsides and difficulties of the daily realities in such a city, but also the positive elements of their own lives there, such as the economic and professional opportunities, leisure activities, access to information and what Paulo referred to as the ability to "breathe."

Ever since the Cuban government was forced to slightly open up the island over a decade ago due to its economic crisis, such stories and the imported consumer goods, popular cultural and fashion trends and dollars they are accompanied by, together with those entering Cuba via tourists and exiled family members, have started to produce fundamental changes in Cuban society. Not only have these transnational influences heightened many people's economic dependence on the outside world, awakened their consumer desires as well as curiosity to experience life outside for themselves, they have also pushed many to ask themselves more critical questions about life on the island and what they have been told about the outside world from their government for the past forty-seven years.

These developments, in turn, have led more and more people to seek out alternative sources of information as well as to create and carve out their own spaces, networks and mechanisms, whether economic, social or cultural, independently from the state. In conjunction with and in large part due to the growing economic problems and continued political repression on the island, the increasing influences from abroad, including those from the international aid workers, are provoking a qualitative change and difference in the way many people think and act. Cubans may not yet be turning to the streets to express their frustrations and discontent, but it is this newfound and growing independence among many that may just turn out to be one of the greatest challenges to the state. Officially sent out to show that a better world is possible, it is ironic that the Cuban doctors and other internationalist aid workers have come to play an important role in this process by showing Cubans on the island that their world could be better too.

Conclusion

Despite the very particular conditions and characteristics of Cuba's social assistance programs, their resulting South-South migration dynamics and transnational practices do not fundamentally differ from the more common North-South and East-West ones. As in the case of most labor migrants, the Cuban doctors primarily migrate, albeit temporarily, in search of economic opportunities and a better life. In the particular case of those in

Mozambique they have, in fact, been able to establish a standard of living and lifestyle akin to what many migrants hope and dream to be able to find in the North-West. This opens up the interesting and important question of what we actually mean by the "North," "West," and "South"?

Despite the difficulties involved in communicating with Cuba, the doctors have been able to establish transnational ties back home. In so doing they are not only influencing their home communities economically, but also, given Cuba's particular political situation, contributing to the slow emergence of a civil society on the island.

Notes

1. This does not however mean that South-South migration and relations are novel phenomena, for a myriad of historical and contemporary ties between the South have and continue to exist. Some of the better known examples include: the coolie labor migrations from China, India, and Japan to both the Caribbean and Africa (Ramdin 2000); Indian Ocean trade links and the many crosscultural currents and dialogues, particularly in the form of music, dance, language and religion that continue to take place between all of these regions (Manuel 1995); the influences of the Indian film and Brazilian soap opera industries in Africa and Asia (Getter 2002); and, the impact of the trade of consumer goods between Asia, Africa and Latin America.
2. To date Cuba's medical and educational aid has been its most important form of assistance. At present there are about 35,000 Cuban health care professionals working in over 80 different countries. Of these about 16,000 are currently working in Venezuela. The numbers of Cuban internationalist workers were provided by the Cuban Ministry for Public Health (MINSAP).
3. According to figures from 2005 there were 15,544 registered foreign students from 110 nations studying in Cuba. The numbers of foreign students in Cuba were provided by the Cuban Ministry of Education (MED) and Ministry of Higher Education (MES).
4. In the particular case of Africa, Cuba's aid, both military and humanitarian, has also been placed in the context of the island's own slave history and African cultural heritage; explaining the aid as a historical debt and duty to the Continent.
5. Costs vary depending on the nature of the aid program as well as the recipient country's economic situation. Scholarships are still free of charge, although students or their governments now pay for their transport to and from Cuba.
6. Before 1975 most skilled laborers and professionals in Mozambique were Portuguese or Mozambicans of Portuguese descent. Most left the country at independence.
7. The other foreign health care workers mainly come from China, India, Pakistan, the former Soviet Union, and Eastern Europe.
8. There are also a number of Cuban doctors in Mozambique who have defected over the years and who thus no longer form part of the formal bilateral aid programs. Most of these doctors have been able to continue to work in the Mozambican public or private health service. No clear numbers were able to be obtained, but estimates range between 30 and 70 defected Cuban doctors in Mozambique.
9. The salary/stipend amount differs from country to country.
10. See: Economist Intelligence Unit Country Report on Mozambique, 2007.
11. To protect the informants all names and biographical data have been changed.

12. It is commonly assumed that CCP members have a higher chance to be sent abroad on a mission.

References

Anderson, B. (2000). *Doing the Dirty Work*. London: Zed Press.
Appadurai, A. (2001). *Globalization*. Durham, NC: Duke University Press.
Caglar, A. (1995). "McDöner: Döner Kebap and the social positioning struggle of German Turku." In *Marketing in a Multicultural World* (pp. 209-230). London: Sage.
Castells, M. (2000). *End of Millennium*. Oxford: Oxford University Press.
Eckstein, S. (1985). "Cuban Internationalism." In *Cuba: Twenty Five Years of Revolution, 1959-1984* (pp. 372-390). New York: Praeger.
Economist Intelligence Unit (2007). *Country Report Mozambique*. London: EIU.
Feinsilver, J. (1993). *Healing the Masses: Cuban Health Politics at Home and Abroad*. Berkeley, CA: University of California Press.
Getter, J. (2002). *The Electrifying Dream: South Indian Film in a Changing World*. Ph.D. dissertation. Middletown, CT: Wesleyan University.
Glick Schiller, N. (2001). *Georges Woke Up Laughing: Long-Distance Nationalism and the Search for Home*. Durham, NC: Duke University Press.
Hannerz, U. (1996). *Transnational Connections*. London: Routledge.
Karim, K. (2003). *The Media of Diaspora*. London: Routledge.
Kearney, M. (1995). "The local and the global: the anthropology of globalization and transnationalism." *Annual Review of Anthropology* 24: 547-565.
Killingray, D. (1994). *Africans in Britain*. Ilford: Frank Cass and Co.
Lozano-Ascencio, F. (1993). *Bringing it Back Home: Remittances to Mexico from Migrant Workers in the US*. La Jolla, CA: Center for US-Mexican Studies.
León-Ledesma, M., and M. Piracha (2004). "International Migration and the Role of Remittances in Eastern Europe." *International Migration* 42 (4): 65–83.
Mahler, S. (1995). *American Dreaming: Immigrant Life on the Margins*. Princeton, NJ: Princeton University Press.
Manuel, P. (1995). *Caribbean Currents: Caribbean Music from Rumba to Reggae*. Philadelphia: Temple University Press.
Ong, A. (1998). *Flexible Citizenship: The Cultural Logics of Transnationality*. Durham, NC: Duke University Press.
Orozco, M. (2002). "Globalization and Migration: The Impact of Family Remittances in Latin America." *Latin American Politics and Society* 44 (2): 41-66.
Østergaard-Nielsen, E. (2003). *Transnational Politics: Turks and Kurds in Germany*. London: Routledge.
Ramdin, R. (2000). *Arising from Bondage: a History of Indo-Caribbean People*. New York: New York University Press.
Rosaldo, R., and J. X. Inde (eds.) (2002). *Anthropology of Globalization: A Reader*. Oxford: Oxford University Press.
Smith, M. P., and L. E. Guarnizo (eds.) (1998). *Transnationalism from Below*. New Brunswick, NJ: Transaction Publishers.
Trouillot, M. (2003). *Global Transformations: Anthropology and the Modern World*. New York: Palgrave Macmillan.
Van der Veer, P. (1995). *Nation and Migration: the Politics of Space in the South Asian Diaspora*. Philadelphia: University of Pennsylvania Press.
Van Hear, N. (1998). *New Diasporas: The Mass Exodus, Dispersal and Regrouping of Migrant Communities*. London: UCL Press.
Vertovec, S., and R. Cohen (eds.) (1999). *Migration, Diasporas and Transnationalism*. Cheltenham: Edward Elgar.

6

Chinese Transnational Entrepreneurs in Budapest and Belgrade: Seeking Markets, Carrying Globalization

Svetlana Milutinovic

China has been a great source of migration since the thirteenth century, when the first significant number of migrants moved to South-East Asia. Today, with its population of more than 1.3 billion and systematic reforms, accompanied by unparalleled economic growth and opening up to the outside world, China could become one of the major actors in global migration processes. Extensive research provides valuable insights into Chinese migration to Southeast Asia, North America, and Australia but much less is known about their migration to Europe. Although Chinese have migrated to Europe for more than a century, their number was comparatively small until very recently. Currently, there are no exact data on the Chinese migrants in Europe. Depending on the source, the numbers vary widely from 200,000 to one million or more (Skeldon 2004), or reports of half a million (Pieke 2005). In general, all the estimates emphasize their rapid migration to Europe during the last few decades.

Scholars have usually focused on the Chinese in West European countries and only a few researchers have explored the relatively recent migration to other European regions. Even more problematic is the fact that research mainly focuses on Chinese migration into individual countries. However, a significant part of this migration has been towards Central and South-East European countries. Besides the lack of information about the exact number of the Chinese who either settle down or migrate further, there is a rather vague picture about their life and connections with the home country. Furthermore, analyses about South-East European countries that are not members of the European Union (EU) or Organization for Economic Co-operation and Development (OECD), such as Serbia, are particularly scarce. The ways in which newcomers have adapted to the receiving societies in the region has yet to be extensively researched. What discussion there has been has focused negatively on problems such as illegal and transit migration, unemployment, impediments to domestic production, or criminality caused by the Chinese. Nevertheless, they should be perceived as part and parcel of the global flow of people, goods and capital. This is what this chapter plans to focus on—the Chinese migrants' close relationship with the new modes of production in China, as well their lives in the receiving societies at the other end of this complex global flow.

The political and economic changes in the region of Central and South-East Europe after the 1990s have led to sizeable migration movements. According to estimates of the Committee on Migration, Refugees and Demography of the Council of Europe (2000), the countries of Central and East Europe have been confronted with large-scale migrations from outside and inside the region, heading for the Western countries. A lot of this migration is illegal, involving a high proportion of trafficking from the Indian subcontinent, China, or the Near East. South-East Europe is sometimes even considered a key area for illegal migration to the West (Widgren 1999). Although migration flows toward Western Europe continue, the Organization for Economic Co-operation and Development sources suggest that the Central and East European countries might be developing into an arena where movements involve far more than a simple westward flow towards the European Union and North America (OECD 2003: 78).

In order to cast light on the insufficiently explored phenomenon of the Chinese entrepreneurial migration in South-East Europe, in this chapter I have tried to: (a) verify whether transnational migration theory is applicable to the Chinese migrants in this world region; (b) understand the economic background of the Chinese entrepreneurial migration and to explore the patterns of their companies' development, which can span the national and economic borders of several countries; (c) reveal the motives for coming to the countries still undergoing economic transitions; (d) show that South-East European countries are not only the transit zone for their further illegal advancement to the Western European countries, but occupy a region where a relatively stable number of the Chinese entrepreneurs live and work; and (e) understand and analyze the considerable number of the Chinese in Serbia as a new and global phenomenon.

Transnational Social Space as Transmigrants' Battlefield

Transnationalism appears to be most appropriate for exploring the contemporary migratory trends, due to its ability to incorporate both the micro- and macro-elements of these trends. This approach overcomes bipolar models of migration by introducing the transnational social space as the main arena of social processes in which and because of which migrants transcend geographic, political and cultural borders. Transnational social space implies that migrants gain *dual embeddedness* through which they simultaneously function in sending and receiving societies. They perform a whole range of activities moving across borders and between cultures, staying at the same time rooted in their places of origin and changing them through the practices performed within the transnational space. Therefore, Chinese migrants in the regions of Central and South-East Europe can be most efficiently approached through transnational migration theory.

Transnational migration is not a new phenomenon in the sense of movements of people across national borders, as well as their simultaneous involvement in social practices within and between nation states. Nevertheless, contemporary migration occurs in distinctively new and rapidly changing environments caused by global economic, political, and cultural processes in both receiving and sending countries. Because production modes play a dominant role in shaping contemporary society, it is necessary to observe changes in capitalism and the capitalist global economy. Nowadays, the flow of people, goods and ideas are shaped by new modes of flexible production and accumulation of capital. Consequently, migration and migrant entrepreneurship should be also examined in relation to these modes of production and the transformation of capitalism from mass industrial production towards the flexible accumulation of capital.

The turning point for contemporary social processes was the disintegration of the Fordist system of capitalist production after 1973, which has initiated new forms of production with flexible labor processes, marketing, and geographical mobility (Harvey 1990: 124). This late stage of capitalism has proved able to contract space in the arrangement of industrial production and the allocation of commodities and services while increasing the speed of production and consumption. The employment of new organizational forms and new technologies in production, such as outsourcing, sub-contracting, de-skilling and re-skilling of laborers, and small-batch production (Harvey 1990: 284-285) has signaled the flexibility and instability of labor and capital markets. These changes have gradually resulted in technological, social and cultural transformations. They have produced innovations in political, economic and cultural life in terms of increased mobility of people, commodities and ideas at the global level. Increasing velocity, uncertainty and fluctuation have thus become the main attributes of all social phenomena today.

The new arrangements of social life, characterized by fluctuation, uncertainty, and rapid change, have inevitably initiated the shift in relations between the spatial and the social. In parallel with traditional social spaces, transnational social space has emerged as an arena for economic, social and political activities, including those of migrants. Now we are observing the political, economic and cultural weakening of the nation-state, in the sense of progressively more social relations that cross its borders. However, we should keep in mind that this by no means implies nation-states' decline but that their container can no longer exclusively encompass the increasing transnational and supranational practices.

Transnational social space is thus becoming a key concept for understanding current international migration. Moreover, in the context of globalization and new communication technologies, it is reasonable to define a new type of migrant—the transmigrant, who simultaneously acts between and within his/her home and host countries (Pries 2001: 56-59). Therefore, transnationalism can also be perceived as the "'lived' and fluid experiences of individuals who act in ways that challenge our previous conflation of geographic space and social identity" (Basch et al. 1994: 8).

For these reasons, migration theory needs to be revised. Showing that there is a growing population whose behavior, socially and politically, evades the traditional bipolar distinction between emigrant and immigrant, Basch and her associates (Basch, Glick Schiller, and Szanton Blanc 1994) argue that conventional explanations centered on nation state are inadequate. They offer a new definition of migrants as transmigrants "whose daily lives depend on multiple and constant interconnections across international borders and whose public identities are configured in relationship to more than one nation state" (1994: 4). Transnational migration is thus "the process by which immigrants forge and sustain simultaneous multi-stranded social relations that link together societies of origin and settlement" (Glick Schiller et al. 1995: 48).

These authors develop several arguments to conceptualize transnational migration (Glick Schiller et al. 1992: 5). First, they argue that concepts such as tribe, ethnic group, nation, society and culture can only reduce the ability of research to analyze the phenomenon of transnationalism. They claim that the transnational perspective of migrant lives stems from the complex interaction of various entities and practices—from diverse historical backgrounds, individual perceptions, as well as from the ideologies both of the receiving and sending societies. Second, being mostly workers, transnational migrants' experience is developed through an intimate relationship with the changing conditions of global capitalism. Third, transnationalism is embedded in the daily lives, activities and social relationships of migrants. This means that social relations materialize within the connections between the host and home-society and are preserved and reconstructed through the affiliation to families, institutions, business and political organizations in both countries. Fourth, confronted with dual ways of life, transnational migrants are forced to reframe their national, ethnic and racial identities. As a result, all aspects of contemporary migration should be observed from a broader perspective that overcomes the traditional bipolar one and considers global, multi-dimensional social and economic processes in both receiving and sending countries at the same time.

Chinese Transmigrants in Europe

We may say that Chinese migration has always had the features of transnationalism. No matter what we call Chinese communities out of China—overseas, diasporic, migrant or transnational—there remains the fact that they have maintained their dual embeddedness for centuries. The number of today's Chinese immigrant population worldwide is approximately 55 million, including Taiwan and Hong Kong overseas Chinese (Cohen 1997: 162). More precisely, it is 33 million outside China, Taiwan and Hong Kong, representing 25 percent of the Chinese overall population, which currently exceeds 1.3 billion (Skeldon 2004).

There have been significant changes in the profile of the Chinese migrants and their destinations after the economic reforms in China in 1979. In addition to traditional destinations in South-East Asia and those in North America and Australia, Europe has recently emerged as an important destination. Pieke has observed that Chinese migration to Europe has entered a qualitatively and quantitatively different phase since the 1980s. He summarizes four general trends that have essentially reshaped this phenomenon (Pieke 2002: 5-20).

First, one of the most observed features of their migratory trend to Europe is the rapid increase in the number of the Chinese in the parts of Southern and Central Europe over the last decade. After the Second

World War, the Netherlands, France, and the United Kingdom received the largest Chinese communities. As a result, they became the nucleus of the Chinese migration across Central and North Europe since the 1970s, South Europe from the 1980s and East Europe from the 1990s.

Second, the new Chinese migration to Europe appeared from the traditional sending areas of southern Zhejiang, Fujian, and Guangdong. The novelty lies in the fact that it quickly went beyond traditional destinations. The previous newcomers from Zhejiang followed the chain migration pattern to the Netherlands, Belgium, Germany, and France, where they already had networks of relatives and friends. Seeking employment and business opportunities nowadays, they started to arrive in Scandinavia, Italy, Switzerland, Austria, and Spain. Finally, they reached the former Communist countries in Central Europe in the 1990s. The migratory flows from Fujian transformed this province into a migration hub in the 1980s and 1990s. In contrast with the migration from Zhejiang, the Fujianese suddenly reached different world regions: Europe, South and North America, Japan and Australia. Besides this, there is another flow of migrants originating from the North-East provinces that suffer from heavy unemployment (Laczko 2003).

The recent flow of emigration from traditional Chinese-sending areas should be observed in a much broader perspective that combines the whole range of social backgrounds, individual experiences and histories. Chinese migrants often move from one category to another in their migratory experience (Pieke 2002: 14). There has emerged an overlap and exchange between students, shuttle traders, skilled professionals, entrepreneurs, and redundant workers from various areas who can engage in trade in parallel to their original occupations.

Finally, Chinese migrants from both traditional sending areas and urban zones are progressively more transnational. They do not migrate to only one particular country any more but, instead, move back and forth and commute between several receiving countries with increasing mobility. We should keep in mind that "Chinese emigration no longer simply is the move to the centers of a world system fully dominated by the West, but is just as much an aspect of the outward extension of a world system centered on China itself" (Pieke 2002: 28).

The impetus to new Chinese migration might be higher income, social status, greater individual freedom, and not only the competition for survival as it was among the traditional migrants (Nyiri 1999: 119). Unlike the traditional Chinese migrants to Western Europe, Chinese migrants today might possess cultural capital, mobility, flexibility to accommodate to local conditions, as well as social capital to develop or maintain ties with enterprises in China. It can be said that economic growth motivates this mobile and upward stratum of the Chinese population that joined the renewed flow of migrants from traditional sending areas (Nyiri 1999: 23).

Chinese Migration to Hungary and Serbia

Transgressing the gender, class, and occupational boundaries of the previous Chinese migration in Europe, Chinese transnational migration in Central and East Europe since the 1990s has set the pattern that Western Europe is following now (Pieke 2002: 16-29). The settlement of heterogeneous shuttle traders, consisting of urban private entrepreneurs and the Zhejiang and Fujianese traders with both urban and rural backgrounds, has signaled the anticipation of new trends currently happening in the whole Europe. The Central and South-East European countries with low ethnic Chinese competition and post-socialist demand for cheap goods, plentifully produced in China, encouraged the arrival of Chinese entrepreneurs. For that reason, the Chinese migration in these regions is more associated with globalizing changes in China itself than to the needs of segments of the receiving states' economies in Europe.

The contemporary phase in Chinese migration to Hungary started in 1989 when the visa requirement for travelers between Hungary and the People's Republic of China was abandoned as a result of the change in the Hungarian foreign policy. Before that, the Communist regimes in Eastern Europe, following the example of the Soviet Union, banned immigration from China. It is interesting that before 1989 only around four hundred Chinese had applied for long-term stay in Hungary since the beginning of the century (Nyiri 1999: 30-47, 123-124).

The absence of the visa regime facilitated Chinese migration to Hungary on a larger scale and by 1991 forty thousand migrants had arrived. At that time those originating mainly from southern provinces of China were attracted by economic opportunities in a newly freed and poorly regulated market, as well as by the easy accessible markets of other East European countries. As a response, Hungarian officials imposed visa requirements in 1992, gradually reducing the number of Chinese migrants to the officially reported number of ten thousand (Nyiri 1999: 32-41).

The Chinese migrant community in Hungary was rather stable and economically prosperous until 1995, when higher tariffs for imported goods were imposed. By then, however, Hungary had become the regional center for the distribution of Chinese goods that were filling the supply gaps on the neighboring countries' local markets. In 1996, the role of Hungary as the hub of Chinese products decreased after they successfully established markets in other Central and East European countries (Nyiri 1999: 47).

Nyiri observes that many of Chinese migrants to Hungary came to pursue independent thinking after 1989 (1999: 31). Many of them have already reached a certain level of income or social status as entrepreneurs, employees or party cadres. The majority of Chinese migrants in Hungary had already moved towards big cities and special economic zones in China and, therefore, had enjoyed upward social mobility even in the home country. Previously Chinese migrants could only achieve social mobility through and after emigration. The survey conducted in Budapest in 1997 reports that most of the Chinese migrants have secondary and many of them tertiary education and that most of them were young: 61 percent were between twenty and forty years old, while 80 percent of the Chinese in Hungary were self-employed (Nyiri 1999: 124). In contrast to the old Chinese diaspora, which predominantly came from Southern provinces, many Chinese in Hungary traveled from North and North-East cities in China that do not have a tradition of international migration.

Data on the Chinese migration to Serbia is scarce. Because the country is not a member of the European Union, it is very often excluded from the EU's official reports. Both Western and Serbian media's rough estimates of the number of Chinese migrants vary from 15 to 50 thousand, even up to one hundred thousand. In order to throw some light on this situation, the next paragraphs will draw on the report of the Serbian Ministry of Internal Affairs prepared for this research.

The citizens of the People's Republic of China started to come in increasing numbers to Yugoslavia after 1997, when the visa regime for them was liberalized. The main reasons for their expanded entry to the territory of the Republic of Serbia at the end of the 1990s are related to the more rigid visa regime imposed by Hungarian authorities. Moreover, Chinese evaluated the Serbian market as favorable, adapting imported goods to the decreased purchasing power of the Serbian population. They first imported costume jewelry and textiles, along with electrical appliances. Afterwards, they started to open restaurants and shops, and to employ their relatives. The Chinese traders' base in Serbia is situated in the "Block 70" shopping mall in New Belgrade. Imported commodities from China are usually shipped to harbors in Montenegro (Bar), Cyprus, or Greece (Thessalonica), from which they are transported by trucks to

Belgrade and other Serbian cities. These products are frequently transferred through illegal channels to both wholesalers and retailers.

Due to the geographical position of Serbia, as well as to the liberal visa regime that existed for the citizens of certain European countries until 2001, migrants from some African and Asian countries, including China, arrived in the country in order to enter Western European countries illegally. As a result, the visa regime toward Chinese was tightened in 2000. However, during 2002 and 2003 Chinese migrants were prevented from entering or leaving the country illegally. At the beginning of 2004, the Serbian police cut the illegal channel of their migration leading from the Pristine airport of "Slatina" across the Kosovo borders, via Belgrade, toward Croatia. Generally, the number of illegal crossings has been gradually reduced: 461 in 2000, 156 in 2001, 39 in 2003 and 25 in 2004. Besides this, there is a constant number of the Chinese migrants who have legalized their status in Serbia by obtaining residence permits for study or business purposes. Finally, according to the data of Serbian Business Registers Agency, there were 1,050 registered Chinese enterprises in Serbia as of 2006 (SBRA 2006).

A Portrait of a Successful Pioneer Migrant

In order to understand Chinese transmigrants' entrepreneurship as part of the global flow of capital, people and commodities, it is necessary to adopt a perspective that transcends the national borders of single receiving countries. The framework of the research, conducted in 2005, therefore included more than one location and focused on a successful Chinese enterprise whose business operations spanned the borders of Hungary and Serbia. I undertook semi-structured interviews in Budapest with the owner of the company and his public relations manager, as well as with three employees in Belgrade, two Chinese and one Serbian.

The owner of the company originated from the Chinese southern province of Fujian. He was 46 and a painter, who graduated at The Academy of Arts in Fujian and had worked as a school teacher before coming to Hungary in 1992. He was a pioneer migrant, married, the father of three children, and lived with his whole family in Budapest. He arrived in Europe in an attempt to go to Italy and paint there but, having experienced the complicated procedure for obtaining an Italian visa, he decided to stay in Budapest. He tried to live from painting in Budapest and even became a member of the Hungarian Fine Artists Association, but gave up. Nevertheless, he always stayed connected to his previous profession and to the idea of introducing Chinese culture to the Europeans whom, he thought, unfortunately perceived China only through the Communist party. Spending almost half of the year in China and regularly commuting between China and Hungary, he was indeed a transnational migrant. He contacted China daily via the Internet and/or telephone, as well as regularly kept in touch with the Chinese employees in the branch offices.

Having realized what the Hungarian market demanded—a medium category of sports shoes for a reasonably low price—he established a company called *Wink* to distribute *Wink Sport* and *Groovy Street* footwear in 1993. All commodities were produced in a rented production line in China. Currently, the enterprise has 27 employees—2 Chinese and 25 Hungarians. *Wink* is basically a wholesale enterprise and owns only four shops in Hungary. The company's range of goods includes more than two hundred sorts of footwear for every season. It is interesting that even smaller Chinese traders in Budapest purchase from the company, which also has wholesale partners in the Czech Republic, Slovakia, Slovenia, Croatia, Romania and Ukraine.

The branch companies are located in Belgrade, Serbia, and Sarajevo, Bosnia and Herzegovina. They are not registered as the company is subdivided according to local laws; their legal owners are local domestic managers. The branch companies function as the major wholesale partners and representatives in their countries, but are supervised by the Chinese employees.

The branch office in Serbia was founded in 1997. The Serbian retailers coming to Budapest to purchase goods from *Wink* spoke of the opportunities in Serbia. The Serbian market lacked domestic footwear producers at that time and consisted mainly of enterprises importing famous foreign brand names, whose prices far exceeded the purchasing power of average Serbian consumers. The opportunity was immediately recognized and *Wink* applied the same marketing strategy as in Hungary. The office had only three employees when it was established but by the end of 1997, seven more workers were employed. At the same time, a representative of the Budapest headquarters went to Podgorica, Montenegro, in order to open an office there also.

During 1999, the Belgrade branch office encountered a crisis, losing some of its buyers for political reasons, while the Kosovo market fell at the beginning of the bombing in 1999. At the same time, the subdivision in Montenegro started to import directly from the headquarters in Budapest due to the unbalanced tariff systems between Serbia and Montenegro that might have caused double taxation. At this time the

Belgrade company had fifteen employees, fourteen Serbians and one Chinese. Another company, *Wink Marketing*, was opened in the same way as the previous one and currently has three employees, one Serbian and two Chinese. Finally, one more branch office in Sarajevo, Bosnia and Herzegovina, was opened through the engagement of the employees in the Belgrade office.

All my Chinese respondents originated from the Chinese southern province of Fujian. One of them came to Belgrade in 1998. He was 43, married, the father of two children and the whole family lived in Belgrade. He had secondary education and spoke no Serbian, unlike his children, who were excellent pupils in a local school, had numerous friends among Serbian classmates, and behaved as though they were fully integrated. He saw political instability in Serbia as the biggest disadvantage of living there, but he wanted to stay and develop his business there. Another Chinese respondent was 31, married, pregnant and was going to give birth in Belgrade. She graduated from university before she came to Belgrade in 2001. Both were relatives of the company owner and both held high-level positions in the Belgrade office.

It is interesting to notice how their brand name, adapted at the beginning in 1993, helped the company to construct an image of a western product. *Wink* is perceived as an American brand name in Hungary, while most of my informal respondents in Serbia think it is a Hungarian product. One of the most distinctive features of the company lies in its sponsoring of numerous sport and cultural activities in Hungary and Serbia. It supports marathons, basketball tournaments, traveling of sport teams abroad, as well as travel to China for employees in both countries.

Furthermore, the company has included a cultural mission in its agenda in order to promote China in a modern and popular way. In order to accomplish this mission, *Wink Culture* as a film production company was established in Beijing in 2004 and employed more than 30 employees. This is an entirely transnational media enterprise for it is oriented toward both Chinese and Central and East European audiences. It is based on foreign direct investment gained from the economic transactions in a transnational social space, which unites the production line in China with markets of several European countries. It has already successfully screened the 20-episode TV series "Some Day, Some Month, Some Year" and a 24-episode TV series "Unforgettable". These TV productions were broadcast in Beijing and other provincial TV stations in China, as well as in Hungary and Serbia. Apart from this, the owner is a shareholder in a mobile telephone and communication company.

Central and South-East Europe: An Arena of Complex Migratory Trends

My research conducted in Budapest and Belgrade reveals that Chinese transnational entrepreneurs, especially those from the southern provinces of China, are deeply integrated with the global flow of people, goods and capital, and linked to the flexible accumulation of capital. Entrepreneurship is always connected to innovation and risk, which are even more important in the case of migrant businesses and global competition. The flexibility and adaptability of Chinese transnational entrepreneurs to these challenges are enabled by the new modes of production in China, their economic transactions, as well as the social networks to which they belong.

The flexibility and adaptability to local demand and conditions are rooted in and caused by their transnational embeddedness in both the receiving states and the home country. These transnational entrepreneurs use their transnational ties to purchase or produce in China those goods that are in demand in the receiving societies' markets. Being able to stay connected with their home country and to take advantage of its economic growth in terms of flexible and cheap labor production, they are able to fill quickly the supply gaps in the receiving states and to carve out or fulfill niches in their local markets. Therefore, the niches filled by Chinese migrant entrepreneurs are integrated within the economic structures of both receiving and sending societies. It is thus true that China has become a central element in the economic success of new migrants, who are eager to exploit business opportunities there (Nyiri 1998).

We can better consider this phenomenon if we focus on global outsourcing, which underlines the growing interdependence of developed and developing countries. Gereffi and Sturgeon (2004: 2) reveal that global outsourcing has given rise to "global value chains" as a new set of economic structures in the world economy. This is a process elaborated through "linkages between economies and firms that participate in highly complex cross-border arrangements that involve a dizzying array of partners, customers, and suppliers". Without doubt, China has become the world's most important global outsourcing foundation for manufacturing. Its mix of economies of scale, industrial diversification, domestically funded infrastructure, together with the world's largest inflows of foreign direct investment, have made China's factories a critical link in global value chains (Gereffi and Sturgeon 2004: 5). The company under analysis provides excellent evidence as to how these remote production locations are connected to favorable markets in South-East Europe.

Wink seems to be representative of the pattern of Chinese economic embeddedness in more than one receiving country. It is clear that the analytical framework focused on a single receiving country does not suffice any more. Chinese transnational entrepreneurship must be observed from a larger regional perspective, the links between the region and China's internal economic growth, and transnational cross-borders production chains.

The company not only connected the local markets with its production modes in China, but also the markets of Central and South-East Europe themselves in different opportunity structures and socio-political environments. There nevertheless remains the question why the Chinese entrepreneurs decided to come to countries that lack political and economic stability rather than only migrating to European Union countries. What attracts them to the countries that are still undergoing difficult economic transformations and where opportunity structures vary not only from one country to the next but also between regions and cities? (See Kloosterman and Rath 2001: 193.)

We may assume that Chinese entrepreneurs are driven by opportunity structures, that is to say, the new markets. Markets are the key point in the opportunity structure. According to Kloosterman and Rath, two dimensions of the opportunity structure are fundamental for an understanding of migrant entrepreneurs' insertion and social mobility within the receiving society. The first dimension is the convenience of markets for newcomers to start a business. The second is the growth potential of the markets where they open the new business and their adaptation to the potential openings of new businesses.

The emergence of opportunity these structures are intimately associated with post-Fordist capitalism, flexible production, and the accumulation of capital. Innovations in technology, consumption and business strategies have encouraged the development of more flexible small businesses, thus increasing opportunities for entrepreneurship. In such an environment, transnational entrepreneurship appears as a strategy for incorporation where migrants negotiate obligations, restrictions and opportunities across national borders (Landolt 2001: 236).

It is not surprising then that Chinese migrants recognize in these transitional economies opportunities for occupying a certain niche and filling the supply gap caused by state decentralization, privatization, or other economic and political measures. It is clear that they are aware of the difficulties and disadvantages of doing business in such an economy. However, it seems that they are ready to take the chance and gradually participate in the newly opened segments of the markets. Additionally, they seem to be aware that it would take much longer for them to enjoy comparable success in the stable economies of Western Europe.

Furthermore, there is a novelty introduced by Chinese entrepreneurs in the regions that alter the old migratory landscapes. Migrants are usually depicted as workers and suppliers of cheap and low-skilled labor, coming from less developed countries to advanced economies. However, more and more attention is being paid to those migrants who start their own businesses and enterprises. By doing this, they become not only self-employed but also employers of their family members and outsiders. This is the case with Chinese migration to Hungary and Serbia that has been entrepreneurial since it began. While creating their own jobs, migrant entrepreneurs can also avoid the barriers they may run into while looking for a job (Kloosterman and Rath 2003: 1). This case study reveals that Chinese migrants are able not only to create jobs for themselves, their relatives, and the locals, but also to solve simultaneously the limitations imposed by local legal regulations. The example is the company in Belgrade that was registered by the locals but has Chinese employees in leading supervisory positions at the same time.

Additionally, if this first migrant generation is successful, the winners might achieve faster upward social mobility than in West European countries where there is a long tradition of Chinese immigration. *Wink* is an excellent example of this. Being the only Chinese trade enterprise in the region that possesses a media production company in the home country, *Wink* also deals with the culture industry by promoting Chinese popular culture in Hungary and Serbia. Without doubt, the success in trade accompanied by the success in the currently booming sectors in China—media and telecommunication technologies—enable transmigrant entrepreneurs to achieve upward mobility in both the receiving and sending countries, as well as eventually to convert their economic capital into social capital.

Finally, we may notice that there may be emerging an interesting connection between cities in the globally dispersed processes of production, management, marketing and consumption. Sassen (2004: 2) argues that one of the strategic working structures enabling the formation of a global political economy is the network of global cities. The economic activities of *Wink* made several cities in the regions mutually connected within the global flow of goods and capital and spanning East Asia, Central, and South-East Europe, namely Fuzhou in China, Budapest in Hungary, Belgrade in Serbia, Sarajevo in Bosnia, etc. Alongside Sassen's claim that the network of global cities also includes secondary cities or regions that possess a limited number of global city functions (2004: 2), we may ask whether Chinese entrepreneurship is making some of the cities of Central and South-east Europe not only interconnected, but, to some extent, also global.

Conclusion

Central and South-East European countries have witnessed the new phenomenon of Chinese transnational migration and entrepreneurship. This case study of a transnational enterprise, which first began in Hungary and then reached out to several neighboring markets, clearly shows that economic globalization is at work in the regions surveyed. Non-EU countries, such as Serbia, proved to be a significant research site that revealed remarkable migratory processes. The new opportunities in Serbia and Bosnia proved attractive to the pragmatic and adaptable Chinese entrepreneurs. Therefore, the perception of the region as only a transit area for Chinese illegal migration to Western Europe is belied by the relatively stable number of Chinese entrepreneurs living and working in these non-EU countries.

Finally, this research has helped to challenge the prejudice about the inevitable development of migration from poorer developing countries toward developed countries through an analysis of South-South entrepreneurial migration driven solely by new and favorable market opportunities that span the political-economic borders of several countries and parts of the world.

References

Basch, L., N. Glick Schiller, and C. Szanton Blanc (1994). *Nations Unbound: Transnational Projects, Postcolonial Predicaments, and Deterritorialized Nation-State.* London: Routledge.

Cohen, R. (1997). *Global Diasporas: An Introduction.* Seattle: University of Washington Press.

Council of Europe (2000). "Transit Migration in Central and Eastern Europe." Report of Committee on Migration, Refugees and Demography, Document no. 8904, http://assembly.coe.int/Documents/WorkingDocs/doc00/EDOC8904.htm.

Gereffi, G. and T.J. Sturgeon (2004). "Globalization, Employment, and Economic Development." Briefing paper of Sloan Workshop Series in Industry Studies Rockport, Mass., http://www.globalvaluechains.org/publications/SloanGVCbriefingFinal.pdf.

Glick Schiller, N., L. Basch, and C. Blanc-Szanton (1992). "Transnationalism: A New Analytic Framework for Understanding Migration." In *Towards a Transnational Perspective on Migration: Race, Class, Ethnicity, and Nationalism Reconsidered* (pp. 1-24). New York: The New York Academy of Sciences.

_____ (1995). "From Immigrant to Transmigrant: Theorizing Transnational Migration." *Anthropological Quarterly* 68 (1): 48-63.
Harvey, D. (1990). *The Condition of Postmodernity: An Enquiry into the Origins of Cultural Changes*. Oxford: Blackwell.
Kloosterman, R. and J. Rath (2001). "Immigrant Entrepreneurs in Advanced Economies: Mixed Embeddedness Further Explored." *Journal of Ethnic and Migration Studies* 27 (2): 189-202.
_____ (2003). "Introduction." In *Immigrant Entrepreneurs: Venturing Abroad in the Age of Globalization* (pp. 1-16). Oxford: Berg.
Landolt, P. (2001). "Salvadoran Economic Transnationalism: Embedded Strategies for Household Maintenance, Immigrant Incorporation, and Entrepreneurial Expansion." *Global Networks* 1 (3): 217-241.
Laczko, F. (2003). "Europe Attracts More Migrants from China." http://www.migrationinformation.org/Feature/display.cfm?ID=144. Washington DC: Migration Policy Institute.
Nyiri, P. (1998). "The Impact of New Chinese Migration on Established Overseas Chinese Communities: Politics and Identity." http://www.ceu.hu/sun/SUN%202001/Downloads/ Nyirisample.doc.
Nyiri, P. (1999). *New Chinese Migrants in Europe: The Case of the Chinese Community in Hungary*. Aldershot: Ashgate.
OECD, Organization for Economic Co-operation and Development (2003). *Trends in International Migration: Annual Report 2002*. Paris: OECD Publications.
Pieke, F.N. (2002). *Recent Trends in Chinese Migration to Europe: Fujianese Migration in Perspective*. Geneva: IOM Migration Research Series.
Pieke, F.N. (2005). "At the Margins of the Chinese World System: The Fuzhou Diaspora in Europe." In *New Approaches to Migration*. Oxford University: Transnational Communities Program. http://transcomm.ox.ac.uk.
Pries, L. (2001). "The Disruption of Social and Geographical Space. Mexican-US Migration and the Emergence of Transnational Social Spaces." *International Sociology* 16 (1): 55-74.
Sassen, S. (2004). "Economic Globalization and World Migration as Factors in the Mapping of Today's Advanced Urban Economy." In *Globalization Research Network*, http://www.globalgrn.org/PDF/Sassen.pdf.
Serbian Business Registers Agency (2006). www.apr.sr.gov.yu.
Skeldon, R. (2004). "China: From Exceptional Case to Global Participant." In *Migration Information Source*, http://www.migrationinformation.org/Profiles/display.cfm?ID=219. Washington DC: Migration Policy Institute.
Widgren, J. (1999). "Southeast Europe as a Key Area for Illegal Migration." http://www.icmpd.org/default.asp?nav=results&folderid=1&id=153&alltext=Widgr. Vienna: International Centre for Migration Policy Development.

PART III

TRANSNATIONAL RELIGIOUS NETWORKS

7

Spiritual Spaces in Post-Industrial Places: Transnational Churches in North East London[1]

Kristine Krause

In the Lea Valley Industrial Park of northeast London there are more than ten transnational churches founded by African migrants. This area is one of the most economically deprived within the capital and consists of large tracts of derelict industrial land, much of which is fragmented and divided by waterways, roads, and railway lines. In recent years more and more churches have rented old storehouses, garages and industrial depots throughout London, due to the difficulty of finding other places, which are financially affordable and tolerant of noisy worship. The churches in this industrial area are difficult to find. Hidden behind scrap metal and next to dealers' garages and repair shops, they share buildings with other migrant entrepreneurs, most of them from Eastern Europe. The East Europeans view these churches suspiciously, but mainly ignore them. The church members themselves use these places as operational bases from which they organize their local and translocal networks. Although migrants from West Africa founded most of the churches, they see themselves mainly not as African but as international churches with a global outreach, not based on ethnicity or country of origin. This is also noticeable in the way in which they emplace themselves. In contrast to other nearby neighborhoods, which are characterized by vibrant markets, where African languages are spoken and signboards and shop names clearly address customers with a specific African background, the churches remain at a first glance strangely disconnected from the neighborhood of the industrial area. They seldom interact with the local entrepreneurs, but even more strikingly, they have little contact with each other. This social disconnectedness has many reasons, some of which will be explored in this chapter by looking at one of these churches.

The chapter seeks to contribute to the discussion about how to ground the description of transnational networks and transnational urbanism within specific places and localities by avoiding both free-floating delocalization and the romanticization of localism (Smith 2001: 102ff., 2005b; Massey 1991, 1993b). To understand the processes of place making I will draw on Massey's understanding of localities, who argues that a locale is not a bounded entity but evolves as a network of social relations and practices. (Massey 1993a: 148ff.). Localities, in her view, are always in the making and contested. They should be understood as "articulated moments" (Massey 1993b: 66), as "*constructions* out of the intersections and interactions of concrete social relations and social processes in a situation of co-presence" (Massey 1991: 277).

Following this understanding of space, which departs from conceptualizing places as bounded entities, I will consider the processes of place-making from three different angles: First, I will look at the ways in which place-making involves finding one's place within a specific spatial-political situation. In the case of the churches this entails meeting certain juridical, political and financial requirements in order to inaugurate a church and struggling to find a place to worship. This aspect will be highlighted by looking at the "spatial history" of one of the churches.

Second, processes of "doing space" will be approached by focusing on the engagement with the place as a social space. Unlike other social actors, such as urban pioneers who have appropriated industrial areas in London for quite some time through gentrification and urban renewal, the churches follow an ideology similar to that of service industries, which has led to the spatial alienation of post-industrial cities and regions such as Greater London. This is apparent in their blatant non-engagement with the industrial area as a social space. The most important social practices, which constitute the church space, are directed towards transnational networks and global Pentecostal media images rather than towards the local industrial area.

Third, I will analyze the performative aspects of place making by focusing on how space is appropriated through aesthetic and ritual practices and how spatial meaning is created within the church. I will argue that it is precisely the size, functionality and "emptiness" of the space, from a spiritual point of view, which helps the church achieve the intensity needed to evoke the presence of the Holy Spirit. In closing, I will reflect on questions raised in recent publications about whether the churches are better understood by avoiding an "ethnic lens" (Glick Schiller et al. 2006; Glick Schiller 2005). This issue is dealt with by looking at when and how churches refer to a shared African background or embeddedness within global Pentecostal Christendom, and how these representational politics are related to the place-making practices and spatial positioning of the church.

Spatial History of "The Destiny Changing Church"[2]

I came across Pastor Solomon and his church during my first stay in London in 2004 on a main street in North East London where I lived just off the main road. The small shop, next to a busy halal butcher, used to be a training center run by an NGO founded by Solomon years ago. Its objectives were to empower people from black ethnic minorities, to bring them back into jobs, and to train them with skills such as computing, especially those who had been hospitalized as mental patients. Now it functions as the church room and office. During the hot summer of 2004 the small room was regularly packed with people for prayer and fasting programs. The Destiny Changing Church is a neo-Pentecostal church, mainly attended by black Africans from Ghana and Nigeria as well as a few from Swaziland, Botswana and Zimbabwe. Apart from one white man, born in Botswana and married to a black woman, I was the only other white person among the black congregation, which attended the church on a regular basis throughout 2004-2006.

Solomon, who is originally from Ghana and trained in Britain as a medical professional, was at that time still working with the National Health Service. He had first founded the NGO at the end of the 1990s and it operated not only in London, but also maintained a satellite mission in Ghana, where it ran Christian clubs at Ghanaian universities and colleges. Through these clubs many young born-again Christians were brought together and at one point in time some of them were invited to come to London by the NGO. Many were able to gain admission to colleges or universities in London and to this day they form the backbone of the church, which was formerly registered as a charity in 2002.

As was obvious during the prayer meetings, the front shop room was too small to host a big congregation. So for its Sunday services the church rented a bigger hall at the local YMCA. Although the hall was comfortable for the number of people who attended the Sunday services and was in easy reach of public transport, it required a lot of work to arrange and clear the place for every service: e.g., arranging chairs, plastic flowers and carpets, installing musical instruments, technical equipment, and the data projector for showing the song texts on a screen. Moreover, there was disagreement with the management of the YMCA about noise and length of worship. By 2005 the church had continued to grow and was able to rent a bigger office space but once more they encountered the same difficulties with neighbors. However, the landlord was sympathetic to the church's needs and offered to let three stories of an old warehouse in an industrial park in East London. The church moved there in 2006, by which time Pastor Solomon had resigned from his well-paid position with the National Health Service. He now dedicates all his time to the church and his mission projects in Botswana, South Africa, Ghana, and the United States. Because the church is unable to provide a full salary, he relies on fundraising among his local and international contacts. He also functions as a guest preacher at other churches and his church frequently receives guest preachers and prophets from befriended churches.

The case of the Destiny Changing Church presents a typical and partly successful "spatial history" for black ethnic minority churches in Britain, which usually observes the following trajectory: first a few people meet in someone's living room or office, then they rent space on an hourly basis from community centers or other churches. The next step is to find a place, which the church can rent on its own until finally they buy or build their own church (Adogame 2004a). Some of the mega-churches in London, such as Kingsway International[3] or Trinity Baptist Church,[4] own the warehouses they worship in and have invested a lot of money in purchasing the premises. Others, which have a different outreach strategy (Ukah 2005a), such as RCCOG (Redeemed Christian Church of God), can be found all over the city as small shop front churches. Older Caribbean and African branches of Baptist churches, established in the fifties and sixties, have been able to acquire abandoned English churches. However, quite a number of them are engaged in strategies similar to those of The Destiny Changing Church, and rent abandoned industrial buildings (Adogame 2004a: 500).

Social and Political Processes of Place Making

The Destiny Changing Church rents an old warehouse in the "Lea Valley Industrial Village"—a rather derelict industrial place. The landscape is scattered with many under-used industrial and commercial facilities and traces of declining light industry. The nearby rail station has been closed and the tracks are overgrown. What attracts attention, however, is the recently redeveloped access route, which has been funded by the European Union, and the presence of several service businesses, such as laundry services, wholesale warehouses, and workshop units for furniture and cars. A closer look reveals how many different actors use, inhabit, appropriate, transform, and redevelop the area. The spot adjoins to the open green fields of Hackney, Leyton, and Walthamstow Marshes, containing the huge water reservoir and water works of the Thames Water Authority. The British Ramblers Association recommends it for its footpaths,[5] the National Cycling Association provides maps with shortcuts and cycling paths through the industrial park and the marshes, while the Inner East Area Partnership and the London Development Agency have published several documents and initiated community participation projects to improve the area. In particular, the London Development Agency has unveiled a Lower Lea Valley "regeneration strategy" to kick off preparations for the Olympic Games in 2012.[6] Ironically, the neighborhood borders on one of the main sites of the yet to be built Olympic Village. Thus, after having been on the fringes of the global hub of the City of London, the industrial village will move into the global arena. However, for the moment, church members still need to be collected by the church's van at meeting points across London and from the nearest bus station, because the place is out of the reach of any tube station. Up to now, it is unclear what will happen to the buildings rented by the churches as a result of the regeneration plan, but it is very likely that the rent will increase, which will be a problem for most of the churches.

Roughly speaking, three groups of actors can be said to be shaping the Lea Bridge area. First, there are people who would classically be involved in gentrification activities, such as the ramblers association and the cyclists. They all agree upon the value of the green marshland and the gritty and "authentic" atmosphere of cycling paths through the industrial village. Second, the small-scale businesses and workshops, which are interested in keeping the area functioning as it is today, also play a role. Third, the London Development Agency, together with its combined forces of civic groups which all aim at urban renewal in the course of the upcoming Olympic Games, wields influence in the area.

Apart from The Destiny Changing Church, there are more than ten other churches in this area founded by African migrants. These include Aladura and neo-Pentecostal churches.[7] Due to ideological differences, these churches hardly interact and regard each other as not pursuing the right Christian practice. Most of them are very difficult to find because there is hardly any proper signposting and entrances are hidden. In some cases there are only sheets of paper attached to fences, bearing the names of the churches. Banners, provisional posters, and signboards for the churches are frequently removed by the other inhabitants of the village, since strictly speaking the churches are not permitted to use fences and entrances for their advertisements. Although all the churches seek to reach out and to win new souls, this aim is undermined by their lack of visibility.

Pastor Solomon's church is located at the rear of a warehouse building, which is surrounded by gray containers and hosts several small furniture workshops in the front. The church inhabits three stories and rents the ground floor to a befriended church. At the moment, another church founded by a Ghanaian pastor is negotiating to rent some of the other available rooms. The middle floor has recently undergone major renovation work, initiated by the church and the plan is to have several offices and to offer capacity-building services to church members. Among other things, the church aims to run computer courses and legal advice on immigration matters.

As already noted, the local space is also used by other migrant entrepreneurs and those operating small workshops, many of them from Eastern Europe. We find wholesalers for Russian food, Bulgarian cabinetmakers, and Polish distributors of East European beverages. From time to time disputes arise over parking space, gates left open by church members, and blocked drains after celebrations. Churches complain that the workers litter passages and do not clean up their bulky waste. None of these disputes have yet evolved into serious conflicts. When I walked around the area on a few occasions, I came across some of the workers and manufacturers in the little café where they meet and relax. It was then that I heard about their suspicions of the churches. They saw me as somebody "from the council" who came "to control" things, possibly because I am white and female and was usually quite formally dressed in order to respect the dress code of the church. Some of the workers, who work on night shifts in the laundry, expressed negative feelings about church services, which lasted all night, and about cooking activities.

Specifically, one white English worker expressed his concern that "our black folks have become so religious overnight" and complained about their cooking on open fires and releasing the fat into the drains, which resulted in blocked pipes. He complained that the problem of cleaning the drains was left to him instead of being dealt with by the churches. A black Caribbean car mechanic told me that one of the churches would sprinkle corn around the parking lot and he strongly suspects that they were involved in voodoo practices and warned me not to talk to them. White Eastern European workers complained about open gates and worship lasting until early in the morning. One of the workers asked me: "What kind of church is that? Singing and drumming until three o'clock, is that normal?"

Strikingly, the white English owner of the building, which is rented to Eastern European workshops and to The Destiny Changing Church, did not regard it as a church but insisted on talking about it as an educational center. On one occasion when I accompanied the pastor, he asked neighbors if they could remove their bulky waste and staff from the shared area because the church was going to celebrate its anniversary. The interaction was very polite and the pastor invited them to the festivity, but, not surprisingly, the men did not show up. On another occasion one of the men approached me curiously and asked if I was "overseeing" the churches and if there were any other white people involved in it. Although hardly any of the churches would define itself as an exclusively "black" church, "white" members are very rare. Yet, the extent to which they are perceived from the outside as black churches becomes noticeable by the very question about white membership. Furthermore, the fact that the workers implicitly assumed that, as a white woman, I was "from the council" or in any other way in a position to control the churches, shows how this racial demarcation becomes charged with other negative attributions.

All in all, the churches exist in a kind of parallel world and are hardly engaged with the immediately surrounding place and people. This emplacement in parallel, transient worlds is underlined by the ways in which church members are escorted to the place by the church vans and how they then move in and out of the building, dressed in their best clothes, passing workshops and heaps of scrap, before immersing themselves in, or emerging from, the ritual space of the church rooms. Everything significant in regard to place making seems to happen exclusively inside and the movement in and out seems to be channeled to reduce contact to the immediate surroundings.

The church's refusal to get involved in public space-making and the perception by its neighbors that the church was an exclusively black congregation, which pursued suspicious practices, stands in contrast to the prevalent celebration of London's religious and cultural diversity within the public space. One of the last examples of this public discourse has been the bid to host the Olympic Games in 2012 with its key phrase "The world in one city."[8] Yet to achieve visibility within the public sphere and to participate in the orchestrated diversity of the global city is not a matter of course for everybody, especially not for born-again Christians who do not easily fit into the multicultural scenario because of their radical views concerning homosexuality and Islam.

However, having reached a certain level of financial power, even black Pentecostal churches have a chance of receiving a share of the huge sums, which are being spent on the Olympic project to buy land for the Olympic Village and stadiums. If a church owns the warehouse it uses for religious services, it may stand to make a sizeable amount of money these days. For example, the Kingsway International Christian Centre (KICC), a mega-church founded by the Nigerian-born Matthew Ashimolo and also located in an industrial depot, has been in the press not only because of misappropriation of money and tax fraud, but also because the London Development Agency has to pay a considerable amount of compensation to the church to have it moved from its premises in Hackney. The site is located in a similarly deprived area as the Lea Valley Industrial Park and directly within the Olympic park development area. The KICC is to receive an alternative plot of land elsewhere and will use this opportunity to build an arena which will host up to 8,000 people. Interestingly, the new site will be again located within a business park. The Destiny Changing Church plays in a lower league than the KICC and does not even own the warehouse it uses for worship. The example of KICC moving from one business park to a similar area, however, shows that location in neglected and rundown places is not only a matter of money, but that such places offer other factors desired by these churches.

One approach, which can help us to understand the appropriation of space by the churches, is to look at aesthetics and representational practices. Coleman has emphasized that although global charismatic Christianity privileges the word, its culture is diffused in a "coherent system of visual, material and embodied aesthetics" (Coleman 2000: 144, 152ff.). Some elements of this system will be explored in the next section when we shall enter the church room to look at the representational and ritual practices of space making.

Doing Space

The church room of The Destiny Changing Church is on the top floor of a three-storey building. If you entered during service time you would see a beautifully dressed congregation gathered together, in stark contrast to the waste bins and iron fences outside the building, which they have passed in order to enter the church. You would further notice that the church is not indifferent to aesthetic matters.

Aesthetics, Media, and Spiritual Renewal

Not only are people's clothes splendid and stylish, but also the decoration and furniture. You would see red and white curtains, blue and red chairs, a red plush carpet which covers the stage, a decorated pulpit, and plastic flowers. The next thing to catch one's eye would be a big screen onto which Bible quotations, song texts, and PowerPoint presentations of the sermon are projected.

Much effort and money has been invested in decoration and technical equipment. We find several microphones and a high tech sound system which enables the place to be filled with "holy noise" when the worshippers speak in tongues or engage in prayer battles. The sound system further serves to record sermons and programs digitally. The technical team is able to duplicate CDs on fast track, so that people can buy the sermon they have just listened to immediately after the service.

Several scholars have noted the central role of media equipment for neo-Pentecostalism and its identification with a global[9] Christian community (Schultze 1991; De Witte 2003; Coleman 2000: 177). Coleman highlights in his work on the World of Life church in Sweden, as does De Witte in her research on the International Central Gospel Church in Ghana, how different types of media have become a constitutive element of ritual practice and performance, and are integrated into the everyday function of churches (De Witte 2003; Coleman 2000: 167ff.). In The Destiny Changing Church media equipment, such as a sound system, a projection screen, and video camera equipment, are prominently displayed. No overseas broadcasts are made of the services at the moment but from time to time the pastor does preach on one of the Ghanaian pirate radio stations. It seems that being on air or on TV to congregations elsewhere is imagined to be more meaningful for place-making practices than location in the industrial area.

Media equipment, therefore, functions beyond its practical use as a symbol for intensified global interconnections. Even though the church has not yet reached the point where it hosts its own TV or radio show, we can note an intricate interplay between global neo-Pentecostal mediascapes (Appadurai 1990: 296ff.) and place-making practices. This becomes more apparent when taking another look at the furniture and decoration in the church, which resemble Pentecostal media representations, especially Christian TV shows that are transmitted via satellite into almost every member's living room. During my research in London I lived in a shared flat with church members on a council estate where we used to watch the regular satellite programs which included, among sports, the Nigerian BEN (Bright Entertainment Network) and Ghanaian OBE (Original Black Entertainment) diasporic channels and numerous religious programs. This gave me a chance to regularly watch some of the prominent preachers on Inspiration Network International and Trinity Broadcast Network. The similarity between decoration, furniture and style of the churches and studios is striking.

Apart from simulating a media reality, which the church still aims to achieve, the presence of cameras, speakers, and microphones results in a reinforcement of the charismata (De Witte 2003), the gifts of the Holy Spirit. The microphones help to preserve the words which have been spoken, inspired by the Holy Ghost, and at the same time create the audibility of its presence in the here and now of the service by amplifying speaking in tongues and words of prayer. The screen functions as a mirror in which the congregation can watch pictures of itself or follow Bible scriptures and key phrases from the preaching.

The highlighting of headlines, mottos and slogans relates to another feature, which fits well into the picture of the churches as globally connected and transnationally organized enterprises (Ukah 2005b). The annual convention in 2005, for example, shows how the church envisions itself as being like a communication-oriented company in business counseling. Under the motto "MOVE 2005—Moments of Opportunity, Vision and Enlargement," the church organized a two-week program with international guests from Canada, South Africa, Botswana, and Ghana, focusing on the motto "Moving into your season of preparation, placing, performance and productivity." At first glance this slogan seems to be in contrast with the spatial marginalization of the church, but if one takes the self-representation of the church seriously it becomes clear that the church sees itself as being at the very center of London's spiritual renewal. This "spiritual renewal" will go hand in hand with economic success and new business opportunities, according to the church's beliefs. To achieve this, the church offers "spiritual services" to their clients, such as teaching, counseling, prayers, and deliverance of evil spirits. At a second glance, then, the location of the church in a post-industrial location seems fitting. Places like the Lea Bridge area have been affected by the increasing shift towards tertiary industries such as service industries. Being based in communication, consulting, and investment, the tertiary industry generates rather ephemeral "products" in contrast to the manufactures produced by secondary industry. The church is also engaged in capacity building, training competences, and empowerment activities and not in traditional social welfare or political activities. The favorite phrase of the pastor "we are a destiny changing church" aims at the individual in his or her life course and does not envision any collective political mobilization.

In concluding this section we can note that the imaginary embeddedness within Pentecostal mediascapes through aesthetics in decoration and language usage is more than a simulation, because it is part of an ideological empowerment program which has effects on a practical level: church members envision themselves as part of a global community of Christians who will not only be successful on the Last Day but also in the here and now. Within the church they find psychological, legal and economic support and a platform for gaining experiences in professional performances, thus creating a link between religion and economic activities in the host country. So far we have seen how the inner decoration and media play a role to emplace the church within the imaginary social field of global neo-Pentecostalism. Keeping in mind these spiritual and practical functions of aesthetics, I now want to take a second look at the warehouse itself and its practical and symbolic meaning for the church.

Warehouse Aesthetics and Ritual Performances

Considering the historical division of urban space in Europe, churches located in industrial areas and warehouses seem to be odd. In Europe, locales[10] for religious practices traditionally have very distinct features, which have been shaped by close interconnections between sovereignty and Christianity. Churches are usually located at the center of the spatial arrangement of a community, recognizable as a shelter and place of refuge. However, they also function as markers of power and authority, dominating a marketplace or indicating the center of a town, which had evolved around a former monastery (Sennett 1994: Ch. 5). In most big European cities, church buildings, recognizable through their distinct features (e.g., a steeple, a bell tower, a churchyard, an impressive entrance), now function as tourist sites and urban retreats, and generally aid in reading the settlement history of the buildings and spaces which form today's metropolis. In contrast, the locale of industrial areas is clearly secular and seems to contradict the purposes of religious interactions, since they were zoned for economic purposes. They are usually located outside the main residential area of a city and provided with adequate transportation access for heavy trucks and railroad.

Usually church buildings are also architectural highlights, serving as markers for a specific period in art history, but warehouses are purely functional. Interestingly, as Coleman reports, several Pentecostal megachurches in Sweden and the United States today, which can afford to construct their own big buildings, have opted for architectural designs which reference "warehouse style" (Coleman 2000: 155, 153). Other examples include churches that actually bought industrial buildings and renovated them for their needs instead of purchasing a different type of building, such as the KICC. Thus there seems to be more of a connection between functional industrial architecture and Pentecostalism than is apparent at first glance.

First, we can note the practical advantages in retaining warehouse elements within mega-church construction. Buildings in "warehouse style" reach "maximum efficiency" in terms of providing seating for a large crowd, employing media equipment, and displaying the power of the word on a huge stage (Coleman 2000: 155). Thus even within the architecture of transnational Pentecostal churches, the reaching out in the world is embodied by being grand and ready to expand (Coleman 2000: 144). For The Destiny Changing Church one of the most important practicalities of the industrial area is that nobody cares about the "holy noise," which is part of the ritual practice of the church: praying, preaching, and music happens always at full blast and through the complete utilization of the sound system.

Apart from the importance of functional space in enabling the embodiment of the Holy Spirit, space matters also spiritually. In Pentecostal ideology every territory has its own spirit, which is in charge of the place. Thus every other spirit wanting to operate in one area needs to ask permission from the territorial spirit or needs to conquer it. Many churches have special prayer groups who deal with territorial matters, such as delivering buildings, parks, and monuments from evil spirits. Especially historic sites or old church buildings are loaded with the spiritual presence of demons. On several occasions I have been told that old church buildings host demons, which have become attached to the structures, because these structures were built in line with occult knowledge. Thus the usage of an old church would require intense spatial deliverance work from the pastors before it became functional for new religious services. As we can see, Pentecostal congregations perceive there to be spiritual advantages in the appropriation of space that has not previously been used as a church.

Time also plays a major role in the religious rituals of these congregations, as shown by scholars who have worked on the ritual practices among West African Pentecostals and have extensively explored the moral meaning of time within Pentecostal ideology. It could be argued that much of the ritual energy is invested in dealing with matters of time rather than space, for example by delivering people from their sinful past and leading them into a new life (see Meyer 1998; van Dijk 2002, 2004). However, evil spirits are still assumed to reside somewhere and to inhabit space in places and bodies. Furthermore, the presence of the Holy Spirit needs space to become embodied. The aim of every ritual activity in the church is to achieve the experience of the presence of the Holy Spirit. Although the spirit moves in whimsical ways and seems to be the paradigm for dislocatedness and deterritorialization (Krause 2006b), the very purpose of coming together in a church place is to experience the spirit spatially, in the "here and now." The importance of space is underlined by the intensity of the bodily techniques, which are part of Pentecostal worship, particularly walking, kneeling, waving, jumping, utterance, sermonizing, singing, and various other ways of being filled with the spirit. Space as lived experience is crucial for Pentecostalism and can only happen through ritual performances. In this sense, Pentecostal space is doing and "does not pre-exist its doing" (Rose 1999: 248). Pentecostal ritual practices rely on the free-floating power of the Holy Spirit. De Witte argues that whilst on the one hand, the Holy Spirit is imagined as "supergalactic power" reaching far beyond any physical boundaries, on the other hand it can only be embodied through fixed patterns of learned behavior, timed practices, and routinized body techniques (De Witte 2003: 175).

In light of the above we can see how an empty space, such as a new building with functional architecture or a vacated space such as an old warehouse, which reflects the performance but does not carry too much own meaning, serves as an ideal church space. However, the difference between our church in the Lea Valley and those mega-churches, which can afford to build their own spaces in a warehouse style, is simply that The Destiny Changing Church has been displaced into the industrial park rather than actively choosing to be there. Yet the continuing tendency to rent space in industrial areas and warehouses among many neo-Pentecostal churches in European cities points to the fact that there are no constraints concerning location in a mundane, purely functional environment. Warehouse aesthetics seem to have become part of the architectonic repertoire within transnational Pentecostalism.

Yet in terms of the hierarchy of urban space, the physical location at the fringes of the city can be seen as indicating the marginalized social status of these churches, not only with regard to their fundamentalist theology, which makes it difficult for them to be incorporated within mainstream Christian institutions, especially as black churches with black pastors. Thus, the practical and spiritual usefulness of a warehouse coincides with the de facto marginalization of African churches. At the same time the church sees itself as part of a global community and uses the warehouse as the base for organizing transnational connections and linkages. Keeping this tension in mind, in the remainder of this chapter I want to come back to a question which I have mentioned so far only in passing: whether or not these churches can be called African and/or transnational churches.

"African" and/or Transnational Pentecostal Churches?

The churches in the industrial park are part of a phenomenon that has recently received increased scholarly attention: the growing number of churches founded by migrants from Africa in Europe. Since the 1960s, branches of so-called African Independent Churches,[11] such as the Celestial Church of Christ, and Aladura Worldwide from Nigeria (Adogame 2004), have been founded by previous generations of migrants. Over the years they incorporated people from varying ethnic and socio-cultural backgrounds and now have an international, pan-African membership (Adogame 2004: 498). However, since the 1990s the transnational networking of charismatic and neo-Pentecostal churches has increased worldwide.[12] In London (Adogame 2004; Hunt 2002; Harris 2006; Daswani 2006; Krause 2006a), as in other European cities such as Amsterdam, The Hague (van Dijk 2002, 2004; Ter Haar 1998), Hamburg (Jach 2005), Berlin (Nieswand 2005a; Krause 2006b), and Copenhagen (Lauterbach 2005), many churches were founded in the late 1990s by migrants from Nigeria and Ghana as offshoots of the charismatic movement, which was sweeping through Ghana and Nigeria at that time (see van Dijk 2002, 2004; Gifford 2004).

The increasing number of new Pentecostal churches can be regarded as a side effect of "new African diasporas" (Koser 2003), which emerged during the 1980s and 1990s, when many Africans moved to new destinations.[13] In the case of the United Kingdom, more and more migrants from African countries without colonial ties to Britain have moved into London such as Congolese and Ivorians (Koser 2003; Vertovec 2006). They patronize the long-established infrastructures of shops, businesses, restaurants and churches of Anglophone West Africans such as Nigerians and Ghanaians. Some of the newcomers might have lived in other European destinations before settling in London, others have come directly from their home countries. black Africans now outnumber black Caribbeans in the UK and the migrant population in London, in general, has undergone an increasing diversification with regard to countries of origin, ethnicities, languages, religions, migration experiences, work and living conditions, legal statuses, periods of stay, individual mobility, and transnational connections.

Consequently, it is more necessary than ever to look at other forms of organization and identification than country of origin or ethnicity to understand this "superdiverse" urbanity (Vertovec 2006). Religious organizations are often used as an example for a research field that fosters a different perspective. For instance, Glick Schiller et al. (2006) use the example of a church founded by a pastor of Nigerian origin in Manchester, New Hampshire, who was able to establish a Prayer Network which assembled twenty different congregations, all aiming at winning the city for God. They explained the divide within Manchester society as being not so much between ethnically diverse congregations but rather between believers and non-believers (Glick Schiller et al. 2006: 620). The authors acknowledge that this form of incorporation might be typical for a small-scale city, but they criticize the "prevailing assumption" within studies on migration and religion "that immigrants live and worship within distinct ethnic communities" (2006: 612). In their view this "ethnic lens"[14] obscures "the diversity of migrant's relationships to their place of settlement and to other localities around the world" (2006: 613). They further argue that many authors see church membership as a measure of whether a church is international or not and do not pay sufficient attention to the self-definition of the churches.

However, I would argue that, in order to reveal the diversity of relationships formed by and through churches, we need to take into account their situational positioning within a specific historical and geographical context, and their engagement in different forms of identification, boundary drawing, and representational practices. Thus, in some situations a church might describe itself as an African church and might act within specific ethnic networks. However, in other situations it might address an international audience and organize its activities within a transnational religious field, which is not grounded in shared country of origin but in a shared belief and a sense of belonging to a global Christendom.

The pastors from our case study, however, would certainly agree with the criticism of Glick Schiller and her associates because they do not like to be pigeonholed as Africans. The Destiny Changing Church is decisively not part of the Council of African and African Caribbean Churches, UK but the Evangelical Alliance, UK. The former is a consortium which actively promotes an African or Caribbean Christian tradition,[15] while the latter brings together a wide scope of evangelical, charismatic and Pentecostal churches in the UK and is part of a worldwide network.[16] The Destiny Changing Church prefers the Evangelical Alliance because it provides access to an international field of contacts and although most of the effective networking with other churches happens with pastors who have a Ghanaian background as well, the church insists on representing itself as international rather than as a Ghanaian or African church. This boundary maintenance towards churches, which identify as African or African Caribbean, is mainly based on their use of certain ritual practices, which they see as belonging to "African traditions" while other churches regard them as demonic.[17] In keeping with this perceived difference, churches, which identify as African, are easily pigeonholed as backward and non-international, and thus as "more traditional" by neo-Pentecostal churches such as The Destiny Changing Church.[18]

Looking at when and how the church leaders and the membership define the church as Ghanaian, black African, black ethnic minority, or as an international church, we see, not surprisingly, that the self-representation varies depending on the context. If asked by a researcher, such as myself or by a journalist, the question is answered by referring to the information available on the church's webpage and other public relations material. Here The Destiny Changing Church is portrayed as an international church with transnational connections, envisioned as part of a Christendom with global outreach. In certain contexts, however, it becomes important to identify as a black ethnic minority church. As mentioned earlier, within the neighborhood of the industrial area, the church is considered to be a black African church: the congregation consists of mainly black members, and the style of worship is perceived as African by the congregation and the neighbors with regard to noise and length.

To call itself an ethnic minority church might be a defiant reaction towards the negative attributes attached to "African" in British society today. This label certainly draws on the British discourse about cultural and religious diversity and also includes Asians and other people classified as non-whites. With this identification the church inhabits a specific social position eligible for protection and funding from public sources within British society, and takes part in a discourse of solidarity among non-white groups. Ethnic minority status works further in the church's favor in its relationship with the English owner of the warehouse, who regards the church as an educational center for black ethnic minorities and is therefore willing to lease the property to the church.

When analyzing the motivation of the members for joining The Changing Destinies Church, it becomes apparent that the Ghanaian origin of all the pastors plays an important role in encouraging migrants to join the church and allowing them to accept the pastors as their spiritual fathers. Furthermore, this shared national background is strengthened by Ghanaian elements that are often noticeable in the service. Phrases and words in Twi—one of the several languages of Ghana—sneak into the preaching and are often jokingly referred to as "pure Hebrew."[19] However, shared ties to Ghana are not the only common denominator among the congregation. Members, who are not Ghanaian, often come to know about the church through personal networks, which rely not only on a shared country of origin but on a black African background. Thus the reference to the shared experience of being from different African countries could be also identified as a major tie binding the congregation together.

Looking at the transnational connections of the church, we find international interconnections of the leadership, which range from kin relations to friendships formed at international Pentecostal conferences, which include pastors with various backgrounds. Additionally the church in London is frequently visited by pastors and traveling prophets from Africa who get into contact with the church through personal networks.

In another paper solely authored by Glick Schiller (2005), she draws on the same case study as above to argue that churches such as The Destiny Changing Church must also be viewed in light of the way in which their Christian fundamentalism feeds into American imperialism. I agree with her that until now the tendency has been to view the transnational engagement of migrants through more accommodating questions rather than focusing on how the migrants participate in a social field of Christian fundamentalism. The ultra-conservative attitudes and body politics of many of the neo-Pentecostal churches are hardly ever mentioned compared with the large amount of work done on the ritual and social elements of these churches. However, limiting oneself to acknowledging the incorporation of these churches within an American-style fundamentalism would ignore the distinct history of African Christian churches.

Many churches founded by Londoners of African background are part of Christian fundamentalist networks but they do have to be understood as coming from a very distinctive historical background. To begin with, they are bound up in the history of African Christianity, which has contributed a great deal to the growing social field of global Pentecostalism

(Gifford 2004; Jenkins 2004). Second, one must consider the history of black people in Europe, which has mainly been a history of rejection and exclusion from mainstream church life and has resulted in the founding of many of the churches present today (Kalilombe 1997; Adogame 2004: 497).[20] Third, within Africa Pentecostal and Aladura churches bear a history, which grew out of the appropriation of mission churches and evolved through conflict with colonialism, new nation-building projects after independence, a transnationalization and reconfiguration of public space, through new media technology and increased emigration of the West African populations (Meyer 2004). It is rather the concurrence of taking part in a transnational social field of fundamentalism, while simultaneously being engaged in ethnic, business, and local social networks which makes many of the migrant-founded neo-Pentecostal churches in Europe and the United States so difficult to grasp conceptually.

Conclusion

In this chapter I have argued that the reason why churches founded by West African migrants in London are often located in industrial areas is greatly influenced by the congregations' difficulties in finding affordable rooms, which are at the same time tolerant of noisy worship. Here they cohabit with other migrant entrepreneurs, but hardly engage with the place as social space. Instead, as shown in the example of The Destiny Changing Church, the spatial practices are more often directed towards an imaginary transnational space in the form of spiritual services, which the church offers to its membership and the city. Based on an understanding of space as a net of social relations and contested negotiations, I have examined the meaningful social interactions in these spaces from the point of view of the church. I have shown that the functionality of the available room in regard to size and spiritual neutrality is relevant for allowing the conducting of ritual performances and for experiencing the presence of the Holy Spirit. Most significant for the appropriation of the industrial places as religious spaces is the reconstitution of Pentecostal mediascapes within them. The imaginary transnational field of neo-Pentecostalism becomes articulated within the warehouse as appropriated place.

As to the question of whether churches such as The Changing Destinies Church are better understood as African churches in Europe or as transnational churches, the answer is that they need to be seen in their shifting positioning depending on the context. The invisibility of the churches in the cityscape, as noted at the beginning, can be understood as an expression of these different positions, reflecting the marginal status as black minority church within British society and the importance of an imagined transnational space for the meaningful actions of the church that take place inside the building.

The church leaders and members can be seen as urban pioneers, who, despite the amount of discrimination their congregations experience, contribute to society by adding a spiritual component to the post-industrial service industry landscape. This spiritual component can be summarized as follows: our service is to transform your life into a better future.

Notes

1. Research during 2005-2006 was made possible by a scholarship from Evanelisches Studienwerk Villigist, an ESRC Center linked studentship with COMPAS, University of Oxford and the German Research Council funded project on Transnational Networks, Religion and New Migration, Humboldt University Berlin. Thanks to Michael P. Smith, Gertrud Hüwelmeier, Viktoria Bergschmidt, Katharina Schramm, Matthias Schwartz for very helpful comments and to Diana Aurisch for correcting my English.
2. The names of the church and its pastor have been changed in order to protect their anonymity.
3. Kingsway International, http://www.kicc.org.uk/. According to the homepage "[t]he church is now seeing over 12,000 members with a vision to double this number by 2010." For special events, the church space is expanded by using a tent seating approximately several thousands. I thank Ann Davies for generously sharing field notes with me on her visit of Kingsway's "International Gathering of Champions" conference in August 2006.
4. Trinity Baptist Church, http://www.trinitybaptist.org.uk/home/index.shtml. The church acquired a former warehouse depot in Norwood.
5. The Rambler Associations, http://www.ramblers.org.uk/info/parks/leevalley.html.
6. Manny Lewis, Chief Executive of the London Development Agency, declared to the press: "The Games will make the Lower Lea one of the City's most exciting places to live and work." (LDA, 16 May 2006. Accessed at: http://www.lda.gov.uk/server/show/ConWebDoc.1494).
7. Aladura churches (in Yoruba: the praying people) were founded in Nigeria during the 1920s and have spread from there throughout West Africa and abroad (Peel 1968: 205; Adogame 2004: 494; Meyer 2004). Pentecostal churches have at the core of their ritual practices the gifts of the Holy Spirit, namely, speaking in tongues and healing, but it makes sense to differentiate different waves of churches. The classical Pentecostal churches were founded between the 1930s and 1950s. Neo-Pentecostal churches are those which were founded in the 1980s and 1990s (Gifford 2004; Meyer 2004). Neo-Pentecostal churches regard Aladura churches as being engaged in malpractice, in particular they accuse them of being too close to so-called African traditional practices (Meyer 1998; van Dijk 2002).
8. http://www.london2012.org/en/city/onecity/.
9. Globalization and transnationalism are often conflated terms (see Smith 2005a; Glick Schiller 2005). To differentiate "global" from "transnational" I refer to global in regard to the imagined community of Born Again Christians who span the planet, and refer to transnational when I speak about actual ties, networks, or networks of networks ("transnational social fields," see Glick Schiller et al. 2006:614).

10. Following Anthony Giddens, locales are characteristic physical settings associated with different types of social interactions, which form specific collectives (Giddens 1979: 206ff., 1984: 188ff.).
11. "African Independent" or "Indigenous" churches have already over a century of history in Africa. They were founded in reaction to the missionary churches and became popular because of their practical approach towards everyday life problems and the inclusion of healing and spiritual protection in their practices (Peel 1969; Meyer 2004).
12. There has been a boom in literature on Pentecostalism, especially in Africa and Latin America, within the last few years. For an in-depth overview on African Christianity see Meyer (2004), on globalization and Pentecostalism see Coleman (2002) and Robbins (2004).
13. Akyeampong (2000). See contributions in Koser (2003) and in Grillo and Mazzucato (forthcoming).
14. The term "ethnic" is rather confusing when applied to migrants from Sub-Saharan countries, because within one country of origin one can easily find up to 40 or more ethnic groups. In some cases, however, it would make sense to use the term "ethnicity." There are churches which are mainly patronized by one ethnic group because of language usage in the service such as Yoruba, Ibo, or Lingala. Glick Schiller et al. (2006) point to the tendency to reproduce the categories of immigration statistics which list country of birth or ethnicity, in line with "methodological nationalism," and to conceptualize only one single possible pathway of incorporation, thereby neglecting other forms of engagement.
15. I refer here to the Council's self-representation. See the documentation of the Consultation of the World Council of Churches with African and Afro-Caribbean Churches (Leeds, 30 November- 2 December 1995. Accessed at: http://www.pctii.org/wcc/jehu95.html).
16. http://www.eauk.org/about/. Within the Evangelical Alliance there is an association for African and Caribbean churches which calls itself "Voice of Black Majority Churches, UK," but the Destiny Changing Church is not a member of this sub-group.
17. There is a considerable body of literature on African Pentecostalism which deals with this question. In particular Meyer (1998), van Dijk (2002, 2004), Marshall (1991) and Gifford (2004).
18. This is despite the fact that many Aladura churches are transnationally organized (Adogame 2004).
19. Recently, the church established a service referred to as "Twi Service." Ironically, it is held by a pastor who speaks Twi only as his second language because he is an Ewe, and thus his preaching is mostly in English. Most of the songs performed are however in Twi. With the establishment of this service, the church seems to follow a trend among other bigger churches which have "second" and "third" services on a Sunday, and which often cater for a specific group within the church.
20. One of the aims of the Councils of Christian Communities of an African Approach in Europe (CCCAAE) is to gain recognition among the "white" mainstream churches in Europe (Adogame 2004b).

References

Adogame, A. (2004a). "Engaging the Rhetoric of Spiritual Warfare: The Public Face of Aladura in Diaspora." *Journal of Religion in Africa* 34 (4): 493-522.

_____ (2004b). "Conference Report: The Berlin-Congo Conference 1884: The Partition of Africa and Implications For Christian Missions Today." *Journal of Religion in Africa* 34: 1-2.

Akyeampong, E. K. (2000). "Africans in the Diaspora: The Diaspora and Africa." *African Affairs* 99: 183-215.
Appadurai, A. (1990). "Disjuncture and Difference in the Global Cultural Economy." In *Global Culture. Nationalism, Globalization and Modernity* (pp. 295-310). London / Newbury Park / New Delhi: Sage.
Coleman, S. (2000). *The Globalisation of Charismatic Christianity*. Cambridge, Cambridge University Press.
―――――― (2002). "The Faith Movement: A Global Religious Culture?" *Culture and Religion: An Interdisciplinary Journal* 3 (1): 3-19.
Daswani, G. (2006). *Between Divine Promise and Practice: Social Change and Transformation Amongst Members of a Pentecostal Church in Ghana and London*. Unpublished PhD Thesis, London School of Economics.
De Witte, M. (2003). "Altar Media's 'Living World': Televised Charismatic Christianity in Ghana." *Journal of Religion in Africa* 33 (2): 172-2002.
Giddens, A. (1979). *Central Problems in Social Theory*. London: Macmillan.
Gifford, P. (1994). "Ghana's Charismatic Churches." *Journal of Religion in Africa* 24(3): 241-265.
―――――― (2004). *Ghana's New Christianity: Pentecostalism in a Globalising African Economy*. London, Hurst & Co.
Glick Schiller, N. (2005). "Transnational Social Fields and Imperialism. Bringing Theory of Power to Transnational Studies." *Anthropological Theory* 5: 439-461.
Glick Schiller, N., A. Caglar, and T.C. Guldbrandsen (2006). "Beyond the Ethnic Lens: Locality, Globality, and Born-again Incorporation." *American Ethnologist* 33 (4): 612-633.
Grillo, R. & Mazzucato, V. (eds.) (forthcoming): "Africa-Europe Linkages." Special issue of *Journal of Ethnic and Migration Studies*.
Harris, H. (2006). *Yoruba in Diaspora: An African Church in London*. Palgrave, Macmillan.
Hunt, S. (2002) "'Neither Here nor There': The Construction of Identities and Boundary Maintenance of West African Pentecostals." *Sociology* 36 (1): 147-169.
Jach, R. (2005). *Migration-Religion-Raum*. Münster, Lit Verlag.
Jenkins, P. (2004). *The Next Christendom. The Coming of Global Christianity*, Oxford, Oxford University Press.
Kalilombe, P. (1997). "Black Christianity in Britain." *Ethnic and Racial Studies* 20 (2): 306-324.
Koser, K. (ed.) (2003). *New African Diasporas*. London: Routledge.
Krause, K. (2005). "'The Double Face of Subjectivity': A Case Study in a Psychiatric Hospital (Ghana)." In *Multiple Medical Realities. Patients and Healers in Biomedicine, Alternative and Traditional Medicine* (pp. 54-71). New York, Oxford: Berghahn Books.
―――――― (2006). "Mobile Prophets and Travelling Pastors: Pentecostal Pathways into Cosmopolitan Male Elites?" Paper for the Panel: Elites and Cosmopolitanism, at the ASA Conference 2006, Cosmopolitanism and Anthropology, 10-13 April, Keele University.
―――――― (2007). "Multiple Medical Practices in Transnational Therapy Networks across Ghana and London." To be published in: *Journal of Ethnic and Migration Studies*, special issue *African-European Linkages*, guest editors R. Grillo and V. Mazzucato.
Lauterbach, K. (2004). *Transnational Religious Networks. A Study of Ghanaian Pentecostals in Europe and Ghana*, 13th Nordic Migration Conference, AMID.
Marshall, R. (1991). "Power in the Name of Jesus." *Review of African Political Economy* 52: 21-38.

Massey, D. (1991). "The Political Place of Locality Studies." *Environment and Planning A* 23: 267-281.

_____ (1993a). "Questions of Locality." *Geography* 78: 142-9.

_____ (1993b). "Power-geometry and a progressive sense of place." In *Mapping the Futures: Local Cultures, Global Change* (pp. 59-69). London & New York, Routledge.

Meyer, B. (1998). "Make a Complete Break with the Past: Memory and Postcolonial Modernity in Ghanaian Pentecostalist Discourse." *Journal of Religion in Africa* 28 (3): 316-349.

_____ (2004). "Christianity in Africa: From African Independent to Pentecostal-Charismatic Churches." *Annual Review of Anthropology* 33: 447-474.

Nieswand, B. (2005a). "Charismatic Christianity in the Context of Migration. Social Status, the Experience of Migration and the Construction of Selves among Ghanaian Migrants in Berlin." In *Religion in the Context of African Migration* (pp. 243-266). Bayreuth: Bayreuth African Studies.

Peel, J.D. (1968). *Aladura: A Religious Movement among the Yoruba*, London, Oxford University Press.

Robbins, J. (2004). "The Globalization of Pentecostal and Charismatic Christianity." *Annual Review of Anthropology* 33: 117-43.

Rose, G. (1999) "Performing Space." In: *Human Geography Today* (pp. 247-259). Cambridge, Oxford: Polity Press.

Schultze, Q. (1990). "Defining the Electronic Church." In *Religious Television: Controversies and Conclusions* (pp. 41-51), Norwood; New Jersey, Ablex Publishers.

Sennett, R. (1994). *Flesh and Stone*. New York, London: WW Norton & Company & Faber & Faber.

Smith, M. P. (2001). *Transnational Urbanism. Locating Globalization*. Oxford, Malden: Blackwell Publishers.

_____ (2005a). "Transnational Urbanism Revisited." *Journal of Ethnic and Migration Studies* 31 (2): 235-244.

_____ (2005b). "Power in Place/Places of Power: Contextualizing Transnational Research." *City & Society* 17 (1): 5-34.

Ter Haar, G. (1998). "African Christians in the Netherlands." In *Strangers and Sojourners. Religious Communities in the Diaspora* (pp. 153-172). Amsterdam: Peeters.

Ukah, A. (2005a) "Mobilities, Migration and Multiplication: The Expansion of the Religious Field of the Redeemed Christian Church of God, Nigeria." In *Religion in the Context of African Migration* (pp. 317-342). Bayreuth, African Studies Series.

_____ (2005b). "Those Who Trade with God Never Lose: The Economics of Pentecostal Activism in Nigeria." In *Christianity and Social Change in Africa: Essays in Honor of John Peel* (pp. 251-274). Carolina: Carolina Academic Press.

van Dijk, R. (2002). "The Soul is the Stranger: Ghanaian Pentecostalism and the Diasporic Contestation of "Flow" and "Individuality." *Culture & Religion* 3 (1): 49-65.

_____ (2004). "Negotiating Marriage: Questions of Morality and Legitimacy in the Ghanaian Pentecostal Diaspora." *Journal of Religion in Africa* 34 (4): 438-467.

Vertovec, S. (2006). "The Emergence of Superdiversity in Britain." *COMPAS Working Paper* WP-06-25, www.compas.ox.ac.uk.

8

Spirits in the Marketplace: Transnational Networks of Vietnamese Migrants in Berlin

Gertrud Hüwelmeier

In the current era of globalization, the flow of migrants from Asia and Africa to Europe has created highly dynamic regions of migration that are globally interconnected. In contrast to the former "guest workers," who moved from Mediterranean countries to northern Europe to work in the industrial and manufacturing sector, mainly through bilateral agreements between governments and employers, the new migrants have found different niches in the European labor market through changes in national immigration legislation. However, due to different policies in various European countries, the legal status of the newcomers is often unclear, with many of them living and working as undocumented migrants.

Religion seems to be one marker of incorporation into the host society, allowing migrants simultaneously to maintain connections with the country of origin and forge new ties with migrant communities in other countries. People, moving to Europe for various economic and political reasons, bring their religious beliefs with them and gathering for religious purposes is one way of setting up a new life in unfamiliar surroundings (Warner 1998: 3). In many cases the organizations, institutions, meetings and gatherings, as well as the religious places and activities of migrants, transform the religious landscape of the host society. At the same time, the architecture of the migrants' places of worship, the names of the spirits they venerate, and the prophets they follow differ from the religious practices in their country of origin.

Many scholars increasingly recognize that religion thrives precisely because globalization provides useful tools for religious actors and organizations. In particular, fluid transnational networks help to project their messages from the local to the global. The emerging literature on the importance of religion and immigration (Tweed 1997; Orsi 1999; Yasbeck et al. 2003; Stepick 2004; Hüwelmeier 2001, 2005a, 2005b, 2007a, 2007b; Mahler and Hansing 2005; Hansing 2005), on religion and pilgrimage (Coleman and Eade 2004), as well as on religion and transnationalism (Hoeber Rudolph and Piscatori 1997), sheds new light on these networks and flows. As for the transnational connections of migrants, specifically those involved in creating and maintaining cross-border relationships, scholars have only recently begun to pay attention to religious networks in the diaspora (Vertovec 2004; Levitt 2003a, 2003b, 2007; Hüwelmeier 2007a).

This chapter will explore how religious place-making in Europe emerges from the ways in which migrants transport and introduce religious ideas, practices, and sacred objects from one place to another, while simultaneously changing or redefining their ideas about belief, ritual, locality and sacred space in the process. In particular, the chapter focuses on the shifting interdependencies between place-making, locality, and religion in the production of diasporic religious identities in Europe. It seeks to understand the importance of these interdependencies for the traveling of religious objects (shrines and altars) and even spirits, but also ventures to investigate religious emplacement as a contested process in contemporary Europe.

Based on anthropological fieldwork with Vietnamese people in Berlin and other places in Germany,[1] I will focus on the migrants' religious experiences in the new country as they simultaneously maintain social and religious ties (Glick Schiller 1992, 1999) to Vietnam. Religion plays a crucial role within the process of settlement for a considerable number of migrants. I will argue that global processes and the liberalization of the socialist economy in Vietnam since the late 1990s have deeply informed the revitalization of religious practices in Vietnam and the Vietnamese diaspora. The global flow of money, the emergence of consumer culture in Vietnam, and the desire to participate in these processes are just some of the reasons for the increasing economic and religious activities in Vietnam and the diasporic communities.

In order to understand the diversity of Vietnamese religious networks in the diaspora, I will outline in the first part of this chapter the different waves of Vietnamese migrants in the two Germanys. After the fall of the Wall, i.e., the unification of the former socialist German Democratic Republic (GDR) and the Federal Republic of Germany (FRG), the religious landscape among Vietnamese migrants changed significantly. The second part of the chapter will concentrate on the relationship between religious activities and their emplacement within the field of immigrant entrepreneurship in Berlin by focusing on altars in shops, snack bars, restaurants and marketplaces. Special attention will be given to spirits and their role in protecting the territory of shops and the wellbeing of the owners. This chapter will focus, in particular, on the places where most of these economic and religious activities take place: in Vietnamese wholesale markets located within remote industrial urban areas.

Vietnamese Migrants in the Two Germanys

During the second half of the 1990s, an estimated 2.3 million Vietnamese were living outside their home country, around 1 million in the United States, 300,000 in France, 200,000 in Australia, 150,000 in Canada, and 115,000 in Germany. There were different groups and different waves of Vietnamese refugees leaving Vietnam after the end of the war in 1975 (Baumann 2000: 38). With regard to the two Germanys the situation was as follows. At the end of the 1970s, the West German government (Federal Republic of Germany) declared it would adopt a contingent of 10,000 refugees from Vietnam, Cambodia, and Laos. During 1979 the numbers were increased to 20,000 and by 1984 up to 38,000 people from Indochina had migrated to the Federal Republic of Germany, the majority coming from South Vietnam. These so-called "boat people" were treated as refugees according to Articles 2-34 of the Geneva Convention and they received a temporary residence permit, which was later changed into a permanent residence permit. "Boat people" participated in language courses and received assistance in finding jobs. Some scholars labeled them privileged refugees (Blume 1988; Jensen 1983, quoted in Baumann 2000: 34), because they received preferential treatment compared with other refugees.

The living and working conditions of the Vietnamese "contract workers" in former East Germany, the German Democratic Republic, were quite different from those experienced by the "boat people" in West Germany. Starting in the 1950s, students from North Vietnam came to live in the GDR, the socialist "brotherland" of Vietnam. Between 1966 and 1986 13,000 Vietnamese students and experts were trained in the GDR. From the 1980s, through contracts established between the socialist GDR and Socialist Vietnam, tens of thousands of Vietnamese migrants, mostly from North Vietnam, came to live and work in East Germany. They stayed for five years and eventually returned to their home country. Incorporation into the host society was not expected. Apart from a German language course of only two months, the contract workers were not "integrated" at all. Living in specially designated housing, they were ghettoized, and watched over by the government and the secret service.

After the reunification of the two Germanys in 1990, new documents in archives—collected by the former GDR secret service—made quite clear that the socialist government of East Germany closely observed the involvement of Vietnamese contract workers before 1989 in smuggling and other "illegal" activities, including sexual relations. Unlike the "boat people," for whom family reunion was quite easy according to West German law, the contract workers (male and female) migrated without their spouses or children. Sexual relations between the contract workers were forbidden and even contact with local people was not allowed. In spite of contract regulations, these contacts took place in manifold ways. As a consequence, pregnant female contract workers, for example, were forced to have abortions or return to Vietnam (Dennis 2005: 38).

Besides the emphasis on the negative treatment of the contract workers, we should realize that they were not passive victims of the secret service—they proactively sought to improve their living and working conditions in the former GDR (Dennis 2005). After the reunification of Germany, they used their personal and economic networks to build up transnational connections with friends and relatives in Vietnam, as well as with former contract workers in East European countries. In the years after the Wall came down, an estimated 40,000 contract workers, about two-thirds of the Vietnamese population in the GDR, were sent home. Many of them returned in the 1990s, legally or illegally, after realizing that living and working in Germany was much easier than in Hanoi or other places in Vietnam (Hillmann 2005). Using their former networks, they forged transnational relations and maintained political, familial, economic, and religious ties between home and the host country (Glick Schiller et al. 1992, 1998). An estimated 115,000 to 120,000 Vietnamese are currently living in the reunified Germany, including about 20,000 (only 10,000 with legal status) in Berlin and its outlying areas.

Religious Networks in the Diaspora

Religious place-making of Vietnamese people in Germany is highly influenced by the political circumstances of their arrival in Europe. Many of those who came as "boat people" to West Germany after the Vietnam War in 1975 were quite critical of the new political regime in Vietnam. Like many migrants in other countries they brought their religion, particularly Buddhism and Catholicism, with them to the new location (Warner 1998: 3). With regard to the "boat people" and their transnational religious ties, it is important to realize that Vietnamese Buddhist monks and nuns cared for them in the refugee camps after their arrival, while other migrants were supported by the Protestant or Catholic Church in West Germany. This led to the foundation of many Vietnamese Buddhist temples and Vietnamese Catholic communities in West Germany. These places of worship were not to be found in East Germany before 1990. Very recently Pentecostalism has begun to emerge among Vietnamese people in Berlin and other parts of Germany as well as in the Czech Republic and Poland. This religious movement has become very popular because of its prosperity gospel and the performance of healing rituals (Hüwelmeier 2006b).

Due to political circumstances, the former contract workers in East Germany and East Berlin, mainly from North Vietnam, had very little contact with the "boat people" in West Germany and West Berlin. This separation is clearly visible in the context of religious networks. For example, although the Catholic Church in Berlin tries to bring together "boat people" and former contract workers, it seems to be difficult to unite them under one roof, since the former contract workers in the GDR mainly come from socialist North Vietnam, while most of the "boat people" in West Germany came from South Vietnam and left the country shortly after the Communist regime came into power in 1975. Apart from these different political traditions, social status within the host society also seems to play an important role with regard to the ongoing separation of the two groups. While the Catholic Vietnamese in the western part of the country have often been able to attain German citizenship and become economically well-established, the residence permits for many of the former Vietnamese contract workers, asylum seekers and undocumented migrants are quite unclear, making it difficult for the two groups to engage with each other.

Although many of the Vietnamese living in East Berlin would call themselves non-religious or atheists, they practice the veneration of ancestors in their homes. According to my interview subjects, these religious performances also took place during the GDR regime, but were practiced only by a minority of Vietnamese contract workers. One of the reasons was that the necessary ingredients, such as incense, were not available to perform the ritual in a proper way. Another reason concerns the age of the contract workers. Many of them came in their early twenties without their spouses and children. They were young and their parents were still alive in Vietnam, so that they did not feel obliged to fulfill any religious duties. As one of my Vietnamese friends put it: "If you are alone, you are not at home. And if you don't feel at home, you would not venerate your ancestors." So it makes sense that the re-emergence of ancestor veneration after the fall of the Wall should be embedded in the context of family reunion processes.

The absence of private space within that society was another reason why the ancestors were not worshipped as much in the GDR. Living cheek by jowl in a small place, without the possibility of a room of one's own for many years, discouraged many migrants from fulfilling their religious duties. Although ancestor veneration was condoned in Vietnam after the war, many Communist households did not practice it any more. According to my Vietnamese informants in Berlin, some of those who continued to practice ancestor veneration in Vietnam, added Ho Chi Minh as a hero to the ancestor altar in their homes. In socialist Vietnam, during and after the war, individual veneration of ancestors was not forbidden, but practicing different religious rituals, particularly *len dong* spirit mediumship, was seen as superstitious and punished by state law (Endres 2000: 123).

Spirits in the Global Trade Center

A recent phenomenon among Vietnamese migrants in Berlin is the veneration of spirits and the emergence of altars in business locations such as shops, snack bars, and global trade centers, especially in the former socialist eastern part of the city. These religious practices were not performed in the decade after the fall of the Wall, but have emerged in the last few years, especially in connection with a similar revival of shrines and temples in Vietnam. This development occurred particularly within the context of the economic liberalization after Doi Moi in 1986 and the expansion of consumer culture all over Vietnam in the last few years.

These events have had important consequences for the religious practices of the Vietnamese diaspora in Germany. Vietnamese migrants in the eastern part of Berlin, especially those owning small shops and snack bars, are performing religious rituals in their places of business, worshipping "spirits of wealth" and "spirits of the place." They place small altars at the entrance of their shops, donating fruits, sweets, cigarettes, and incense to the spirits every day, while praying for good business. The altars are also to be found in the newly opened "global trade centers" in East Berlin, localities where people from many different parts of Germany, especially the east, forge networks of different kinds. Vietnamese traders from Rostock and Schwerin, cities in northeastern Germany, as well as those from Erfurt, Cottbus, and Leipzig, south of Berlin, visit the Vietnamese "global trade centers" every week to buy goods and to transport them back to their own places of business.

Places of Business

To understand better the economic situation of Vietnamese migrants in East Berlin and their new religious activities, I will briefly discuss the fact that most of these migrants are embedded in the labor market as self-employed small business owners. For many of them this is the only way to survive economically. After the reunification of Germany in 1990, living and working in Germany became quite difficult for the former Vietnamese contract workers. Before 1990, East German enterprises were responsible for organizing every aspect of the migrants' daily lives, from housing and employment to medical treatment. Nearly all GDR enterprises collapsed after the reunification and about 70 percent of the Vietnamese immigrants lost their jobs (Hillmann 2005: 91). Former contract workers were forced to find new sources of income. Due to special state regulations during the time of transition, former Vietnamese contract workers were allowed to become independent small business owners. Many of them opened grocery shops and worked in importing and exporting goods between Germany and other countries, such as Vietnam, China, and Poland.

One "business"—the smuggling of cigarettes and the emergence of a "cigarette mafia" in Berlin—dominated media discourse during the mid-1990s. Cases of murder among competing gangs labeled simply "Vietnamese" were widely discussed in the press and gave Vietnamese migrants a bad image (Bui 2003). To illustrate the production of anti-Vietnamese sentiments by the media, I quote from an article written in the FAZ (*Frankfurter Allgemeine Zeitung*), an internationally renowned daily newspaper:

> The illegal cigarette sales in Berlin, if they ever were innocent, no longer are and haven't been so for a while now. Most recently since Vietnamese gangs from the north of the country [Vietnam] and from the Czech Republic penetrated the market and underscored their claim to protection money with targeted murders, the naivety is gone. The Central Vietnamese avenged themselves by murdering the leaders of the mafia but took on their structures themselves. Today, one can guarantee that every spot in Berlin where [smuggled] cigarettes are sold has a protection fee attached to it [and] that every participating Vietnamese is bound up in a larger organization. Escape is very difficult. (FAZ February 25, 1995. Quoted in Bui 2000: 54.)

These reports about smuggling and thirty-five cases of murder among rival Vietnamese gangs in Berlin during August 1996 alone (Bui 2003: 64), coincided with the mid-1990s negotiations between Hanoi and the German government about the repatriation of "tens of thousands of 'illegal' Vietnamese migrants living in the city" (Bui 2003: 58). Exaggerations about the numbers of "illegal" migrants, for example, were part of a general racist mood. With regards to "unregistered" Vietnamese and the closing down of dormitories in some East Berlin suburbs, German newspaper articles talked about 40,000 Vietnamese migrants "who are actually not supposed to be there" (Bui 2003: 59). An article entitled "Three official renters, twenty-one toothbrushes" reported on the living conditions of the migrants:

> Twenty-one tooth brushes stand in cups on the shoe-box. In this apartment of the former dorm for Vietnamese contract workers of the GDR, there are three people registered. How many people really live in the sixth floor of the prefab building in Berlin's Zingster Street is not ascertainable. Suddenly no one understands Germany more when the question is posed (Bui 2003: 59-60).

After the repatriation agreement signed on July 21, 1995, which provided for 20,000 Vietnamese to leave eastern Germany during the following four years, many of them returned to Vietnam. The German government paid the flight ticket and a sum of money was given to each person leaving the country. However, according to my interview subjects, a considerable number of those, who left for Vietnam, returned to Germany in the late 1990s, many of them as "illegal" immigrants (see also Weiss 2005: 81).

Only a few of the Vietnamese migrants were involved in the "gang wars" of the mid-1990s. Most of the former contract workers tried to become successful in small businesses and by opening shops and snack bars they "discovered" economic niches in East Berlin. Pipo Bui, when starting to conduct interviews with Vietnamese entrepreneurs in some parts of eastern Berlin in 1999, found at least "one Vietnamese-run snack bar every five blocks on average. The work permits issued to former contract workers in the early 1990s prohibited them from starting businesses outside of the territory of former East Germany and Berlin" (Bui 2003: 182). Like immigrant entrepreneurs in other parts of the world (Kloosterman and Rath 2003) the opening of small shops and snack bars was one way of making a living in the new surroundings.

However, unlike migrants elsewhere, the economic opportunities for Vietnamese people in Germany were quite unique. As a result of the complete breakdown of the economy in East Germany, as well as in many parts of East Berlin after 1989, there was almost no infrastructure—just some shops to buy food or fresh vegetables, milk or bread. Germans, as well as Vietnamese and people from other countries, had to walk or ride long distances to find a place to buy food. The shortage of food and other goods was compensated for by the economic activities of Vietnamese migrants. Already experienced in some kinds of business during their years as contract workers—for example, from tailoring jeans and shirts during their leisure time and selling these products to the people of the GDR (Dennis 2005: 26), Vietnamese migrants sold their goods, in particular textiles, in the streets as mobile traders and in small weekly markets after the fall of the Wall. Former contract workers opened snack bars and restaurants, which were not labeled Vietnamese snack bars at that time, but "Chinese snack bars" or "Thai restaurants," although the owners as well as the staff were Vietnamese. The owners often chose not to label their snack bars as "Vietnamese," because Chinese or Thai food was already well accepted in the western parts of the city (Bui 2003: 209) and the Vietnamese migrants hoped to profit from this already existing popularity.

As I realized during my fieldwork in 2006, the situation changed during the last few years and many Vietnamese-owned restaurants have begun to self-confidently label themselves as "Vietnamese restaurants." A newly opened restaurant in 2005 in the tourist zone of East Berlin—the "Prenzlauer Berg," near Kollwitzplatz—even raised the Vietnamese flag in front of the entrance. This is quite a recent phenomenon, but seems to be part of a new national consciousness of Vietnamese people in East Berlin.

Altars in Shops and Wholesale Markets

In the snack bars and restaurants, as well as in the small shops and spaces where business takes place, including offices, hairdressers and especially the "global trade centers," (wholesale markets), where Vietnamese from various regions in Germany and Berlin buy food, vegetables, fruits, and textiles, I noticed small altars. Some of the owners brought the altars and the religious objects and figures, representing the spirits, from Vietnam to Berlin. Other shop owners bought their altars in East Berlin's global "trade markets," and now they are also sold in Vietnamese supermarkets.

During the last few years, alongside the global flow of money and political and economic liberalization in Vietnam, these altars have started appearing in the streets and shops of Hanoi and Ho Chi Minh City. One of the largest Vietnamese wholesale markets in eastern Berlin opened in 2004 is called "Dong Xuan" market, named after the Central Market in Hanoi. The choice of this name and the establishing of transnational connections between traders and clients in Hanoi and Berlin clearly show the imaginative power of being here and there at the same time.[2] This imaginative power of economic place-making is also important in the context of new Vietnamese arrivals in Berlin. New migrants already know—via the Internet and phone calls with friends and relatives in Berlin—about the "global trade centers" long before their arrival. "Dong Xuan" is the first place where undocumented migrants will find work, where they can make contacts, and find themselves among fellow Vietnamese migrants. This place, therefore, plays an important role in the economic, religious, and social lives of migrants in Berlin.

The religious objects that I call "snack bar altars" or, alternatively, because you will find them in all kinds of shops, "business altars," are placed at the entrance of a shop and consist of two figures sitting in the middle of the altar. One is called *ong tho dia* (spirit of the place), protecting the owner and her or his family from evils such as diseases, thieves, and so on. The second one is called *ong than tai* (spirit of wealth), guaranteeing economic success and the accumulation of capital.

To be successful in business is very important for Vietnamese migrants in Berlin. In many cases whole families are involved in the business and are highly dependent on the income. Remittances are sent back to Vietnam, where relatives are constantly waiting for financial support. The sending of money "back home" is a characteristic feature among transnational families (Bryceson and Vuorela 2002). To protect the shop and to be protected by the spirits, an altar has to be installed before the grand opening. In order to guarantee economic success of the shop owners, the spirits must be fed. Food, drinks, and incense are offered regularly. In many cases I noticed cigarettes on the altars, given and burnt as offerings. The manager of an expanding wholesale market in eastern Berlin, who gives fresh food to the spirits every day and puts money and red wine from different countries on the altar, explained to me that the spirits at his site enjoy the smell of good and expensive perfume. For this reason he sprays *Armani* perfume on the altar several times a day.

Before opening a shop, the "spirit of the place" (*ong tho dia*) must be satisfied, so worshippers, some of whom pray every morning before opening for business, offer certain donations which they believe the spirits will like most. In many cases I noticed alcohol given to the spirits. Interestingly, they were offered "typical" former East German products such as special Russian vodka or a sparkling wine called "Little Red Riding Hood." By offering products such as Armani perfume and Marlboro cigarettes, but also products associated with the GDR, former contract workers do not just participate in western consumer culture, but seem to identify simultaneously with the newly emerging "Ostalgie," a term invented after the fall of the Wall to characterize an East German nostalgia, an identification with an imagined past. Consuming "relics" of the socialist period is part of the "Ostalgie." In addition to eastern and western consumer products, Vietnamese shop owners offer "typical" Vietnamese food like *banh chung*, a special cake made from rice.

Part of the offerings made by Vietnamese migrants in Berlin involves money, such as fake U.S. dollars in imitation of western money. Nowadays, to offer money to the spirits is also quite common in Hanoi, as I discovered during interviews. There is a street in Hanoi with many shops where people can buy votive paper objects, such as fake dollar notes as well as small cars like Mercedes and houses built in a western style, all made from paper board. People buy these products and give them to the spirits through burnt offerings; they want the spirits to participate in modern consumer culture.

Spirits do not only protect the shops and snack bars, but also offices, located in a separate building of the territory of the Vietnamese "global trade center" in the eastern part of Berlin. There I noticed "computer altars," placed in an office under the desk, just near the server, the printer, and the Internet connection of the computer. In this way, every message sent and received while ordering new products from Vietnam or elsewhere may be "blessed" by the spirits.

Conclusion

An attention to place and an understanding of how people adapt social relations to novel settings can show how contested beliefs and practices are mediated. The emphasis on dislocation, disembedding and deterritorialization is but one side of theories on globalization and localization. Emplacement "builds on earlier insights into flows and circulations in a global space, and it recognizes specific sites and terrains as the conditions of their existence and transformations" (Englund 2002: 268). It dissipates distinctions between the local and the global by recognizing places as both material and imaginative constructions engendered by global forces and migrant agents. What we need concerning religious sites and places of worship is to ground globalization through the documentation of its spatial effects, focusing on the regional and local production of the experience of globalization, as well as taking into account the manifold transnational connections of migrants.

Emplacement is a process, therefore, where people re-embed social relations that have been "distanciated" and "disembedded" (Jacka 2005: 654). As for the religious place-making of Vietnamese migrants in Berlin and other locations in Germany after the reunification, it is clear that forging and maintaining economic and religious activities is one of the ways of creating a stable life outside of the country of origin.

Due to political and economic processes of liberalization in Vietnam, as well as political transformations in Germany, religious activities seem to have become more prominent in both the home country and the diaspora. In Vietnam, cadres of the Communist party now visit Buddhist temples and new pagodas in Vietnam and other Southeast Asian countries are built with money collected by Vietnamese migrants in Germany (Hüwelmeier and Krause 2006). *Ong tho dia*, the "spirit of the place," is venerated in Hanoi, in Ho Chi Minh City, and other places in Vietnam where business has become increasingly important over the last few years.

Because of global processes and frequent travel between the sending and receiving countries, the entrepreneurial and religious activities of Vietnamese migrants in Germany are closely connected with the political and economic liberalization in Vietnam. Within these global processes, especially the increasing trade of goods and the opening of restaurants and snack bars in the diaspora, spirits are busier than ever before. They are connecting the people to a particular place, protecting the territory and its owner as well as his or her family from diseases and misfortune, while simultaneously guaranteeing economic success. As neither the German nor the Vietnamese state will provide social and economic security for many of the former contract workers and non-documented Vietnamese living in Germany, these migrants rely on the support of spirits and the transnational links, which these spirits help create between "back home" and the various diasporic communities so that the migrants can live a better life in the host country.

Notes

1. This paper is part of my ongoing research project on "Transnational Networks, Religion and New Migration", financed by the German Research Foundation and affiliated with the Humboldt-University Berlin, Department of European Ethnology.
2. Rijk van Dijk (2006) discussed this point with regard to Ghanaian migrants in the Netherlands and people in Ghana.

References

Baumann, M. (2000). *Migration—Religion—Integration. Buddhistische Vietnamesen und hinduistische Tamilen in Deutschland.* Marburg: Diagonal Verlag.
Bryceson, D., and U. Vuorela (eds.) (2002). *The Transnational Family.* Oxford: Berg.
Bui, P. (2003). *Envisioning Vietnamese Migrants in Germany.* Münster: Lit Verlag.
Coleman, S., and J. Eade (eds.) (2004). *Reframing Pilgrimage: Cultures in Motion.* London and New York: Routledge (EASA Series).
Dennis, M. (2005). "Die vietnamesischen Vertragsarbeiter und Vertragsarbeiterinnen in der DDR, 1980-1989." In *Erfolg in der Nische? Die Vietnamesen in der DDR und in Ostdeutschland* (pp. 7-49). Münster: Lit Verlag.
Endres, K. W. (2000). *Ritual, Fest und Politik in Nordvietnam. Zwischen Ideologie und Tradition.* Münster: Lit Verlag.
Englund, H. (2002). "Ethnography after Globalism: Migration and Emplacement in Malawi." *American Ethnologist* 29 (2): 261-286.
Glick Schiller, N., L. Basch, and C. Szanton Blanc (eds.) (1992). *Towards a Transnational Perspective on Migration. Race, Class, Ethnicity, and Nationalism Reconsidered.* New York, New York Academy of Sciences.
_____ (1999). "From Immigrant to Transmigrant: Theorizing Transnational Migration." In *Migration and Transnational Social Space* (pp. 73-103). Aldershot, England: Ashgate Publishers.
Hansing, K. (2005). "Rastafari as Counter-Hegemonic Culture and Discourse in Post-Revolutionary Cuba." In *Caribbean Narratives* (pp. 179-202). London: Macmillan.
Hillmann, F. (2005). "Riders on the Storm: Vietnamese in Germany's Two Migration Systems." In *Asian Migrants and European Labour Markets* (pp. 80-100). London: Routledge.
Ho, L. (1999). *Vietnamesischer Buddhismus in Deutschland. Darstellung der Geschichte und Institutionalisierung.* Hannover: Pagode Vien Giac.
Rudolph, S. H., and J. Piscatori (eds.) (1997). *Transnational Religion and Fading States.* Oxford: Westview Press.
Hüwelmeier, G. (2000). *Women's Congregations as Transnational Communities.* Publication of the "Research Programme on Transnational Communities": http://www.transcomm.ox.ac.uk.
_____ (2005a). "Ordensfrauen unterwegs: Transnationalismus, Gender und Religion." *Historische Anthropologie* 1/2005: 91-110.
_____ (2005b). "'Nach Amerika!' Schwestern ohne Grenzen." *L'Homme. Zeitschrift für feministische Geschichtswissenschaft* 2/2005: 97-115.
_____ (2006b). *Vietnamese Pentecostalism in the Diaspora.* Unpublished paper.
_____ (2007a). "Global Sisterhood—Transnational Perspectives on Gender and Religion. In *Untangling Modernities: Gendering Religion and Politics* (forthcoming).
_____ (2007b). "Women's Congregations as Transnational Networks of Social Security." In *Social Security in Religious Networks: Changes in Meanings, Contents and Functions.* Berghan (forthcoming).
_____, and K. Krause (2006). *Gods and Spirits in the City.* Paper presented at the Humboldt University Berlin, Institute of European Ethnology, June 20.
Jacka, J. K. (2005). "Emplacement and Millennial Expectations in an Era of Development and Globalization: Heaven and the Appeal of Christianity for the Ipili." *American Anthropologist* 107 (4): 643-653.
Kloosterman, R., and J. Rath (eds.) (2003). *Immigrant Entrepreneurs. Venturing Abroad in the Age of Globalization.* Oxford: Berg.

Levitt, P. (2001). *The Transnational Villagers.* Berkeley, CA: University of California Press.

_____ (2003a). You Know, Abraham was Really the First Immigrant: Religion and Transnational Migration. *International Migration Review,* Fall 2003, 37(143), 847-874.

_____ (2003b). *Between God, Ethnicity and Country: An Approach to the Study of Transnational Religion.* WPTC-01-13: http://www.transcomm.ox.ac.uk/working.papers.htm (downloaded February 23, 2003).

_____ (2007). *God Needs No Passport: Immigrants and the Changing American Religious Landscape.* New York: The New Press.

Mahler, S. J., and K. Hansing (2005). "Toward a Transnationalism of the Middle: How Transnational Religious Practices Help Bridge the Divides between Cuba and Miami." *Latin American Perspectives* Issue 140, 32 (1): 121-146.

Mai, M. (2006). "Ein Geschäft, das Glaubenssache ist." *Die tageszeitung,* January 21.

Orsi, R. A. (ed.) (1999). *Gods of the City. Religion and the American Urban Landscape.* Bloomington and Indianapolis: Indiana University Press.

Stepick, A. (2004). "God is Apparently not Dead: The Obvious, the Emergent, and the Still Unknown in Immigration and Religion." In *Immigrant Faiths: Transforming Religious Life in America* (pp. 11-37). Walnut Creek, CA: AltaMira Press.

Tweed, T. A. (1997). *Our Lady of the Exile: Diasporic Religion at a Cuban Catholic Shrine in Miami.* Oxford: Oxford University Press.

van Dijk, R. (2006). *Cities and Linking Hot Spots: African Migration, Sensibilities and the Fragmentation of Urban Spaces.* Paper presented at the Humboldt University Berlin, Institute of European Ethnology, June 23.

Vertovec, S. (2004). "Religion and Diaspora." In *New Approaches to the Study of Religion* (pp. 275-304). New York: Verlag de Gruyter.

Warner, R. S. (1998). Immigration and Religious Communities in the United States. In *Gatherings in Diaspora. Religious Communities and the New Immigration* (pp. 3-34). Philadelphia: Temple University Press.

Weiss, K. (2005). Nach der Wende: Vietnamesische Vertragsarbeiter und Vertragsarbeiterinnen in Ostdeutschland heute. *Erfolg in der Nische? Die Vietnamesen in der DDR und in Ostdeutschland* (pp. 77-96). Münster: Lit Verlag.

Yasbeck Haddad, Y., J. L. Smith, and J. L. Esposito (eds.) (2003). *Religion and Immigration.* Walnut Creek, CA: AltaMira Press.

PART IV

TRANSITIONAL DIASPORAS AND IDENTITIES

9

A Diasporic Sense of Place: Dynamics of Spatialization and Transnational Political Fields among Bangladeshi Muslims in Britain

David Garbin

There has been, for more than a decade now, a profusion of sociological or anthropological studies focusing on "transnational communities," shedding light on the use of social, economic, political and religious networks by migrants or ethnic minority groups across nation-state boundaries (for example Basch et al. 1994; Levitt 2001; Portes et al. 1999). Many of these studies have, implicitly or explicitly, introduced a distinction between a "space of flows," constituted by supranational agencies, multinational corporations and other powerful actors of global capitalism, and a space of symbolic and material mobility whose boundaries are closely linked to the transnational scope of migrants' activities. Indeed, this particular conceptualization has produced binary oppositions, between, for instance, processes of globalization/transnationalism "from above" and "from below" (Smith and Guarnizo 1998) or between the formal/visible and informal/invisible aspects of transnational networks (Cesari 1999; Tarrius 2002). While the relative institutionalization of transnational studies has led more and more sociologists and anthropologists to consider how and why migrants and ethnic minorities maintain or create networks between places, there is still a heuristic need to take into account the heterogeneity of these transnational practices. As suggested by Levitt (2002) and others, a relevant way to avoid simplification or reification is to take into consideration the scope, intensity and frequency of transnational practices within the migrant/ethnic groups studied. Using the Bangladeshi diaspora as a case study, one of the objectives of this chapter is to make sense of this heterogeneity, particularly with regard to the relationship to diasporic space and spatialization.

The post-modern conceptualization of the social construction of identity and difference in terms of "hybridity" or "creolization" (Bhabha 1994; Gilroy 1997; Hannerz 1996) has highlighted the increasing complexity of cultural productions shaped by globalization and "time-space compression" (Harvey 1989). Yet one could argue that such approaches have not really attempted to question the links between diasporic belonging and dynamics of hierarchy and power relations. As Glick Schiller (2005) pointed out, the use of the Bourdieusian concept of "field" can be helpful here as transnational practices often involve the unequal distribution of social and symbolic capital, as well as an intense competition for representation, legitimacy or positionality. Similarly, Werbner (2002) indicated the need to go beyond a depoliticized paradigm of cultural hybrid identities in her analysis of the Pakistani diasporic public sphere. Indeed, she showed that the power dynamics at the heart of a political economy of honor (*izzat*) not only operated within the local space of co-residence, but also included the imagined and material realms of the Pakistani diaspora. In following up these suggestions, I will also explore in this chapter the ways in which transnational social fields are sites of struggle where processes of *distinction* operate and where accumulation of social/symbolic capital, strategies of status and competing politics of representation influence diasporic practices and identifications.

To address these issues of politics of transnationalism, space and power, I will differentiate between several distinctive, yet sometimes overlapping and interrelated, social fields within a broader Bangladeshi diasporic sphere. Translocal networks connecting groups and localities in Bangladesh with British Bangladeshi urban enclaves heavily determine the first one. While this sphere is characterized by a relative autonomy vis-à-vis mainstream British politics, the second field I examine is shaped by competing diasporic constructions of imagined identities in a local urban context of ethnic and religious institutionalization. Finally, I will explore the diversity of Bangladeshi religious dynamics, especially the different socio-spatial scales of Islamic activities.

Migration and the Bangladeshi Diaspora

The fact that the majority of the Bangladeshis in the United Kingdom originate from several *thanas* (administrative sub-districts) in the northeastern rural district of Sylhet is the result of the well-documented process of "chain migration" (Gardner 1995). To some extent, it is also due to geographical factors, such as the proximity of the Surma and Kushiara rivers, which linked Sylhet to Southern Bengal and to Kolkata (Calcutta), from where Sylheti *lascars* (seamen) were recruited to work in British-owned ships during colonial times. Moreover, the distinctive regional land tenure system may have played an important role in creating what is sometimes presented as a Sylheti "tradition" of migration and travel (*jatra*) (see Adams 1987). Indeed, in the Sylhet region, which formed part of Assam from 1847, the British favored the development of a *Talukdari* class (small landowners) whose lineages had enough resources at their disposal to finance the initial departure of one or several young male members to Kolkata, thus establishing the first chain migration network to *bidesh* (abroad) (see Gardner 1995).

It is important to note that this process of "chain migration" to Britain has had a twofold impact on both sides of the transnational continuum. It has produced a highly localized "geography of prosperity" in rural Sylhet and, at the same time, it has shaped Bangladeshi settlement across Britain. For instance, in Tower Hamlets, families from Beani Bazar *thana* can be found in the Whitechapel and Shadwell areas, while around Brick Lane (within Spitalfields ward and "Banglatown") families originating from Jagonnathpur and Bishwhanath tend to dominate. In Camden (North London) Bangladeshi families originate mainly from the Maulvi Bazar *thana*. It should be noted that, in the case of East London, the spatial distribution of the Bangladeshi community had also been influenced by the discriminatory housing policies of the 1980s which forced entire families to reside in specific zones of the borough, often in the worst and older council properties (Phillips 1985).

The largest settlement of expatriate Bangladeshis is in Britain, but communities have also emerged elsewhere, for instance in the Middle East from the 1970s and in North America, Italy, or Southeast Asia more recently. These communities are more heterogeneous than those settled in Britain since they comprise individuals and families originating predominantly from the districts of Dhaka, Chittagong, Comilla, and Noakhali, as well as from Sylhet. Bangladeshis in Britain are a largely young population and in Tower Hamlets, the third-generation Bangladeshi population—those "born and bred" in the area—constitutes approximately half of the community. As an increasing number of these British Bangladeshis has entered higher education, the prospects of employment, for a long time restricted to the restaurant and textile industry, have changed. Yet despite having access to local white-collar jobs, mainly in public organizations, many young British Bangladeshis still experience long periods of unemployment or occupy low skilled or unskilled jobs at the margins of the service economy.

Diaspora, Translocalism and the Strength of "Strong Ties"

It was mainly from the 1960s, when sizeable Bangladeshi communities began to form in Britain, that the political situation in the *desh* (homeland) started to influence significantly the organization of Bangladeshis in *bidesh*. First generation migrants were actively involved in the mass movement of resistance to the Pakistani government leading to the 1971 "Liberation War" (*Mukto Juddo*) in Bangladesh. These migrants in Britain mobilized to support the *Mukti Bahini* ("freedom fighters") and the Awami League, the main pro-independence party, principally through fundraising, public protests, and an intense lobbying of the British government, institutions and media. As described by Nurul Islam, a Bangladeshi writer and intellectual who was involved in nationalist activities in Bangladesh and later in London, this mobilization can provide a relevant and interesting illustration of a "long-distance nationalism" before the age of global technologies:

> At that time, everything was kept secret by the Pakistani government, but information came with people. People circulated, information circulated, it was not globalisation like now, no Internet, no fax and few telephones, but people travelled by plane, they came with their stories in mind, stories from villages, stories from cities. A lot of activists in London went to India, to the war front and then came back to London with new messages and information.

The politicization of Bangladeshi migrants through the independence struggle paved the way for the institutionalization of an ethno-national identity based on secular, nationalist and socialist values. Promoted by the Awami League and its leader Sheikh Mujibur Rahman (assassinated in 1975) these values were central to the affirmation of an utopian "Bengaliness" transcending national, caste/class and religious boundaries. As we shall see later, this particular "narration of the nation" had a key role to play in the maintenance of a diasporic collective memory linking the "Liberation War" in Bangladesh to strategies of resistance to racism and discrimination in the British Bangladeshi urban enclaves.

However, one should not assume that the political construction of a specific "imagined community" was the only element contributing to a sense of diasporic belonging among Bangladeshis in *bidesh*. Indeed, the importance of Bangladeshi politics among *probashis* ("expatriates") in Britain was sustained by a set of networks and practices connecting groups and localities across national boundaries and by the movement and circulation of people between *desh* and *bidesh*. It is essential to take into account these processes to understand how, by the mid-1980s, nearly all the Bangladeshi political parties were represented in Britain.

While it is difficult to "measure" the influence of these groups, it seems that the Awami League has enjoyed and still enjoys a dominant position in terms of membership within British Bangladeshi communities. For many, this is explained by the great aura of his founder, Sheikh Mujibur Rahman, "Father of the Nation," the role played by the party during the "Liberation War," as well as during the mass mobilization against the General Ershad who seized power after a military coup in 1982. One of the ways the Bangladeshi political elites from the Awami League or other parties in Britain maintain (or even create) links between *bidesh* and the homeland is through the activity known as *jonokollan* ("development") carried out by hundreds of small associations across Britain. These groups operate within the boundaries of a translocal *desh-bidesh* sphere connecting villages in Bangladesh with kin groups (*ghusti*) in Britain. Their role in terms of "development," but also in terms of social and political dynamics within this translocal space, has to be considered against the backdrop of the ideological, symbolic and material power of the "miracle of migration," as coined by Gardner (1995).

Indeed, the *bideshi taka* ("the money from abroad") has dramatically altered the economic and local landscape in Sylhet (Garbin 2002). In the context of intense competition for status and *izzat* (prestige), mobility to *bidesh* has become a strategic resource, a crucial source of power. It has allowed families, which contain *probashis*, to improve rapidly their socio-economic position and to strengthen their role in the *shomaz*—the community moral and social order. As a result, because connections (*lainta*) with *bidesh* constitute a precious social capital, a polarization has emerged between families/lineages enjoying these connections (or whose status can lead to a matrimonial alliance with *probashi* groups) and those that do not. The local ideological hegemony of migration as a strategic source of economic wealth and social/symbolic success has, therefore, been produced and reproduced by the visibility of the "*bideshi* miracle," in particular the improvement of collective facilities and infrastructures (e.g., mosques, schools, madrassahs, roads) conducted by migrant lineages in Sylhet. It was from the mid-1980s that this local-scale development work has been institutionalized by a myriad of village and *thana* associations emerging across Britain in the Bangladeshi "*faras*" (neighborhoods) of cities such as London, Luton, Birmingham, or Oldham.

Apart from improving educational and religious facilities in the homeland, these groups also perform an important social function in *bidesh*. They enable members of the same Sylheti village or *elaka* ("locality") to socialize mainly through the organization of regular meetings or cultural or religious gatherings, which are usually advertised in the Bengali newspapers published in Britain. Moreover, for many Bangladeshi parents whom I met during fieldwork among these groups, a recurrent concern appeared to be the transmission of a set of values based on a Bangladeshi "culture" and "heritage" to their children born and/or raised in Britain. They believed that the social environment, provided by the village associations, reinforced a sense of rootedness to an ancestral and authentic "home" and contributed to the feeling of "nostalgia without memory" which is sometimes associated with the representation of the "country of origin" by second- and third-generation sons and daughters of migrants (Maira 2002: 113).

To some extent, then, the process of chain migration between *desh* and *bidesh* has shaped the constitution of the translocal field within which these groups operate, since a geographical sector of an urban British Bangladeshi area usually corresponds to a specific regional or sub-district (*thana*) affiliation. Furthermore, in British Bangladeshi enclaves, local networks of sociality are greatly influenced by these Sylheti local affiliations. This is reflected, for instance, by marriage preference or by mutual support for business projects between kin or people from the same *elaka* in Sylhet.

It is important to note that the emergence of these translocal groupings in the diaspora coincided with a sub-regional decentralization of governance in Bangladesh during General Ershad's regime. Indeed, the creation of newly elected positions at local level in Sylhet led some first generation *probashis* (expatriates) to return to the *desh* to compete for these positions in their *thana* of origin. The connections maintained or reactivated with the village and/or the broader locality in Sylhet could be strategically mobilized for this electoral purpose. The improvement of collective facilities, converted into symbolic capital, could also reinforce the *izzat* of a candidate, who could then manipulate more easily kinship-based local factions. The networks established across the diasporic space, in turn, provided a political platform for Bangladeshi leaders coming to Britain, who could, for instance, raise funds among families belonging to these groups to help finance political campaigns in their Sylheti constituencies.

While they may not all be involved directly in Bangladeshi politics, the individuals who control these associations are highly respected figures.

They are *matbors*, lineage elders, traditionally responsible for the community social order. A great number of them circulate regularly between *desh* and *bidesh* and some are engaged in both the local economy of the ethnic enclave (catering, garment sector, travel agencies, import-export), and in Sylhet through retail, restaurant, hotel or real estates businesses. As Ballard (2001) shows in the context of Pakistani entrepreneurship, the emergence of diasporic transmigrant elites is linked to the transnational management of economic and social resources primarily based on kinship arrangements. Contrary to some assumptions that "globalization from below" entails the increasing mobilization of multiple "networks of weak ties" (see Badie 1995:137), the "strength of strong ties" and the maintenance of reciprocity between the communities divided by migration represent crucial aspects of transmigrants' activities. Thus, for the majority of those who have economic interests in Bangladesh, a mutual co-responsibility is sought after. For instance, business properties are managed commonly or land (*zommi*)—a powerful status symbol—remains undivided between male kin.

However, increasing financial constraints faced by many families in *Bidesh* (and also conflicts between members of a same lineage) has led to a reinterpretation of the links with the ancestral homeland, undermining the "ideal" unity and solidarity of the translocal kinship group. Therefore, the reproduction of practices through strategies of mobility linking localities transnationally appears to be more and more dependent on power dynamics as first-generation community elites tend to monopolize the politic/economic resources within an encompassing diasporic space.

Diasporic Territorialization and Identity Politics

Within the translocal sphere described above there are endless rivalries between competing groups whose role cannot, therefore, be fully understood without referring to a broader diasporic field where business interests, participation to Bangladeshi political parties, regional and *elaka* (locality) belonging are embroiled. While tensions are also salient in the political field, I wish to turn now to the relationship to spatiality where the "diasporic sense of place" is not so heavily dependent on translocal networks. Strategies of territorialization, shaped by collective memory and dynamics of identity, play a central role in this sphere. Whereas the analysis above suggested the autonomy and institutional invisibility of *desh-bidesh* translocal dynamics, the tensions I will examine now revolve around issues of public space, political and "community" representation in a context of multicultural policies and urban regeneration.

Among the main actors in this field are secular Bangladeshi leaders who were involved in the youth movements of the late 1970s, partly in response to endemic harassment and racism in Britain. This second generation of Bangladeshi activists were keen to move away from a first generation preoccupation with translocal activities ("village politics"), even though they were influenced by the secular values initially promoted by the Awami League in Bangladesh and in the diaspora. Challenging their elders as "community representatives," their prime consideration was to enter the local political arena through the Labour Party. They also forged alliances with white activists in order to fight discrimination in the housing, educational and cultural spheres while creating community organizations supported by local and central state funding. By the end of the 1980s, many of these second-generation Bangladeshis, who were at the forefront of the anti-discrimination struggle 20 years earlier, became elected Labour Party councilors, or occupied white-collar jobs within the council or other public services in the health, housing, or employment sectors.

Since most of them were born in Bangladesh during the early 1960s and came to Britain during the mid-1970s, they were exposed to both the "Liberation War" in Sylhet and discrimination in the streets and schools of the East End. A secular community activist who came to Tower Hamlets in 1976 at the age of 17 explained:

> For me it was natural to get involved, because I had this double frustration in Bangladesh and in London, anger in Bangladesh and anger in London ... In Bangladesh I saw the war, I saw it with my own eyes, and I saw the birth of Bangladesh at the time of independence. And in London, no jobs, no housing, and racial attacks every day—it was a real struggle for us.

During the anti-discrimination struggles in Britain, the articulation of both social experiences was central in creating a link between a Bangladeshi nationalist heritage and a Bengali cultural identity, on the one hand, and the mobilization of class and ethnic identity on the other (Eade 1989). A wide range of initiatives reflecting a commitment to transmit a secular/nationalist Bengali heritage was undertaken: organizations of festivals, youth cultural "awareness" programs, commemorations of the independence movement key dates, etc. From the end of the 1980s, many Bangladeshi cultural and community projects were also funded by urban regeneration agencies or government initiatives such as City Challenge, the Single Regeneration Budget or the more recent New Deal for Communities. In this context, the secular leaders established alliances with Bangladeshi entrepreneurs and regeneration agencies and City businesses to create a new spatial identity, "Banglatown," in Spitalfields, the western ward of Tower Hamlets. "Banglatown" was seen by Bangladeshi leaders as an opportunity to attract tourists and to boost the Bangladeshi-run "Indian" restaurants along Brick Lane. The "exotic" reinvention of the locality, included in the socio-economic development of the area promoted by a public-private partnership, Cityside Regeneration, was intended to enable Brick Lane and its surroundings to compete with other ethnic enclaves, especially Chinatown, in the West End of London.

The local Bengali "culture," described as an important capital for the revival of the area, was enhanced by various projects, which reflected the particularity of the local ethnic community. An essential part of the implementation of the strategy of the Banglatown was the organization of the Bengali New Year (*Baishaki Mela*), on Brick Lane, which is celebrated in Bangladesh at the start of the monsoon (*baishak*) season. During this festival Brick Lane is turned into a pedestrian zone, with stalls selling homemade food and small handicrafts, and stages where different artistic events are performed. Even if the performances reflected a wide range of genres (traditional folk music, Bengali dance, drama and pop music with DJs), the Bangladeshi secular leaders and organizers of the event were keen to describe the event as an "authentic" cultural celebration linking Bangladeshis in Britain with their country of origin (Eade, Fremeaux, and Garbin 2002; Eade and Garbin 2002).

This urban reinvention of the Banglatown and the associated street festivals related to a spatial and diasporic sense of "Bengaliness" was criticized by members of local Bangladeshi Islamist groups who stressed their commitment to a religious ethos and identity transcending national boundaries. They deplored the "lack of morality" characterizing, in their eyes, the *Mela*, since the event encouraged "unrespectable" behavior influenced by western secular values and Sikh/Hindu practices. In other words, Muslim identity, rooted both in the complete code of conduct that Islam has to offer and in the "authenticity" of moral universal values, was contrasted with a set of "syncretic" cultural practices. Moreover, many were clearly challenging the ethno-national project behind the cultural commodification of the place, such as this young British Bangladeshi female member of a group based at the East London mosque:

> [- What do you think of "Banglatown"?] Again it's nationalistic isn't it? They say they want to improve the area and make the Bengali culture more diffused. But you see, why call it Banglatown? They promote nationalism and it stops the Muslims to think Islamically. Muslims start to identify with Bengali rather than Muslim.

These criticisms by leaders of the East London Mosque and members of young Muslim organizations were legitimized not only in terms of a positive Islamic universalism, but also by the increasing role these actors played in the local arena. Thus, during the 1990s and especially after Labour's general election victory in 1997, the influence of secular Bangladeshi professionals and politicians has been offset by the growth of Islamic community activism encouraged by Government policy involving "faith communities" in urban regeneration. In Tower Hamlets groups loosely associated with the East London Mosque started to collaborate with public bodies on issues such as drug addiction, family breakdown, housing and employment. The East London Mosque, like other mosques, also benefited from funds sent from the Middle East and Bangladesh so that local concerns became linked to global Muslim issues and to political and religious development in the country of origin (Eade, Fremeaux, and Garbin 2002).

It is important to point out that this competition for social and political control, mediated by the appropriation of local spaces, has revolved around the mobilization of two different "imagined communities" situated beyond the local ethnic enclave: on the one hand, a Bengali cultural/nationalist diasporic space and on the other hand, a global religious space—the *umma*, the universal community of Muslim believers (Garbin 2001). This situation of tension can illustrate the performative constitution of a diasporic public sphere as conceptualized by Werbner (2002), since different narratives of cultural, moral and religious aesthetics are produced, which entail the elaboration of strategies of power, external recognition and community representation. These discourses are also highly dependent on collective memory and historical reinterpretations surrounding the "Liberation War," given for instance the current links between the East London Mosque and the *Jamaat i Islami* (a Pakistan-based Islamic political party, member of the governing alliance in Bangladesh) or the participation of some secular leaders to the *Nirmul Committee*, an organization founded in Bangladesh to promote the trials of *razakars*, collaborators of the Pakistani regime during the war, among them *Jamaat i Islami* members (Eade and Garbin 2002).

Politics, Religion and the Bangladeshi Islamic Diasporic Field

The debates around the Banglatown and the *Mela*, linked to an intense struggle for the appropriation of community space, have reflected the tensions between Islamist and secular nationalist ideologies, which greatly influenced the political definition and expression of a Bangladeshi identity after the "Liberation War" against Pakistan. In Tower Hamlets the YMO (Young Muslim Organization) is one of the Islamist groups most strongly opposed to the promotion of a cultural and nationalist "Bengaliness." When it was created at the end of the 1970s, it sought to provide an alternative to the then dominant secular Bengali youth movements. The YMO was initially controlled by the *Dawat'ul Islam*, a group founded just after the Bangladesh "Liberation War" by Bangladeshi settlers and strongly influenced by the Islamist political party, the *Jamaat i Islami* (Andrews 1993). These religious actors had little influence on Tower Hamlets community politics until the opening of the purpose-built East London Mosque in 1985, when they began to gain more legitimacy and the issue of religion started to appear at the center of local debates about "community needs." In 1988, after a factional conflict, members of the *Dawat'ul Islam* left the East London Mosque management structure and a new group, the Islamic Forum Europe (IFE), was created. The IFE not only built up its local base, but established several branches across Britain, including Oldham and Birmingham, working closely with the YMO, from which several of their key members originated. As we have already seen, the East London Mosque has been highly successful at building alliances with local government officials and its recent expansion, which resulted in the creation of the London Muslim Centre—used for prayers, recreational facilities and housing—has also strengthened its position at a time when funding for secular groups significantly declined.

As described in the previous section, the competition for territorial representation in the East End of London illustrates the complexity of global/local dialectics and what appears to be local identity politics is actually shaped by more global, diasporic forces. Furthermore, these dynamics are inscribed in a context of rapid urban change where different groups—Bangladeshi and non-Bangladeshi—produce various narratives about a "multicultural," "working-class" or "local" area (see Eade and Mele 1998; Jacobs 1996).

The conflict surrounding the extension of the East London Mosque in the late 1990s also reflected this articulation between different sociospatial scales. The mosque was then engaged in a large-scale extension on its adjacent site, previously owned by a private developer. The planning permission for the extension was secured after an intense campaigning against the secular Bengali councilors on the grounds that religion provided the unique basis for community identity. For the East London Mosque activists the successful conclusion of a two-year conflict over the disputed land demonstrated their strengthening position both within the community representation sphere and in the struggle for local resources. Moreover, in the discourses associated with this mobilization, the issue of practicing Islam in a secular local context was linked to broader concerns about a global "Westernization," Islamophobia in Britain, and the problems faced by other Muslim populations across the world. Rather than being directly projected onto the local arena, diasporic Islamic issues were reinterpreted according to a specific community context. They were also discussed according to a number of other elements, such as the visible local presence of more radical Islamic groups like *Hizbut-Tahir* or *Al-Muhajiroun*.

Outside London the partnership between Bangladeshi-dominated groups, such as the YMO or IFE, and local authorities through community-based activities has been less significant. For example, in Birmingham, the Handsworth-based IFE has started some educational and drug awareness initiatives among young British Bangladeshis, but its influence remains limited, mainly due to lack of membership and resources. In Oldham, however, Islamist activists have managed to acquire a piece of land in the Bangladeshi enclave of Westwood where they were planning to build a new center (Oldham Muslim Centre) with religious and recreational facilities and inspired by the East London Mosque's high profile London Muslim Centre. Since the 1990s the Oldham IFE and YMO have also successfully undertaken small projects targeted at local Bangladeshi youth, in partnership with local authorities and the police.

Some senior members of the IFE were involved in the *Jamaat i Islam* or its student wing (*Islami Chatra Shibir*) in Bangladesh before coming to Britain during the 1980s and 1990s. They share the same ideological orientations based upon a scripturalist approach of Islam, which aims to cover every aspect of social and political life. This vision involves the construction of clear-cut boundaries in order to preserve an "authentic" religious ethos free from the traditions of *Pirs* (saints) and Sufism, which were seen as encouraging such "un-Islamic" tendencies as *shirk* ("association") or *bida* ("innovation"). Furthermore, given the importance attached to politics at local, national and transnational levels, Islamists affiliated to the IFE and *Jamaat i Islami* are also keen to distance themselves from the *Tabligh Jamaat*, which has been influential in the Indian sub-continent and the South Asian diaspora. Indeed, while the *Tabligh Jamaat* also rejects *Pir* and Sufi traditions, it concentrates on missionary and preaching work and tries to avoid any involvement in politics (Metcalf 1996).

Groups associated with the East London Mosque and the London Muslim Centre are seen as offering a positive role model by the YMO/

IFE activists in Birmingham and Oldham, mainly because these London groups have managed to legitimate their claims to represent the "Muslim" community in a local public sphere dominated by secularists for decades. The London groups are also admired for the partnership, which they had forged with government institutions and the way they have voiced their concerns about religious needs and Islamic identity in the debates about multiculturalism, both locally and nationally.

Conclusion

My research, both in British Bangladeshi enclaves and in Sylhet, Bangladesh, where the majority of British Bangladeshis originate, suggest not only that individuals and groups use, produce, or perceive space in many different ways, but also that there is an analytical distinction to be made between different articulated "scales" of the socio-spatial experience, between for instance village, regional, national and broader diasporic scales. As well as social status and the uneven access to translocal political networks, inter-generational differences represent a key factor in the evolution of the Bangladeshi diaporic sphere.

At a political level the claim that Bangladeshis needed to occupy a strong position in British mainstream politics through their participation in local authority institutions led the second-generation secularist leaders to re-examine the role of their older elites. The latter were criticized mainly for their inability to mobilize their political resources and the strength of their social networks for the social advancement of the local "Bangladeshi community" in Britain. For the Islamic actors linked to the East London Mosque, rejecting both the "syncretic" and "backward" religious practices that characterized first-generation migrants and the "traditional" patron-client relationships of their political activities, the prime concern was to assert a British Muslim citizenship mainly through a moral commitment to Islamic values.

Another aim of this chapter was to show how the local/global dialectics of spatialization among Bangladeshis in Britain related to different political and community contexts. While the tensions between Islamists and secularists over the reinterpretation of the 1971 "Liberation War" have been projected in a relatively similar way in several Bengali urban enclaves, the degree of institutionalization of cultural and religious political projects is clearly not the same in the different localities. While we must be careful not to analyze these tensions only in terms of a simple binary opposition (Islam vs. secularism), it is also important to say that the quest for institutionalization has encouraged actors and "community leaders" to establish sharp distinctions and clear-cut boundaries. Finally, it should be noted that the "purity" and "authenticity" of these dominant categories of identification, which rely on a diasporic collective memory and belonging, are challenged by young British Bangladeshis in their "hybridized" politics of everyday life (see Alexander 2000; Desai 1999).

References

Adams, C. (1987). *Across Seven Seas and Thirteen Rivers*. London: THAP Books.
Alexander, C. (2000). *The Asian Gang: Ethnicity, Identity and Masculinity*. Oxford and New York: Berg.
Andrews, A. (1993). "Sociological Analysis of the Jamaat-I-Islami in the United Kingdom." In *Religion and Ethnicity*. Kampen: Kok Pharos.
Badie, B. (1995). *La fin des territoires*. Paris: Fayard.
Ballard, R. (2001). "The Impact of Kinship on the Economic Dynamics of Transnational Networks: Reflections on Some South Asian Developments," *Transnational Communities Working Papers*, WPTC-01-14, University of Oxford.
Basch, L., N. Glick Schiller, and C. Szanton-Blanc (1994). *Nations Unbound: Transnational Projects, Postcolonial Predicaments and Deterritorialized Nation-States*. Amsterdam: Gordon and Breach Publishers.
Bhabba, H. (1994). *The Location of Culture*. London and New York: Routledge.
Cesari, J. (1999). "Le Multiculturalisme Mondialisé: Le Défi de l'Hétérogénéité," *Cultures et Conflits, les Anonymes de la Mondialisation* 33.
Desai, P. (1999). *Spaces of Identity, Cultures of Conflict: The Development of New British Asian Masculinities*. Unpublished PhD Thesis, Goldsmiths College, University of London.
Eade, J. (1989). *The Politics of Community: The Bangladeshi Community in East London*. Aldershot: Avebury.
Eade, J., and C. Mele (1998). "Global Processes and Customised Landscapes: The 'Eastern Promise' of New York and London." *Rising East* 1 (2): 52-73.
Eade, J., and D. Garbin (2002). "Changing Narratives of Violence, Struggle and Resistance: Bangladeshis and the Competition for Resources in the Global City." *Oxford Development Studies* 30: 137-149.
Eade, J., I. Fremeaux, and D. Garbin (2002). "The Political Construction of Diasporic Communities in the Global City." In *Imagined Londons* (pp. 159-177). Albany, NY: State University of New York Press.
Garbin, D. (2001). "Politiques Identitaires Musulmanes et Représentation Communautaire Bengali dans l'East End de Londres." *Journal des Anthropologues* 87: 183-194.
Garbin, D. (2002). "Bideshi Taka: Argent, Migration et Politiques Transnationales entre Banglatown (Londres) et Sylhet (Bangladesh)." *Journal des Anthropologues* 90-91: 55-77.
Gardner, K. (1995). *Global Migrants, Local Lives: Travel and Transformation in Rural Bangladesh*. London: Clarendon Press.
Glick Schiller, N. (2005). "Transnational Social Fields and Imperialism: Bringing a Theory of Power to Transnational Studies." *Anthropological Theory* 5 (4): 439-461.
Gilroy, P. (1997). "Diaspora and the Detours of Identity." In *Identity and Difference*. London: Sage.
Hannerz, U. (1996). *Transnational Connections: Culture, People, Places*. London: Routledge.
Harvey, D. (1989). *The Condition of Postmodernity*. Oxford: Blackwell.

Jacobs, J. (1996). *Edge of Empire: Postcolonialism and the City*. London and New York: Routledge.

Levitt, P. (2001). *Transnational Villagers*. Berkeley, CA: University of California Press.

Levitt, P. (2002). "Redefining the Boundaries of Belonging: Thoughts on Transnational Religious and Political Life." *Working Paper 48; Center for Comparative Immigration Studies*. San Diego: University of California.

Maira, S. M. (2002). *Desis in the House: Indian American Youth Culture in New York City*. New York: Temple University Press.

Metcalf, B. (1996). "New Medinas: The Tablighi Jama'at in America and Europe." In *Making Muslim Space in North America and Europe*. Berkeley, CA: University of California Press.

Phillips, D. (1985). *What Price Equality? Report on Allocation of GLC Housing in Tower Hamlets*. London: Research and Policy Report (9) GLC.

Portes, A., L. E. Guarnizo, and P. Landolt (1999). "Transnational Communities." Special issue of *Ethnic and Racial Studies* 22 (2).

Smith, M. P. and L. E. Guarnizo (eds.). (1998). *Transnationalism from Below*. New Brunswick, NJ: Transaction Publishers.

Tarrius, A. (2002). *La Mondialisation par le Bas*. Paris: Balland.

Werbner, P. (2002). *Imagined Diasporas among Manchester Muslims: The Public Performance of Pakistani Transnational Identity Politics*. Oxford and Santa Fe: Currey/SARP.

10

Practicing Identities Across Borders: The Case of Bulgarian Turkish Labor Migrants in Germany[1]

Mila Mancheva

In his bestseller novel "Russian Disco" the German-writing author of immigrant background, Wladimir Kaminer, acquaints us with two attendants at a Turkish snack bar in Berlin whom his protagonist, upon entering the place for a quick midnight dinner, finds listening to popular Bulgarian music. Having inquired why Turks appear to be listening to Bulgarian music, he is told by the snack bar attendants that they are actually Bulgarians pretending to be Turks: "Berlin is already too diverse. One should not complicate the situation unnecessarily. The consumer is used to being served by Turks at a Turkish snack bar, even if they are actually Bulgarians."[2]

This episode is the inspiration for the story called *Business Camouflage* which, funny and shrewd as Kaminer's stories on Berlin are, touches upon the issue of the pragmatic nature of identity formation. During the casual midnight encounter, described by the author, what appears to be "discovered" is as much as what is "covered" since the two snack bar attendants must have been Bulgarian Turks rather than simply Turks or Bulgarians. Since the early 1990s Bulgarian Turks have been a useful labor resource for the relatively young, small ethnic businesses of German Turks in Germany. German Turks, on the other hand, have served as a powerful resource for Bulgarian Turks in their search to diversify income and employment opportunities through migration in conditions of harsh economic transition at home.

Kaminer's story helps us to understand how Bulgarian Turkish migrant experiences in Germany are marked by the (dis)advantages of continuous identity negotiation at the everyday level. Introducing us to numerous other cases of business camouflage among representatives of other immigrant groups throughout Berlin, the author ironically calls the city "mysterious," referring to the infinite dynamic between the voiced and the hidden sides of people's identity and the infinite (im)possibilities for its recognition. The story fits within this particular perspective of contemporary social science that approaches identities—ethnic, national or cultural—in terms of social interaction rather than content, as multiple and situationally defined rather than unified and centered, as the outcome of continuous process of negotiation among different actors, rather than as natural and self-perpetuating (Barth 1969; Jenkins 1996, 1997).

Migration Patterns of Bulgarian Turks in Retrospect

Ethnic Turks are the largest minority in Bulgaria amounting to 9 percent of the overall population. They are an old minority, one of the main legacies of the Ottoman Empire that once encompassed all territories of the Balkan Peninsula (sixteenth to nineteenth centuries). Ethnic Turks have traditionally been considered the country's most important minority, not only because of their numerical strength, but also because of their Muslim religion and the close proximity of their kin-state Turkey, which lies to the south. Ethnic Turks today enjoy full minority rights and are politically represented at the levels of Parliament, government and state administration. They are bilingual as Bulgarian is the official language of instruction at public school level and they profess a moderate form of Balkan Islam (Popovic 1986).

Since the late nineteenth century ethnic Turks practiced either internal seasonal labor migration or kin-state based ethnic migration. The kin-state of Turkey traditionally played the role of symbolic homeland for the Turks in Bulgaria and has attracted migration waves with various levels of intensity throughout the twentieth century. With the exception of rare cases of individual migration Bulgarian Turks never headed to other parts of the world until the early 1990s. During the transition period (1989-2006) the traditional patterns of migration became diversified with new trends and destinations. The migration of Bulgarian Turks during the transition period was initially directed to Turkey with the forced emigration of 300,000 people resulting from the serious human rights abuses by the pre-1989 socialist government (Vasileva 1992). Although about half of these people (154,937) returned to Bulgaria as a result of dissatisfaction with demands for adaptation to the host society (Vasileva 1992; Zhelyazkova 1998), for many other Bulgarian Turks Turkey remained a powerful destination throughout the 1990s with complete migration being gradually substituted for seasonal and circular migration.

From the early 1990s Western Europe began to attract Bulgarian Turkish migrants for the first time in their social history. Migration to Germany, in particular, was initiated by those Bulgarian Turks who, for various reasons, were unable to join the first massive migration wave to Turkey in 1989 or who were part of the subsequent return wave which was dissatisfied with the conditions of life or the social adjustment prospects there. A powerful channel for migration for both ethnic Turks and ethnic Bulgarians to Germany in the early 1990 was the asylum regime, which provided generous social benefits. Between 1990 and 1995 a total of 79,003 asylum applications from Bulgarian citizens, Bulgarians and representatives of various minority groups alike, were submitted in Germany (Federal Statistical Office, Germany). Asylum seekers from Bulgaria, like those from other countries of Eastern Europe, were really economic migrants, who combined social benefit entitlements with regular and irregular employment during their application procedures (Wenning 1996: 173). Being allowed to stay in the country for periods of six months to several years, they were able to establish a skeleton of migrant networks in Germany, which was used by labor migrants from Bulgaria throughout the whole transition period.

Migrants and asylum seekers from Bulgaria were, in fact, a small component of the vast inflow of immigrants from Eastern Europe who headed to Germany after the fall of the Berlin Wall. Between 1989 and 1993 a total annual inflow of between half a million to 700,000 people entered Germany from Hungary, Poland, the Czech Republic, Romania, Bulgaria, and the former USSR (Hönekopp 1995: 224). The overall net migration during the same period amounted to 4 million people, including asylum seekers, ethnic Germans and citizens of former East Germany, family immigrants, contract workers and illegals (Angenendt 1999: 188).

This vast inflow of people provoked changes in the German border, immigration, and asylum regime designed to limit further immigration and to fight illegal migration. The German government revised the asylum regime and the foreigners and citizenship laws. It also concluded bilateral readmission agreements with countries like Poland, Romania, the Czech Republic, and Bulgaria that were considered major sources for migration at the time. While these measures led to a considerable decrease in the overall number of asylum applicants in Germany, they contributed to a shift towards illegal immigration (Münz and Ulrich 1998: 42). Labor migrants throughout the 1990s resorted to various practices of irregular entry and irregular residence for the purposes of work, and largely evaded the restrictive border and residence regime, introduced by the German government.

Bulgarian Turkish Labor Migrants in Germany: The Circumstances of Migration

Today migration and labor practices among Bulgarian Turkish labor migrants in Germany are affected by three important developments. First, with the abolition of the Schengen Visa Regime for Bulgaria in April 2001 Bulgarians obtained the right for visa free entry and visa free stay of up to three months as tourists in European Union (EU) countries. These new border regulations affected the predominantly seasonal character of Bulgarian Turkish migration. Migrants now had to shuttle between Bulgaria and Germany in 3-month cycles to comply with this new visa regime. Second, the economic stagnation of the German labor market and the decreased demand for labor in the construction sector, in particular, resulted in lower wages for irregular migrants. Third, stricter labor market regulations aimed at restricting illegal employment were introduced by the German government. In particular, the new *Act Intensifying the Fight Against Illegal Employment and Ensuing Tax Evasion* (July 2004) and the *German Social Code* introduced imprisonment for up to 3 years and fines of up to €500,000 for employers who employed foreigners without permission or without residence title, compared with fines of up to €5,000 and in special cases imprisonment of up to 1 year for illegal employees (Sinn, Kreienbrink, and Loeffelholz 2005: 49-50). Many authors have disputed the effectiveness of German border controls and labor market regulations in the fight against illegal migration and the irregular labor market. In the case of Bulgarian Turks they contributed to a greater caution on the part of employers in hiring illegal workers. Bulgarian Turks, who occupied a weaker position in the German irregular labor market than immigrant groups with stronger infrastructures, reported that employment opportunities since 2002-2003 became less readily available. This in turn rendered their penetration into the irregular labor market more difficult and their position vis-à-vis employers more precarious.

Bulgarian Turks are to be found predominantly in the less protected sectors of the German labor market associated with ethnic businesses that require higher flexibility and tougher working conditions. They appear to rely for employment predominantly on co-ethnic networks established by German Turks. Many of them, however, also worked for German, Arab, or Afghan employers. The typical Bulgarian Turkish (regular and irregular) employment niches for men are the construction business and the service sector (grocery shops, fast food places, coffeehouses, wedding salons, public laundries and restaurants). Cleaning and cooking in the service sector are the main occupations for women. Bulgarian Turks usually work in German-Turkish small businesses that employ up to 3 employees. These businesses are still the majority (53.8 percent in 2001 and 43.7 percent in 2005) in an otherwise diversifying and internationalizing German-Turkish economy (Şen and Sauer 2005: 30). They are usually family-run businesses (Hedwig and Hillmann 1998: 144; Şen and Sauer 2005: 31) where irregular labor has been an important factor in withstanding the highly competitive and volatile economic environment that small entrepreneurs face in Germany.[3]

An important characteristic of the Bulgarian Turkish irregular labor market in Germany is that it operates without the help of recruiters or intermediaries. Jobs on the informal market are found through private networks. The prices of such services are not paid in cash and a service is usually reciprocated by another service. This, in turn, makes trust very important in the process of establishing and maintaining migrant networks. The conditions of precariousness and economic vulnerability that often characterize German-Turkish small businesses shape the unfavorable working conditions for Bulgarian Turkish migrants. In general, migrants work between ten and twelve hours a day with no or occasionally one free day a week. Work conditions for irregular migrants and for new arrivals are even worse. Those who have been in Germany for some time and have established wider social networks, especially those with work permits, are in a stronger position to request better pay and more favorable work schedules.

Since 2001-2002, the labor market for Bulgarian Turkish irregular migrants in Germany has become less flexible, wages lower, and the market more difficult to penetrate without an already close relationship with an employer. Jobs on the irregular labor market remain available, although under less favorable conditions. Irregular migrants from Bulgaria still come as part of strategies to maintain livelihoods and support families back home.

Migrant Networks and Trajectories

The current group of Bulgarian Turkish labor migrants in Germany is composed of both regular and irregular migrants. They are predominantly male, but there is a significant proportion of female migrants. Both men and women arrive in Germany solely for the purposes of work and the most leave their families behind. The group of irregular migrants is composed of either seasonal workers shuttling between Bulgaria and Germany in three to six-months cycles or long-term migrants who have stayed and worked in Germany for seven to ten years or more. A sub-group within this group consists of regular migrants who legalized their status largely through marriages of convenience to German citizens. Some members of this group have managed to bring their children to Germany and place them in German public or professional schools. There is also a smaller number of people who have given birth in Germany and whose children are being wholly raised in Germany. Although already legal, members of this group maintain close connections with co-ethnic irregular migrants and tend to remain within their ethnic networks. Some Bulgarian Turks were able to join relatives who had had migrated from Bulgaria to Turkey during the 1960s and 1970s and subsequently arrived in Germany on the back of the Bilateral Guest-Worker Contracts between Germany and Turkey. This helped them achieve legal status and relative economic stability more quickly than those without such support, since they enjoyed better access to local networks and were employed in businesses run by relatives under more favorable conditions. Another group of migrants has already completely returned to Bulgaria. They either invested migrant savings in small family businesses sufficient to cover living expenses or found jobs that provided satisfactory wages.

Overall, both regular and irregular labor migrants, whether seasonal or long-term, support households and families back home. While some of them combine their occupations in Germany with jobs in Bulgaria, others work only in Germany in order to send money to their families back home. Thus they appear to maintain livelihoods across two or more countries with the aim of improving social status back home. Many, if not all the interviewees in Berlin, appear to be deeply involved in migration and their families are linked transnationally to towns all over Europe. Migrants refer to relatives who live in countries outside Germany or Bulgaria, such as Turkey, Belgium, The Netherlands and the United Kingdom. International locations such as London, Paris, Kiev, or Berlin now figure in migrants' daily conversations as often as the names of their home towns or villages. Thus a process of transnationalization of Bulgarian Turkish families appears to be developing as family structures and ties of support and control now seem to persist over several countries. Moreover, family forces appear to play an important role across borders not only as source of material support but also as units of gender and age hierarchies where key life decisions are made.

Migration and mobility between the host and the home society have become normal for Bulgarian Turkish migrants. While family life in Bulgaria is structured around the cyclical leaves and returns of family members from work abroad, the life of migrants abroad is framed by livelihood strategies back in Bulgaria. Thus the practice of earning money in Germany and spending it in Bulgaria translates into the cultural formula of "working here, living there" (Karamihova 2003: 207). The notion of home remains primarily linked to the home country, as households in Germany appear to be supplementary (temporary, shared, rented) to the migrants' prime households back in Bulgaria that are owned, renovated and well equipped for the whole family.

It is worth noting, however, that Bulgarian Turkish labor migrants in Germany do not share the same migration strategies, life trajectories and embeddedness in the home and the host society. Their narratives reveal a multiplicity of personal experiences, pre-migration biographies, educational and professional backgrounds as well as family situations back home or elsewhere in Europe or Turkey. Thus any attempt to analyze and typologize their personal accounts of migration has to be undertaken in full awareness about the diversity and fluidity of their experiences and situations.

Practicing Identities

I had the chance to meet Fatima through a friend of mine who, while on a short visit to Berlin, came across her accidentally entering the Turkish snack bar where she worked. After having served him a small lunch she would hear his "thanks" uttered in Bulgarian and would initiate a short cordial conversation saying that she too was from Bulgaria and was always happy to meet people from Bulgaria. Upon our first meeting at the snack bar she would mention almost immediately the "backwardness and laziness" of the German Turks and would support her words by pointing in direction of her colleagues. She would then add: "it is nice to talk a little with someone from Bulgaria, communication among us is a different thing." Fatima is 43, she is divorced and has two children in Bulgaria to whom she regularly sends money. When I met her she had been in Germany for 15 years and most of that time she had worked illegally in Turkish snack bars across Berlin.

At the snack bar where I found her she worked as a cook and was responsible for preparing various types of *bureks* and traditional Turkish warm dishes. Her closest colleague was the owner's nephew, who took care of the counter and the clients. Fatima, however, often combined his duties with hers because of his frequent absences. The owner himself, together with either his sister or wife, would spend time in the restaurant working on the accounts or talking with friends or regular customers. Fatma worked 10 hours a day and had 1 free day a week. She was central to the functioning of the restaurant as she was a good cook—she "learned the craft from the best *Imbiss*[4] keepers in Berlin." She was highly trusted and was often allowed to take care of the counter. In addition, she was placed in charge of the business when the family took their regular summer vacation to Turkey.

All her comments about her employers and about German Turks in general, however, emphasized their cultural dissimilarity and conservatism and their arrogance towards those like her coming from Bulgaria. They could not understand her sense of humor and her openness with male customers. They would voice doubts about her piety and faith and would question the fact that pork was not a taboo for her. During the fourteenth year of her stay in Germany she obtained residence and a work permit (through marriage to a German citizen) and for some time considered the idea of starting a job with Germans. She did not make a change, however—"After all, I don't want to change profession—this is what I am good at" was her explanation. So, for the time being, she continued her daily routine, which remained closely intertwined with that of German Turkish employers, colleagues and acquaintances. Small stories, complaints and jokes about her daily interactions with them remained a continuing theme of our conversations.

The case of Fatima is representative of the social reality of Bulgarian Turks in Berlin, which is based on a dynamic that is distinguished by the close pragmatic association with German Turks on the one hand, and ongoing symbolic tensions created by claims concerning the cultural distinctiveness between the two groups, on the other. Thus their experiences in migration are narrated as a constant process of negotiating "difference" and "sameness." Migrants seem to be under constant pressure to justify certain aspects of their identities, which they feel to be perceived by others as inconsistent, insufficient or contradictory. They are "Muslims" but they "eat pork and drink alcohol"; they are "Turks" but they "are from Bulgaria" and their "women behave as equals to men"; they are "Bulgarian passport holders" but their "language is Turkish" and they work with Turks.

The way in which Bulgarian Turks experience their identity is revealed in their stories about how are they approached and perceived by the various social environments they confront in the process of migration.

These stories are usually told in relation to the German Turks (including Kurds), to family and local situations and developments back in Bulgaria and elsewhere in Europe and, to a lesser extent, to perceptions and experiences related to German society and the Germans. German Turks see them as "inferior," "not belonging to them," "Bulgarians," "not true Muslims," "Christians," "women are easy and frivolous." German immigrant authorities approach them as Bulgarian citizens and holders of Bulgarian passports—their "Turkishness" is irrelevant for them and in situations where it comes to the fore, it is seen (and often not without justification) as an attempt to manipulate the system. Bulgarian border officials approach them as "rustic" and "uneducated" people who can be taken advantage of and asked for unauthorized border fines.

These incomplete identity validations that Bulgarian Turks encounter in migration involve them in an ongoing process of negotiation about belonging, way of life and honor. Within this process the notions of being Bulgarian, Turk and European appear to constitute the major sources for identity configurations. These identity markers are commonly mentioned and used as ways to describe or refer to oneself. While Turkish is the *origin* and the *mother tongue*, being Bulgarian involves the *passport*, the *home country* and the *home place*. Bulgarian identity is also associated with the *air*, the *earth* or *the soil*, while being European entails a mentality, which is *modern*, *open* and *free*. These three self-identifiers keep Bulgarian Turkish transnational reality strong through being emphasized or silenced according to the various social contexts within which people interact.

Being Turkish

> In Turkey and here (in Germany) the Turks call us Bulgarians, in Bulgaria we are called Turks—tell me what is one to do? (Male respondent, 21).

While "Turkishness" has always been the primary identification of/and for Bulgarian Turks in the public realm of Bulgaria, once in Germany they find the notion confronted by their ethnic kin from Turkey who have different understandings about its religious, linguistic and cultural dimensions. So although ethnic networks appear a powerful mechanism for migrant accommodation in the host country, they also serve to affirm co-ethnic difference. However, neither Bulgarian Turkish involvement with German Turks nor the mutual refusal of the two groups to acknowledge "sameness" are to be understood and explained within the framework of solely cultural or ethnic arguments. The two processes are deeply intertwined and produced by a complex set of factors related to migration and employment in Germany.

"Being Turkish" does not explain why Bulgarian Turks enter and remain within German Turkish networks. The answer lies in their adoption of a pragmatic strategy and response to restricted opportunities rather than pursuing a deliberate choice based on ethnic principles. First, the irregular labor market in Germany is dominated by immigrant groups such as Poles, Turks, citizens of former Yugoslavia, or the Russian Federation that are longer established in the country and enjoy much stronger infrastructures (Sinn, Kreienbrink and von Loeffelholz 2005: 35). As a result, the smaller groups of newcomers, such as migrants from Bulgaria, face limited opportunities in terms of industries, employers, and pay. Secondly, the state of irregularity in conditions of highly controlled labor market pushes Bulgarian Turks into the networks of German Turks where they feel safer and "less visible." It is not the lack of knowledge of the German language but their irregular status that Bulgarian Turks offer as their main reason for working mostly for German Turks. Moreover, many of the long-term migrants have acquired a command of German sufficient for everyday interactions. Therefore, it is not surprising that attempts to leave the network for German employers are observed mainly when certain forms of legalization are achieved. Bulgarian Turks, in fact, do work for German employers when conditions such as residence status, personal desire, and employment opportunity allow. In the early 1990s, for example, when most Bulgarian Turkish immigrants resided in Germany as asylum applicants, employment with German employers was a common practice, since under certain conditions legal work was allowed as part of the social benefit package to which they were entitled. However, those who have residence and work permits and have full-time jobs with German employers, may also have semi-regular jobs on the side with German-Turkish employers that are not reported to the social benefit and insurance authorities. Thirdly, for German Turkish employers, the availability of cheap labor by co-ethnics, who speak the same language, but are perceived as inferior (and therefore exploitable), is a good structural opportunity within a labor market that is highly restrictive and inflexible. As a matter of comparison, the situation of Bulgarian Turkish migrants in The Netherlands is somewhat different. In spite of the marked presence of an old Turkish immigrant community, Bulgarian Turks work largely for Dutch employers.[5]

The nature of the relationship with German Turks and the differences between the two groups are a dominant theme in migrants' personal accounts. Interactions with German Turks are felt by Bulgarian Turks as a rather stressful experience due to cultural differences perceived as essential by both groups. Differences in language, religious practices, and gender relationships—not least in the practicing of humor—are reported to be constant sources of tension, mistrust, and lack of acceptance on both sides. In their accounts of German Turks, Bulgarian Turks repeat "'they are different from us...we are different from them,' 'they don't accept us and we don't accept them,' 'they think that we are below them and we think that they are below us'" (female respondent, 43). These mirror-formulas, however, function in social circumstances that are hierarchical and serve to overcome the subordinate and dependent position that Bulgarian Turks maintain in relation to German Turkish employers. The seemingly mutual consent between the two groups of not belonging together is to be explained partially with the structural organization of German Turkish businesses which are predominantly organized as family enterprises.[6] Bulgarian Turks thus find themselves employed among family members, who are bound together by particularly strong ties of trust and interdependence. Thus their position as outsiders is structurally defined rather than exclusively culturally conditioned.

While the fragmentation and diversity of the German Turkish community(s) is not reflected in the accounts of Bulgarian Turks, a recurring distinction is being made between them and the Turks in Turkey. While speaking about German Turks, Bulgarian Turks would often make sure to point out that they have little in common with Turks in Turkey. German Turks are the "poor," the "uneducated," and the "misfits" of Turkey who, back in the past, had no other alternative but to migrate to Germany.

> Those (Turks) that were coming here in the '60s were the poor ones from Anadola[7] who did not have much. A man with a store and a good life there (in Turkey) will never come here... here you will never meet someone to tell you that [he or she] comes from Istanbul because nobody from Istanbul comes here (Male respondent, 36).

> The Turks—I hate them... those that were coming here earlier were misfits and terrorists, Kurds that were persecuted by the state (Turkey) (Female respondent, 47).

The distinction that is constantly being made between the German Turkish diaspora and the Turks in Turkey proper has the symbolic meaning of emancipating Bulgarian Turks from a co-ethnic environment that perceives them as inferior. In fact, the ethnic kin in Turkey appear to be incorporated as the positive equation of a construct that includes good and bad, backward and civilized Turks. The implied existence of other

Turks, who are cultured, educated and socially well off, serves to reconcile the disputed contents of Bulgarian Turkish ethnicity and is also an indication of the positive symbolic meaning that Turkey retains as an ancestral homeland for them.

Sometimes migrants' accounts affirm differences with German Turks in a positive way:

> Before coming here I did not know this… the Turks, the Germans—the music, the songs (of the German Turks). I only spoke Turkish and that was all. I did not know that there are different Turks some from the coast, other from Asia or from Istanbul (Male respondent, 36).

The encounter with German Turks is thus being represented in a less contested way as a culturally enriching experience in the culturally diverse social context of Berlin. Accounts of this type are to be observed mostly among male migrants who have lived longer in Germany and have well established contacts and work experience with German Turks, representatives of other immigrant groups and Germans alike.

The culturally justified tensions with German Turks appear particularly visible in the accounts of Bulgarian Turkish single female migrants, who strongly resist the gender realities of German-Turkish society. These realities are informed by traditional cultural norms, which define their social position through the authority of male figures, such as father, husband, or brother. The survival strategies employed by Bulgarian Turkish female migrants, however, involve both the manipulation of this reality and resistance at the everyday level. Living single, having jobs, joking in public, communicating with men on equal terms—in all those they perceive themselves to challenge the culturally rooted understandings of what it means to be a woman in German Turkish society.

Being European

"We speak Bulgarian, German, Turkish—many languages, we are European women." This comment by a female respondent over 50 with the name of Zakrie, whose German was very poor, is typical of the way Bulgarian Turks talk about themselves as migrants. The practice of resorting to self-ascriptions outside the framework of ethnicity, such as "Europeanness," "Bulgarianness" or "modernity," appears widespread among them. It serves to counteract the inferior image maintained towards them by German Turks but it is also triggered by the diverse cultural milieu of Berlin that allows them to connect in various ways with their versatile social and cultural surroundings.

The notion of Europe is used by Bulgarian Turks in a practical and symbolic sense. In pragmatic terms, Bulgaria's entry into the European Union is seen as making European space easier for legal access. In symbolic terms the awareness of being "European" is activated by Bulgarian Turks as a response to a co-ethnic social environment that does not accept them as equal. In this context 'European" is employed to mean "cultured," "modern," "liberal" as opposed to "backward" and "conservative. "We are Europeans" is the answer to German Turkish perceptions that serve to degrade Bulgarian Turks as "second-rate people" in social, cultural and religious terms. "We are Europeans" is opposed to German Turks, who are "savage," "jealous," and "uneducated" and have a "rigid sense of humor."

Self-identifications with the notion of "Europeanness" only rarely appear to trigger pragmatic choices to break away from the co-ethnic networks of German Turkish employers. Such was the case of Zakrie who had spent about 7 years in Germany. She first left Bulgaria in 1989 and prior to her arrival in Germany, her migration history included travels and work in Sweden and Austria. Everywhere she would be in close contact with Bulgarian Turk relatives and acquaintances who would help her out upon arrival and secure work placements for her in the networks of local Turkish immigrants. After several years of irregularity in Germany, however, soon after she obtained a work permit through a marriage to a German citizen, she made a deliberate choice to avoid employment with German Turks. Since then she had worked for about four years as a maid at a German-run hotel. The hotel is located in the Berlin quarter of Spandau with a rather small German Turk population as compared to other parts of the city.[8] The chosen place of employment, which was also her area of living, to a great extent reduced her encounters with both German and Bulgarian Turks. Like most of her Turkish compatriots from Bulgaria she was readily sharing stories about previous interactions with German Turks accompanied by jokes about their conservatism and traditionalism. She would always make sure to contrast her previous experiences with her present situation which she viewed as very favorable. She would usually say "I have my calm now" referring to her nice one-room apartment, in close proximity to her working place and to her German co-workers whom she would invariably see as "nice" and "cultured."

Zakrie and Fatima, whose story I presented earlier, were close friends. Although they used to meet rarely they had respect for each other and a lot in common to talk about. They shared the same opinions about

German Turks, similar levels of acknowledgement as being "modern" and "European" and an equal standing as legal immigrants at the German labor market. They had resorted to different employment strategies however. Paradoxically, Fatima, whose German was much better than that of Zakrie, had chosen to stay "with her profession." Her contentment with her craft and her pride in the quality of her dishes were central to her understanding of what was bringing meaning and dignity to her life. This involved a choice that placed her in close interaction with a German Turkish social environment. Her sense of "European-ness" was thus expressed verbally in conversations with other Bulgarian Turks or was continuously negotiated and defended in her daily interactions with German Turk employers. Zakrie's sense of dissimilarity with her host co-ethnic surrounding on the other hand, resulted in her decision to reduce contacts with and dependence on German Turks. She would often say, "I would never go back and work for those people," thus expressing her choice to break away from the power induced cultural codes that relations with German Turks entailed. She opted for working with Germans and the hotel of her choice seemed just the right place for her. Her strategy however, did not involve severing of ties with Bulgarian or German Turks in principle. While she kept friendships and acquaintances from both groups, she also made efforts to maintain friendships with Germans as well. Her particular approach aimed at securing independence from the networks of German Turkish employment. The spatial and occupational choices that she made in this direction provided her with the opportunity to experience her sense of being a "modern," "European woman" free of tensions and constraints.

The stories of Zakrie and Fatima point to a complex reality where migrants face various accommodation possibilities, dictated not only by the prevailing structural realities of the host-country labor market, but by migrants' specific professional preferences, individual situations, and stances towards work, dignity, and honor. Migrants' individual choices appear to be determined by the combined forces of these factors that in turn play an influence over their identity practices. For Fatima, being a good cook was the most important, irrespective of the long working hours and the tough conditions that employment at the German Turkish-run small business gastronomy sector in Berlin entailed. What was valued by Zakrie, on the other hand, was the quiet of life with favorable employer-employee relations, better working conditions and less stressful job schedules. By evading the power relationship with German Turkish employers, Zakrie chose to dictate her own terms of participation in the co-ethnic network. She believed to have secured herself the opportunity to live the various facets of her identity in a less contested way, while Fatima had to constantly negotiate them through.

Being Bulgarian

"Bulgarian" is the ascription used not only by German Turks when referring to Bulgarian Turks but by Bulgarian Turks among each other. This is a reflection of a situation where civic identifications, associated with the notion of belonging to the home country, often come prior to ethnic identifications both at the everyday and the institutional level.[9]

At this stage, migration to Germany seems to reinforce the civic Bulgarian identity of Bulgarian Turks in several ways. Firstly, they are treated by the German state as Bulgarian passport holders. Their Turkish ethnic origin plays no role in their interaction with German immigrant institutions and EU states at large. Their Bulgarian citizenship gives them the chance to travel freely across the European space. Secondly, their modern "European" identity is also a Bulgarian identity—one that gives them cultural advantage with respect to the "backward" German Turks. Not least their migration experience results in the feeling that one's life is lived best in Bulgaria. "What is there to like in Germany? I don't like it neither here nor in Turkey. It is nice only in Bulgaria" (male respondent, 21). Thirdly, Bulgarian Turkish migrants' experiences seem to trigger a stronger feeling towards Bulgaria and increase its value as a homeland. Throughout the whole transition period their livelihood strategies are geared towards return. Once beyond the border they stress much more their commonness with ethnic Bulgarians ("beyond Kalotina[10] we are all Bulgarians"). Although ethnic Bulgarian and ethnic Turk irregular labor migrants occupy different zones in the German irregular labor market, they come into contact in certain public spheres (for example, in Bulgarian restaurants and the Bulgarian Orthodox Church). Moreover, in moments of crisis (sudden loss of job or lodgings) they turn for help to an extended network that encompasses both groups based on shared home country and citizenship.

The self-ascriptions of being European and Bulgarian have a powerful positive effect in the process of identity negotiation by Bulgarian Turks in Germany. Contrary to their ethnic ascriptions, the notions of "Europeanness" and "Bulgarianness" appear much less disputed as Bulgarian Turks are less frequently exposed to immigrant groups other than German Turks or to the German majority.

Conclusions

The migration of Bulgarian Turks to Germany is predominantly organized along ethnic networks. Bulgarian Turkish migrants share information and support predominantly within extended family, kinship, and co-ethnic circles. Furthermore, they tend to rely for employment on the older and better established networks of German Turks. Analysis of Bulgarian Turkish migrants' personal accounts, however, demonstrates that ethnicity as such is not at the center of this development—it is the outcome of a complex set of factors related to the specificities of the irregular labor market and the overall border and migration regime in Germany. Not least it is the outcome of political and institutional attitudes towards irregular migration and irregularity generally in Germany.

In a situation where the "price" of network services is rather high due to a highly controlled and restrictive labor market and a weak infrastructure of the Bulgarian immigrant group, they are being provided exclusively within the family/kinship and regional/ethnic circles which, in turn, reinforce the importance and prevalence of these units among these migrants. In addition, the restrictive policies of German government towards irregular migration and illegal employment push Bulgarian Turks into the niches of the German Turkish economy because migrants face both restricted employment opportunities and a need to remain invisible in order to avoid the threat of arrest and return. This heightens the dependence of Bulgarian Turk migrants on the ethnic economy and reinforces their inferior and subordinate position within German Turkish networks. Thus their marginal position in German society is exacerbated and the potential for incorporation beyond the borders of the ethnic economy, with the cultural and social stratifications it entails, is hindered.

The "us" of Bulgarian Turks in migration appears to be constructed mainly as the outcome of the tight social relationships they maintain with German Turks who play not only the role of their closest social partners but their most immediate "other" as well. Despite the constantly reported cultural differences and dislikes between Bulgarian Turks and German Turks, which seem to be perceived as strong and important by both groups, a strong pragmatic relationship operates between them—a relationship based on mutual interest and mutual need. It is the hierarchical nature of this relationship that exacerbates feelings of mutual dislike and it is the perceptions of cultural difference that serve to justify the hierarchical nature of the relationship. While ethnicity in conditions of migration appears to be experienced by Bulgarian Turks as if in a state of tension or as a failure of sameness in everyday practice, it is the silent spaces of pragmatic interest that make their migration strategies possible.

The notions of being Bulgarian and European are closely intertwined and intensively resorted to by Bulgarian Turks in Germany as they appear a powerful resource of symbolic opposition to the culturally justified tensions with German Turks. The transnational character of migrants' experiences and their strong commitment to the home country, in particular, provide a strong additional resource for resistance with respect to the culturally justified confrontation they face from their most immediate German-Turkish environment in Germany.

Notes

1. This chapter is based on field research conducted in Berlin during 2006, based at the Institute for East-European Studies, Free University and funded by the Alexander von Humboldt Foundation. The main methods used included collection of life-course interviews with migrants and participant observation.
2. Author's own translation from German (Kaminer 2000: 97-98).
3. The question of the use of irregular labor by German Turkish small entrepreneurs in Berlin and its impact for the development of the German-Turkish economy has not been given sufficient attention in the literature.
4. "Imbiss" is the German term corresponding to the English "fast food" or "snack" and is widely used to label snack bars across Germany.
5. Due to the different organization of the irregular labor market in The Netherlands, representatives of the Turkish community there form just a segment of the networks that Bulgarian Turk labor migrants establish there. Semi-legal work bureaus of Kurdish intermediaries who introduce Bulgarian Turkish irregulars to Dutch employers under false identities of Greek, Spanish or other EU citizens appear important for their entry into the labor market. Many Bulgarian Turks, however, establish direct contacts with their employers in the course of time that allow them evade the intermediary work-bureaus of the local Kurds.
6. The percentage of small German Turkish businesses that employ family members was 41.2 and 54.9 in 2001 and 2005 respectively (en and Sauer 2005: 31).
7. *Anadola* is the Bulgarian transcription of the standard Turkish name *Anadolu* for the Asian Anatolian part of Turkey. Used in vernacular speech, however, the Bulgarian transcription has a semi-pejorative meaning being generally associated with backwardness.
8. According to statistical data from 2003 the administrative quarter of Spandau hosted 7,258 inhabitants with Turkish citizenship who formed a share of about 3 percent of the total population there. In comparison, other Berlin quarters such as Mitte, Friedrichshain/Kreuzberg or Neuköln had shares of Turkish populations of respectively 9.5, 9.4, and 8.7 percent (Ohliger and Raiser 2005: 13).
9. Very interesting accounts on the situational attitudes to the ascription of being "Bulgarian" by the Bulgarian Turkish emigrants in Turkey are to be found in two recent independently conducted field research studies by Parla (2005) and Maeva (2006).
10. The main border checkpoint on the northwestern border of Bulgaria.

References

Angenendt, S. (ed.) (1999). *Asylum and Migration Policies in the European Union.* Bonn: Europa Union Verlag.

Barth, F. (ed.) (1969). *Ethnic Groups and Boundaries. The Social Organization of Culture Difference.* Oslo, B-T: Universitetsforlaget.

Brettel, C. (2003). *Anthropology and Migration. Essays on Transnationalism, Ethnicity, and Identity.* Oxford, New York: AltaMira Press.

Caglar, A. (1994). *German Turks and Their Quest for Social Mobility.* (Dissertation Thesis). Montreal: Department of Anthropology: McGill University.

Cohen, R. (ed.) (1996). *The Sociology of Migration.* Cheltenham, UK, Brookfield, US: Edward Elgar Publishing Limited.

Eichenhofer, E. (Hrsg.) (1999). *Migration und Illegalität.* Osnabrück: Rasch Druckerei und Verlag.

Jenkins, R. (1996). *Social Identity.* London, NY: Routledge.

_____ (1997). *Rethinking Ethnicity. Arguments and Explorations.* London, ND: SAGE Publications.

Hedwig, R. and F. Hillmann (1998). "How Turkish is the Donar Kebab? Turks in Berlin's Food Sector." *Scottish Geographical Magazine* 114 (3): 138-147.

Hönekopp, E. (1995). "The East-West Migration in Europe: Normalization after Some Years of Growth." In *Migration Policies: A Comparative Perspective* (pp. 221-241). Stuttgart: Enke.

Kaminer, V. (2000). *Russendisko.* München: Wilhelm Goldmann Verlag.

Karamihova, M. (ed.) (2003). *Da jiveesh tam, da se sanuvash tuk: Emigracionni procesi v nachaloto na XXI vek.* [Living There, Dreaming Yourself Here: Emigration Processes in the Beginning of the XXI Century]. Sofia: IMIR.

Maeva, M. (2006). *Balgarskite Turci-Preselnici v Republika Turcia.* [Bulgarian Turkish Settlers in the Republic of Turkey]. Sofia: IMIR.

Massey, D. (1998). *Understanding International Migration at the End of the Millennium.* Oxford: Oxford University Press.

Münz, R. and R. Ulrich (1998). "Germany and its Immigrants: A Socio-Demographic Analysis." *Journal of Ethnic and Migration Studies* 24 (1): 25-56.

Ohliger, R. and U. Raiser (2005). *Integration und Migration in Berlin: Zahlen — Daten — Fakten.* Berlin: Beauftragte des Senats von Berlin für Integration und Migration.

Parla, A. (2005). *Terms of Belonging: Turkish Immigrants from Bulgaria in the Imagined Homeland.* (Dissertation Thesis) New York University: Department of Anthropology.

Popovic, A. (1986). *L'Islam Balkanique: Les Musulmanes du Sud-Est Europeen dans la periode post-ottomane.* Berlin: Osteuropa Institut.

Pecoud, A. (2002). "Contemporary Trends in Berlin's Turkish Economy." In *Dve Domovini Razprave O Izseljenstvu/ Two Homelands Migration Studies* (pp. 89-105) Ljubljana: Zalozba ZRK.

Schiller, N., L. Basch, and C. Blanc-Szanton (1995). "From Immigrant to Transmigrant: Theorizing Transnational Migration." *Anthropological Quarterly* 68 (1): 48-64.

_____ (eds.) (1992). *Towards a Transnational Perspective on Migration: Race, Class, Ethnicity, and Nationalism Reconsidered.* New York: Annals of the New York Academy of Sciences, vol. 645.

Scönwälder, K., D. Vogel, and G. Sciortino (2004). *Migration und Illegalität in Deutschland.* Arbeitstelle Interkulturelle Konflikte und gesellschaftliche Integration (AKI): WZB.

Şen, F. and M. Sauer (2005). *Türkische Unternehmer in Berlin: Struktur—Wirtschaftskraft—Problemlagen.* Berlin: Beauftragte des Senats von Berlin für Integration und Migration.

Sinn, A., A. Kreienbrink, and H. v. Loeffelholz (2005). *Illegally Resident Third-Country Nationals in Germany, Policy Approaches, Profile and Social Situation.* Nürnberg: BAMF.

Vasileva, D. (1992). "Bulgarian Turkish Emigration and Return." *International Migration Review* 26 (2): 342-352.

Vertovec, S. (2001). "Transnationalism and Identity." *Journal of Ethnic and Migration Studies* 27 (4): 573-582.

_____ and R. Cohen (eds.) (1999). *Migration, Diasporas and Transnationalism.* Cheltenham, UK, Northampton, MA, USA: Edward Elgar Publishing Limited.

Wenning, N. (1996). *Migration in Deutschland. Ein Überblick*, Münster, NY: Waxmann.

Wilpert, C. (1998). "Migration and Informal Work in the New Berlin: New Forms of Work or New Sources of Labor?" *Journal of Ethnic and Migration Studies* 24 (2): 269-294.

Zhelyazkova, A. (ed.) (1998). *Between Adaptation and Nostalgia: The Bulgarian Turks in Turkey.* Sofia: IMIR.

Contributors

Kathy Burrell is a senior lecturer in modern history at De Montfort University. Her doctoral work considered post-war Polish, Italian, and Greek-Cypriot migration to the United Kingdom. She is now researching migration from Poland to Britain during and after the Communist regime. Her key publications include the books *Moving Lives: Narratives of Nation and Migration among Europeans in Post-war Britain* (Ashgate, 2006) and co-edited with Panikos Panayi, *Histories and Memories: Migrants and Their History in Britain* (I. B. Tauris: 2006). She is also the list owner for the 'immigration-history-uk' jiscmail list. She can be contacted at: kburrell@dmu.ac.uk.

John Eade is professor of sociology and anthropology at Roehampton University, London and executive director of the Centre for Research on Nationalism, Ethnicity and Multiculturalism (CRONEM) at Roehampton and Surrey universities. His most recent books include: *Placing London* (2000), *Understanding the City* (with C. Mele, 2002), and *Reframing Pilgrimage* (with S. Coleman, 2004). He can be contacted at: J.Eade@surrey.ac.uk.

David Garbin is a research fellow at the Centre for Research on Nationalism, Ethnicity and Multiculturalism (CRONEM-Roehampton University). His doctoral research on the Bengali diaspora and transnational networks involved three years of transnational ethnographic fieldwork in London (Tower Hamlets) and Bangladesh (Sylhet). He is currently involved in the study of black Christians, Muslims and Hindus in London and is conducting fieldwork among British Bangladeshis in East London and French-speaking Africans, mainly Congolese refugees in London and in the Democratic Republic of the Congo. He is the author of several articles on migration and transnationalism and is preparing a book on diasporic religion in London with John Eade and Ann David. He can be contacted at: davidgarbin@yahoo.com.

Peter Geoghegan is a doctoral candidate at the Institute of Geography, University of Edinburgh. He has broad research interests in social and urban geography and is currently writing his doctoral thesis on the politics and policy of anti-racism and race relations in contemporary Northern Ireland. He can be contacted at: p.geoghegan@sms.ed.ac.uk.

Katrin Hansing is an anthropologist and has predominantly worked on issues of migration, transnationalism, race/ethnicity and civil society in relation to Cuba. She is currently the associate director of the Cuban Research Institute at Florida International University. She can be contacted at: hansingk@fiu.edu.

Gertrud Hüwelmeier is an anthropologist and research fellow at the Humboldt University, Berlin in the Department of European Ethnology. She is currently working on religious networks of Vietnamese and Ghanaian migrants in Berlin and elsewhere. Her research project reported in this chapter was financed by the German Research Council (DFG). She has also done research on "Transnational Religion—women's congregations as actors in the process of globalization." She can be contacted at: gertrud.huewelmeier@rz.hu-berlin.de.

Kristine Krause studied social anthropology and religious studies at the Free University in Berlin. She is a doctoral student in social anthropology at the Centre on Migration, Policy and Society, University of Oxford, and a research fellow in the German Research Foundation project on Transnational Networks, New Migration and Religion at the Humboldt University Berlin. She is currently completing fieldwork among migrants from Ghana in London and Berlin. She can be contacted at: kristine.krause@anthro.ox.ac.uk.

Mila Mancheva is currently affiliated with the Osteuropa Institute, Free University, Berlin as an Alexander von Humboldt Fellow working on a postdoctoral project studying the relationship between ethnicity and migration in the case of irregular Bulgarian Turk migrants in Germany. She holds a doctorate in history from the Central European University, Budapest (2003). Between 2001 and 2005 she worked for the International Organization for Migration (Sofia Mission) as project developer and research associate. Her main research interests are in the area of ethnicity and nationalism, minority-majority relations and migration. She can be contacted at: mila_mancheva@yahoo.com.

Svetlana Milutinovic is a researcher working on Chinese migration in Southeast Europe. Since completing her M.A. in sociology and social anthropology from the Central European University she has been based at the Forum for Ethnic Relations in Belgrade. She can be contacted at: svetamil@gmail.com.

Giulia Sinatti is a post-doctoral fellow at the University of Milan-Bicocca, Italy. She holds a Ph.D. in urban sociology and her work focuses on the spatial dynamics associated to migrations. She has been collecting research material on Senegalese migrants for many years. She has studied and spent research periods at the University of Trento, Italy, Trinity College Dublin, Ireland, Cheikh Anta Diop University and Institut Francophone d'Afrique Noire in Dakar, Senegal, and the London School of Economics. She can be contacted at: giulia.sinatti@yahoo.it.

Michael Peter Smith is professor and chair of the Community Studies and Development Program at the University of California at Davis. His most recent books on transnationalism and cities are: *Transnational Urbanism: Locating Globalization* (2001) and *Citizenship across Borders* (with M. Bakker, 2008). The last three co-edited volumes in his CUCR Book Series are: *Transnationalism from Below* (with L. Guarnizo, 1998 and 1999), *City and Nation* (with T. Bender, 2001), and *The Human Face of Global Mobility* (with A. Favell, 2006). He can be contacted at: mpsmith@ucdavis.edu.

Index

A8 Accession countries, 54
Africa
    and foreign aid, 79-80, 82
    churches, 109-127
    HIV/AIDS, 84
alienation, 23
anti-racism, 5, 40, 45-52
Anti-Racist Network (ARN), 45 see also West Against Racism Network (WARN)
Appadurai, Arjun, 62-63
assimilation, 7-8
asylum seekers, 165-166

Bangladesh,
    Bangladeshi migrants, 147-150
    Bangladeshi Muslims, 10
    Bangladeshi organizations in Great Britain, 157-159
    "Bengaliness," 150-151, 154-156
    "Liberation War," 150-151, 155-157
Banglatown, 154-156
banlieues, 64, 66-67
Belfast. *See* Northern Ireland
Belfast Agreement, 39, 43
Berlin Wall, The, 134
Bhabha, H., 40-41
black market, 81, 83, 85
"boat people," 133-135
Brick Lane, 149, 155
British Poles, 18-35
Bulgaria, 164, 168
Bulgarian Turks,
    in Germany, 165-169
    past migration patterns, 164-166
Burrell, Kathy, 4, 15-36

capitalism, 78, 93-95, 103, 147
Catholic/Protestant binary, 39-40, 50
China, People's Republic of
    Chinese entrepreneurship, 6-7, 92

Chinese migration trends, 95-96, 103-105
Chinese migrants in Europe, 91-92, 95-99
Chinese migrants in Hungary, 6-7, 97-98
Chinese migrants in Ireland, 42, 52-54
Chinese migrants in Serbia, 92, 98-99
citizenship,
    Bulgarian, 159
    for Vietnamese migrants, 133
Cold War, The, 12, 18, 20, 28-29, 34, 78
Coleman, S., 116-117, 120
collective memory, 8, 150, 153, 156
colonialism, 126
Committee on Migration, Refugees and Demography of the Council of Europe, 92
communism,
    fall, 10, 27, 29, 79
consumer culture, 132, 136, 140-141
co-presence, 31, 67, 110
creolization, 148
Cuba
    assistance programs, 6, 77-80
    Cuban Communist Party (CCP), 83-86
    Cuban doctors in Mozambique, 79-87
    economic crisis, 81
    maintaining identity in Mozambique, 85-86
    medical professionals in Mozambique, 6
cultural pluralism, 7

Dakar. *See* Senegal
Destiny Changing Church, 111-127
De Witte, M., 117-118, 121
diasporas,
    Bangladeshi Muslims, 147-160

communities, 8, 10-11, 148
Pakistani, 148
Polish, 15-35
religious networks, 132-136
Dong Xuan market, 140-141
dual embeddedness, 93, 95

Eade, John, 3-12
East Berlin,
Vietnamese businesses, 137
East Germany, 133-139, 165
economic liberalization, 9, 132, 136-142
email, 31-32, 87
emplacement, 41, 62, 74, 132-133, 141-142
"ethnic lens," 111, 123
ethnicity, 43
European Union, 19, 34
exile, 24-27, 88
expatriates, 150-152

Filipino nurses, 43, 46
fundamentalism, 125-126

Garbin, David, 10-11, 147-160
gentrification, 110-113
Geoghegan, Peter, 4-5, 39-54
Germany
Bulgarian Turks community, 9, 11, 165-169
German Turks, 11, 167
immigrants in East and West Germany prior to reunification, 134
labor market, 166-167
reunification, 134
Vietnamese community, 9, 131-142
Ghana, 111-114, 117, 122-125
Glick Schiller, Nina, 9-10, 125
globalization
discourses on, 77-79
Good Friday Agreement of 1998, *see* Belfast Agreement
Great Britain,
2012 Olympic Games, 113, 115-116
African migrants, 9-10, 109-127
Bangladeshi community, 9, 11
Polish community, 16-20, 22-35
secularization debate, 8
Tower Hamlets, 11, 149-150
guest workers, 131, 168

Hannerz, Ulf, 62-63
Hanoi, 138-142
Hansing, Katrin, 6, 77-89
Havana, *see* Cuba
Ho Chi Minh City, 138-142
Home Office's Worker Registration Scheme, 33
Hungary, 6-7, 97-98
Hüwelmeier, Gertrud, 10, 131-142
hybridity, 148

identity politics, 11-12, 153-157
identities, 169-178
illegal immigration, 92, 99, 168
imagined communities, 156
instant messaging, 31, 35
Internet,
genealogical web sites, 23
Italy,
Senegalese in Italy, 69-73
Zingonia, 5, 69-73
Ireland. *See also* Northern Ireland

Jewish people
in Ireland, 39, 42-43

Kaminer, Wladimir, 163-164
Kingsway International Christian Centre (KICC), 116, 120
Krause, Kristine, 109-127

labor migration, 81, 164, 166-167
"Little Senegal," *see* Zingonia
London Development Agency, 116
long-distance nationalism, 150

Mancheva, Mila, 11, 163-179
Maputo, *See* Mozambique
migrant groups
historical contexts for, 3-5
in Northern Ireland, 41-44, 50-54
participation in anti-racism movements, 51-52
Polish, 15-35
Vietnamese, 131-142
workers, 45
migration
and modern technology, 19
and communication to homeland, 29-33

chain, 148-149
motivation, 17, 68-69
transnational, 15
Milutinovic, Svetlana, 6, 91-105
MOVE 2005, 118-119
Mozambique,
   Cuban life in, 6, 79-87
multiculturalism,
   European backlash, 7-8
Murid Islamic brotherhood, 72-74
Muslims, 72-74

Northern Ireland,
   Belfast,
      anti-racism movements, 5, 40, 45-52
      racist attacks, 40, 44
      sectarian divisions, 39-40
      transnational migration to Belfast, 5
   economic development, 43
   Peace Process, 43
   Portuguese, 43
   West Belfast, 45-49
nostalgia,
   for former migrant homelands, 4, 16-17, 20-21
   stuck in the past, 24-25
Nyiri, P., 98

OECD (Organization for Economic Cooperation and Development), 92
outsourcing, 94, 102

Pakistan, 148-150, 153, 156-157
Pentecostalism, 111, 117-121
Poland,
   Communist period, 18-19
   Polish migration to Great Britain, 4, 15-35
   return of British poles, 23-24
Police Service of Northern Ireland (PSNI), 45, 47
Polish migrants,
   Communist regime émigrés, 18, 26-28
   first generation, 17-18, 22
   patriotism, 24
   post 2004, 19-20, 32-34
   pre 2004, 21
   reasons for migrating, 29
politics of representation, 148

Racial Equality Strategy for Northern Ireland, 45
racism,
   in Germany, 137-138
   in Northern Ireland, 5, 40, 44-50
Rahman, Sheikh Mujibur, 150
religion,
   Buddhism, 9
   Christianity, 8-9
   Islam, 8-9, 11-12
roots tourism, 21-22
routes, 68-69
Rushdie, Salman, 16

sectarianism, 40, 53
Senegal
   Dakar, 64-69
Senegalese migrants, 5-6, 63-69
sense of place, 10, 23, 62
Serbia,
   Chinese migrants living in Serbia, 92
Sinatti, Giulia, 5-6, 61-74
Smith, Michael Peter, 3-12
smuggling
   of illegals, 134
snack bar altars, 139
"space of flows," 147
sojourners, 61
Solidarity activism, 18, 22

temporal detachments, 33-34
Tower Hamlets, *see* Great Britain
translocalities, 5-7, 62-64
transnational
   actors, 113
   families, 65
   churches, 109-127
   cities, 69-72
   communities (diasporas), 10-12
      Bangladeshi Muslims, 147-160
      Polish, 15-35
   defining, 22, 25
   entrepreneurs, 6-7, 9, 92, 114, 153
   links, 23, 29-33
   media, 101
   migration
      after end of World War II, 7, 17-18
      aid factors, 6
      defining, 41-42, 93
      in Ireland, 42-44

religious factors, 5
socio-cultural factors, 4
networks
   commercial, 67, 102-105
   ethnic, 110-129
   family, 6
   migrant, 61
   religious, 8-10, 109-127, 131-142
social fields
   social space, 93-95
   urbanism, 5, 110-111, 121-123
   visits to homeland, 28-29

transnationalism
   and the role of time, 15-17, 22-23
   Polish, 4
transnational ties
   East-East, 6-7
   South-North, 5-6, 7
   South-South, 6, 77-89

"Troubles," The, 39, 42-44

umma, 156

Vietnam,
   Catholics/Buddhists, 135
   contract workers in Germany, 9, 131-142
   Vietnamese migrants, 133
   War, 134-135
visa requirements, 19, 99

West Against Racism Network (WARN), 45-49
Wink, 100-101
World War II,
   Polish migration to Great Britain after the war, 17-18

Zingonia, *See* Italy.

Printed in the United States
207770BV00001B/1-51/P